Rainbow of Indian Civilization

Attention Authors

'We Convert Fighters into Writers'. That's the motto of Manas Publications since more than four decades. Our message to the world is that India can win the battle not only by the bullet but also by the pen. There is no dearth of intellectuals in our country, but their knowledge is confined only to them. No sincere effort has been made by any other publisher to channelise their knowledge in national interest. That is why the talent of a large number of intellectuals remains latent. An author transforms his knowledge into a manuscript, and it is our job to spread his/her knowledge by converting it into a beautiful book. For over four decades, Manas has been motivating the intellectuals by publishing their manuscripts and would like to publish your manuscript too. If you or your colleagues have any manuscript ready for publication or are working on it, kindly contact us with detailed synopsis and list of contents. We will transform your work into a valuable publication. If you wish, we can also suggest you the suitable subjects for writing the books related to your area of expertise. Manas is known for its publishing quality and commitments. We take utmost care in production and give wide publicity to the book as well as its author through our national and international distribution network.

Rainbow of Indian Civilization

Niraj Kumar

Foreword by

Swami Paranand Tirth

Manas Publications
(We Convert Fighters into Writers)
New Delhi-110002 (INDIA)

MANAS PUBLICATIONS
(We Convert Fighters into Writers)
(Publishers, Library Suppliers, Importers & Exporters)
4402/5-A, Ansari Road (Opp. HDFC Bank)
Darya Ganj, New Delhi-110 002 (India)
Off. 23260783, 23265523, Fax: 011-23272766
E-mail: manaspublications@gmail.com
manaspublications@yahoo.com

ISBN 978-81-7049-475-1
₹ 995/-

Designed at
Manas Publications

Printed in India at
RK Print Services, Delhi
and Published by Mrs Suman Lata for
Manas Publications, 4402/5-A, Ansari Road
(Opp. HDFC Bank),
Darya Ganj, New Delhi-110 002 (INDIA)

Contents

Foreword

The illustrious author comes out with marvelous semiotics in each of his works. *Rainbow of Indian Civilization* is no exception. The book is an unparalleled admixture of aesthetic and esoteric perspectives specially that of a culture which has seen myriad vicissitudes during the course of its eons of evolution.

Owing to its traditional nomenclature '*sanatan*' or eternal through the thick and thins of its evolution and changes, there has always been an undercurrent of a stream of consciousness that is defined in terms of existence and bliss. Bliss or *ananda* is also known as *anantam* or infinitude. This is owing to phonetic combinatorics of Vedic revelations. Aldus Huxley chose to call it 'perennial' instead of 'eternal' may be because this culture never sheds the leaves of its peculiar ilk i.e. a sound metaphysical footing. There must be a substratum of truth or let's say metaphysical truth interlacing our civilization that has been safeguarding it from extinction unlike innumerable contemporary cultures Occidental as well as Oriental which have passed into oblivion long since. It took a keen mystic and aesthetic insight aided by scholastic exuberance and discursive caliber of Neeraj to experience this phenomenon.

He has compiled his vision into this great volume in order to share it with all of us. Without going into the detail of the "ultra violet" of the ancient Vedic culture, the author begins his work straightway with Shiva. The first canto is analogous to the first violet strand of the VIBGYOR of the Rainbow. Each chapter of the seven cantos provides us with a most sophisticated reservoir of knowledge.

Rama has been enunciated in a pragmatically innovative way that decides the story of Rama as *a posteriori* of the great grammarian Patanjali. This dispute between discursive and traditional aspects of many such concepts is ages old. The author has delved deep into the etymological depths of Rama and Ravana which to me meant only as-one in whom the world rejoices and one who causes every one to cry. After reading this passage new vistas of word-meaning relationship unfurled. Same with the syllable *kha* or void, the second consonants of the Sanskrit alphabet on which the edifice of entire Buddhist metaphysics is caricatured has been scholastically analyzed by the author. Neeraj's industrious exposition has made the innate and intimate relationship between the Vedic and the Buddhist metaphysics easily comprehensible to his readers.

His specification of the four fold evolution of culture viz. aphoristic encryptions, commentary, gloss and notes is a produce of deep intellectual insight. An elaborate deep and exhaustive canto devoted to Tantra is worth reading and assimilating.

His reflections on the esoteric import of the beheaded goddess help readers get an idea of how important it is to reject the conventional and conditioned experience to be in unison with the complete universal principle.

Some verses in Sanskrit from *Panchastavi*, a popular book of psalms along with their meaning add to the theistic and mystic touch of the book. Colours of this rainbow get more brilliant and vivid as the author goes on to elaborate the aesthetic master pieces of classical Sanskrit specially the manuals of dance, drama and poetry, details of *auchitya* and *rasa* schools of poetry and dramaturgy.

His view point takes this multifarious ultra beyond Asiatic geographic restrictions. Neeraj sees the reflections of his culture-rainbow throughout Asia and beyond. Owing to his mystic affiliation with void or Shunya the concluding chapter of his laborious compendium comprises the infra red of this masterpiece.

I recommend this to both a novice dilettante as well as a person well versed in this lore. The former will get initiated due to the mystic charm of this book whereas the latter will appreciate the labour that this genius of a writer has put in as much in studying what it took to write and in writing too.

With sincere benediction

Swami Paranand Tirth
(Founder Principal and CEO)
YTA Yog Tantra and Agama (Inc)

Preface

In the autumn of 2010, the journal *Praznath*: A discourse on Kashmiri Identity and Politics published a paper of mine titled "*Spanda*: *the Signature of Existence*". The article was my first attempt into exploration of the infinite continuum of Indian civilization. The healthy feedback led me to contribute more papers on Kashmir Shaivism and Indian aesthetics. I was tempted to purchase complete volumes of *Tantraloka* by Abhinavagupta. Reading the work in Sanskrit-Hindi prompted me to dive into the study of an important *vedanga, Nirukta* (Etymology). Yaska's work became my torchlight to fathom connections and correlations among distant categories.

In Indian tradition, *Shabda* is one of the most powerful categories to be reflected upon by illuminative mind. The world is viewed as concentric sheaths of materiality with *Shabda* occupying the inner layer of manifestation. *Shabda* emanates from the subtler vibration and the physical universe is considered as mere consequence of condensation of *Shabda*. The material universe dissolves back into *shabda* through rarefaction. It is like the changes of state of same set of atoms from gas to liquid , liquid to solid and vice versa.

Shabda is enshapement of the primordial vibration, *Spanda*. The universe is seen as interconnected, nested whole where a single vibration can influence the outcome at the grosser level of reality. This is the principle underneath powerful mantra tradition in India. The greatest contribution that India has made to the world civilization is the technique of miniaturization of thoughts into mantras. In fact, mantra has been a perennial export item from India for millennia. To decode mantras require extensive knowledge of etymology, cultural specificity and geo-cultural imagination. There have been numerous studies in recent times to explore mantras. I have attempted to contribute a little in this book towards this evolving subject.

India is a *karmabhumi* as well as a *punyabhumi*. Four great religions-Hinduism, Buddhism, Jainism and Sikhism- originated in this majestic land. The historical personality of Buddha is one of the finest treasures that we possess. I have added a section on Buddha. There are reflections over Rama and Tantra, the art of dialogue, aesthetic delight and voidness of categorical thinking.

This book is not intended to be a work of cultural history of India. It is a multi-dimensional lucid interpretation of cognitive structure of Indian civilization. Writing a book on Indian culture was never my goalpost. But, exploring Asian history and cultures led me to peep into the core of Asiaffinity viz. Indian civilization. Since I never had a regular study at college/university level, I am lucky to have survived the paradigm-centricity of thinking. The way my life has unfolded in last two decades has also turned me into a liberal maximalist. Liberty to think must be open-ended. Speculation is the very essence of thinking. Mere facticity neither leads to scientific innovation nor to the enrichment of humanities. This book is akin to hyperbola asymptote of open-ended thinking.

The openness of mind and heart to let the voidness penetrate my being could not have been made possible without the care and concern showered by my wife, C.N. Biak. My two daughters, Nidhi and Priya, are masters of homonyms and puns. Often, their deconstruction of words would lead me to surprising results. I am grateful to my parents for allowing me to dropout from the race of getting rich. My brothers, Dheeraj and Pankaj, stand by my side during the recurrent period of crisis.

I am immensely grateful to following friends and guides for encouraging me to pursue multiple ideas simultaneously: Rambahadur Rai, Priyadarshi Dutta, Late M.K. Dhar, K.C. Ajit Doval, Lallan Prasad, S.S. Toshkhani, Rashneek Kher, Dileep Singh, Yatish Yadav, O.P. Tiwary, Rakesh Singh, Himanshu Shekhar, Aneel Patil, S.K. Arya, Ghulam Mustafa, Rahul Kashyap, Manoj Jha, Soumya

Chattopadhyay, Raju Parulekar Kshitij Mohan, Sakib Jamal, Lama Chosphel Zotpa, Professor Vinay Kanth, Profesor Daisy Narayan, Professor S.S. Prasad, Late Professor Vijay Thakur, Late Professor R.S. Sharma, Late Professor H.S. Pradhan, Akhilesh Suman, Binod Singh, Dr. Ashok Gadiya, Swami Satyamayananda, Swami Amleshananda, Swami Chandrananda, Swami Shashankananda. Foremost, my sincere thanks to Swami Paranand Tirth for writing the foreword for this book.

I extend my gratefulness for inspirational role played by the editors at Manas Publication for making the book much better than it would have been if left in the hands of this 'fragile-thinker'. The errors and remaining shortcomings are entirely my responsibility.

Writing a book without financial support from institutions is a tough exercise. I owe my existence to this *karmabhumi*, Bharat, where Ma Annapurna feeds me and my family uninterruptedly. May I take birth in this holy land time and again and witness transmutation of residents into multi-hued rainbows shedding materiality and short-circuiting the undramatic route of leaving their bodies intact without *spandan*. Nothing should be permanent, not even our certain destiny of death. May this book be a primer on impermanence of mortality itself!

Niraj Kumar

Acknowledgement

I wish to express my gratefulness to the Editors of following magazines and journals for permitting me to reproduce my papers for parts of this book: *Praznath* for Spanda: Signature of Existence (Vol.1, No.2, July-September, 2010); Padmasambhava-a Pan-Asian Avatara from Kashmir? (Vol.1, No.3, October-December, 2010); Anandavardhana and His Theory of Poetic Suggestion (Vol.1, No.4, January- March, 2011); Panchastavi and Abhinavagupta (Vol.2, No.1 & 2, April-September, 2012); Abhinavagupta's aesthetics and the Concept of Camatkara (Vol. 4, No. 1-4, April, 2013-March, 2014) and *World Buddhist Forum magazine* for Buddha's Dharma Chakra Pravaratan-Philosophy of Action (June, 2013).

Introduction

Indian civilization stands out for its ceaseless creativity, continuity and unity in diversity. What is the source of the non-senescence of Indian civilization? The Himalayas is Asia's *kamandal.* It is the source from which South Asia's four major river systems—the Ganga, Indus, Brahmaputra and Sutlej—originate in the Himalayas. Other major rivers being fed by the Himalayan water includes the Amu Darya, Yellow River, Yangtze, Sutlej, Nu/Salween and Mekong. Water in a sage's *kamandal* is considered auspicious and represents the amrita (ambrosia). The Himalaya's water is an elixir for the Indian sub-continent. The combined river basin of the Indus, Ganga and the Brahmaputra constitute 43.8 per cent of India's total surface area. The Himalayas provide 63 per cent of India's fresh water.

If one charts out the path of these river systems originating from the Himalayas, one can discover the pattern of lotus petals spreading from its pericarp centred around Mount Kailash, the perennial abode of Gods in Indian mythology. The Ganga and Brahmaputra originate in the Himalayas. Both run eastward. The Brahmaputra takes a great bend in Tibet and flows southward towards the Bay of Bengal. The two meet at Goalundo in Bangladesh. Their flow path appears to generate a lotus petal on relief map. Similarly, the Indus and Sutlej originate from the vicinity and forms another petal on the western half of Indian subcontinent. These four rivers constitute two southern petals of Indian geo-imagination. Since everything is believed to be generating the mirror image, for every *bimba*, there is a *pratibimba*; the anticipation of two more petals in the north of the Himalayas might have encouraged Indian thinkers to propose for Indian geography a model of the pericarp of a lotus with four petals. This is the Jambudwipa. The lotus is now the national flower and the symbol of a political party which espouses ancient wisdom and national pride. But, the lotus is also found everywhere. In rituals, in the yogic parlance, in the simile for the charm of women, in the mythology, in the hagiography of saints; lotus plays the role of a womb, creatrix, sheath, purity and prosperity.

The Himalayas act as the site upon which utopias and fantasies are projected. Much of it is still a *terra incognita* and the geo-imaginative articulation by different Asian communities provides a structurally coherent meaning as well as reflects the centrality of the Himalayas in their practice of topopiety. For an Indian observer, the Himalayas appear as a crescent Moon dotted with fourteen highest mountain peaks (the eight-thousanders) as stars on a relief map. The Mount Kailash would appear as the sixteenth digit of the Moon, the dot of immortality in Tantric parlance. The Kailash holds a special place as the *axis mundi* of the Universe, the manifestation of the mythical *Meru* in the Asian imagination of the sacred landscape.

The Himalayas have always been viewed as the abode of immortals. There are various myths about the existence of Dmuthang, the rope to the heaven. Hindus believe in the hidden land of immortals in the Himalayas, siddhashrama, while for the Buddhists there are 108 similar hidden abodes, *beyuls,* across the Himalayas; Pemako being the most sacred site. From Tibetan side, the Himalayas appear as a rainbow. And it is not a strange coincidence that the rainbow holds the highest importance in the Tibetan view of immortality. The rainbow for Tibetans is the body of immortals. There is an ancient tradition of Zhang Zhung where trekchod and togel practices lead one to attain rainbow body of deathlessness in which the master practitioner leaves behind no flesh after death and transforms into rainbow bodies.

A fourth or fifth century Chinese poet, *Tao Qioan,* wrote about an earthly paradise hidden in the Himalayas. For the Chinese, the Himalayas appear as a mighty dragon. The range that separates Tibet from India appears like the body and wing of a dragon and the range that curves out from Sichuan to Chiang Mai in Thailand appears as the foreleg and the neck. The curve that extends from Afghanistan to northern Iran appears as the hind leg and the tail of a dragon. In the Chinese mythology, the dragon symbolizes immortality, fertility and creativity. Thus, the Himalayas become the source of life and immortality for sacred imagination across Asia. Though constituting only 0.3% of the planet area, the Himalayas contain 10% of the global bio-diversity, many seemingly related to the belief in immortality ranging from jambu fruit, tea, caterpillar mushroom (Buddha mushroom) and soma leaves. The Himalayas represents an index of immortality.

The strength of our civilization lies in this inter-connected thinking. For us, everything is alive. Indian history is not a buried history. A Buddha can emerge through *avataran.* Shiva can emerge as a *svayambhu.* Everything pulsates with presence, transcendence and bliss. Therefore, even if a part gets diseased, the other parts support the renewal and regeneration. The Himalayas, Ganga, lotus, Kailash are our record keepers and also actors in unknown ways. The mechanical and secular world view that arose in the West from Francis Bacon onwards has endangered the diverse pool of cognitive thinking within a short span of time. We have compartmentalized thinking. When the present age is a network society, the cocooned thinking does not aid the blooming of holistic thinking. That is why we have not been able to produce a world-class thinker in the last five decades. The national movement leaders were the last generation who contributed to the pride we had in our civilization. Now, we have doctorates from the westoxified centres, who are mostly dumb when it comes to thinking in real situation within India. Until and unless we start to look at our history, geography, mythologies and various other knowledge traditions as an imaginary grid with potential solutions, we are likely to fail again in pushing top down policy prescriptions.

This book is aptly titled *Rainbow of Indian Civilization.* The book has been divided into seven sections to represent India's variegated civilization as a rainbow. Rainbows are connected with the power of immortality in the Himalayan tradition. This book seeks to explore the unceasing flow of Indian culture. Indian civilization continue to renew in spite of seamless constraints. The power does not come from the state or the political philosophy. This is the result of our historically integrated approach towards belief systems, ethnicities, topographies. The holistic thinking is now endangered under the flux of the post-modern posturing of the west by imposing the engagement with marginalities as the panacea for the developing world. We must reclaim our holistic thinking. This book is an attempt to capture the ethos of Indian civilization from the present goalpost. There is ample fusion of science, mysticism and poetry. The seven parts of the book correspond to the colours of a rainbow. Each section opens up a new possibility to explore our civilization from a-temporal, non-chronological integrated perspective. The elements move from present to past and from, place to place. Many features may appear duplication of arguments. But, that is where the possibility of power of renewal springs forth. The seven sections deal with the most fundamental persisting aspects of Indian civilization. It is neither the binarised thinking nor the deconstructionist approach. The book engages with the centres as much as peripheries. The first section opens with reflection on Kashmir Shaivism and Shiva at the centre of philosophy of void. Other sections concern with Rama, Buddha, Tantra, Samvad, Camatkara and Shunya. Our theistic world view can be covered under the first four sections and fundamental issues of cultural aspects like poetry, drama, music, painting, literature etc under the next two sections. The last section is an exploration of void and emptiness.

A fresh understanding on Indian civilization at this juncture is required. Today, when polity, security as well as economy, appears paralysed, only from the civilizational womb can we retrieve some hope to build the future of our dreams. There is no alternative to integrated thinking.

SHIVA

Chapter 1

Spanda: Signature of Existence

The concept of '*spanda*' is at the heart of the remarkable doctrine of Kashmir Shaivism. Etymologically speaking, Spanda is a 'throb', a vibration, an oscillation between manifestation and disappearance or between emergence and dissolution. Now, modern science is finally grappling with the United Field Theory and eagerly waiting to examine the voluminous data emanating from the collision of sub-atomic particles in the Large Hadron Collider (LHC) Project, Geneva. The interest of the philosophers who seek to formulate meta-narrative, is bound to deepen in the glorious legacy of the *spanda* doctrine that constitute one of the pillars of the non-dualist Kashmir Shaivism.

There are two schools of thought in modern physics that are at loggerhead. While adherents of the Standard Model pitch for the 'field theory' of physical universe, in recent years the bandwagon of chaos/fractal theorists have gained prominence who posit the idea of 'scalar invariance of structures' in a dynamic universe. The field theory presupposes 'vibratory mode' as the fundamental nature of the universe. Fields are produced by oscillatory movement and the quantum theory presupposes linear oscillators at work at sub-atomic level. Particles invariably have quantum numbers like spin number. The String theory postulates the existence of one-dimensional strings that consist of oscillating loops vibrating as various sub-atomic particles like electrons and protons. The String theory that considers varying oscillation of string as the cause of manifestation of different particles lies at the extreme end of this dominant paradigm. The whole universe gets reduced to mere vibration, mere throb of 'physical nothingness', since physicality itself is merely an appearance of vibration.

Neuroscientists have discovered in the last decade the phenomena of synchronous oscillation of neurons in the cerebral cortex and have proposed that this pattern of synchronous pulsation in the brain generates a mechanism whereby various sensory data contribute to the perception of 'wholeness' of observed phenomena. There cannot be a perception of unified object without this mechanism. Heart beat, breathing, and similar kind of internal rhythm are present across biological world. Pulsation in biological system is explicitly visible if one observes a beheaded chicken. Muscles continue to expand and contract rhythmically even though the body is cut off from the head. Rhythm precedes the birth but continues even after death. Scientists at the Blue Brain Project at Geneva which is building artificial mammalian brains including that of the human beings were surprised to observe a bizarre phenomena. Artificial silicon neurons respond to external stimuli and pulse and flash synchronously. Vibration seems to exist even beyond biological world.

All living beings survive by the process of glycolysis, i.e. glucose is broken down and energy is produced. Now, the glycolytic cycle itself has been found to be pulsating. Discovery of temporal oscillation at the level of chemical processes at sub-cellular level shows the ubiquity of *spandan*. The case of Belousov-Zhabotinsky reaction in chemistry where the concentration of chemicals pulsates with different colours is often cited by theorists of the dynamic system.

Physicists are surprised to observe certain interesting phenomena. There is a set of particle called 'neutrino'. Neutrinos have no charge and insignificant mass. Neutrinos form a shadow universe since these don't interact much with the matter that constitutes us. Therefore, millions of neutrinos from the sun or the cosmic rays are continuously passing through us without causing any interaction. Proton-proton collision creates new particles that immediately decay into neutrinos. LHC at Geneva is experimenting with the behaviour of neutrinos even. There are three families of neutrinos (muon, electron, tau). Scientists are perplexed to find that one type can oscillate into another. Therefore, oscillation/pulsation seems to be an inherent characteristic at much deeper level than even beyond the appearance of our type of 'universe'.

On the other hand, the fractal theorists discover reiteration of self-similar structure/form at various scale of the universe like Russian Matryoshka dolls where self-similar dolls are nested one inside the other. The hierarchy and nesting of self-similar structure is easily discernible in cauliflower or broccoli where tiny pieces look much like the whole vegetable. The fractal paradigm can be summed up in philosophical term as 'microcosm reiterates macrocosm'. The only difference is in the scale of seeing. Fractals are found in every dynamic system. In reality, everything in the universe is in flux. There is no absolute rest or changelessness in the phenomenal universe.

The future of science depends upon the experimental result at the LHC. If the elusive Higgs boson is discovered, the Super Symmetry (SUSY) theory, the String theory and dozens of hypothesis based on the presupposition of 'wave/field/oscillation' at the root of physical universe will get a fresh lease of life. But, if the nature of Higgs particles itself appear 'fractal', the whole world of science and technology and the future of human civilization will take an unprecedented turn. The discovery of Higgs boson is merely a comma in further quest for fractality of fundamental particles.

The *Spanda Shastras* unify the two conflicting paradigms of contemporary times. The *Spanda* doctrine espouses 'vibration' as well as hierarchy, nesting and recurrence of self-similar structure of the Being. *Spanda Shastras* contain the seeds of future civilization.

Emergence of Spanda School

The origin of Spanda doctrine can be attributed to Vasugupta (c 800 AD). In his *Spandanirnaya,* the commentary on the Spandakarika, Kshemaraja (11th century), the cousin and pupil of Abhinavagupta, mentions how the *Shiva Sutras* were revealed to Vasugupta by Lord Shiva himself in a dream. He went to the sacred Mahadeva Mountain and found the *Shiva Sutras* engraved on the surface of the rock. The *Shiva Sutras* contain 78 sutras or aphorisms. There is a difference of opinion on the authorship of *Spandakarika,* the 51-verse commentary on the Shiva Sutras. Kshemaraja, Maheshvarananda and Daniel Odier attribute the composition of the *karika* to Vasugupta. Bhaskara and Utpala mention Kallata, the disciple of Vasugupta, as the writer of *Spandakarika*. Jaideva Singh opines that Vasugupta composed the karikas and taught to Bhatta Kallata who only publicized them.

The revelation of *Shiva Sutras* to Vasugupta seems to be determined by the criss-crossing religious and philosophical trajectories prevalent in Kashmir during his time. Shankaracarya (788-820 AD) had visited Kashmir and reinvigorated Vedanta philosophy by incorporating the then dominant conception of Reality as a form of non-dual Absolute as propounded by Nagarjuna in the *Madhyamika* school of Buddhism. Around 760 AD, King Trisong Detsen of Tibet invited Padmasambhava and Santarakshita (705-762 AD) to Tibet. Santarakshita was the abbot of famous Nalanda University. Both of them introduced Buddhism into Tibet and translated *Dharmic* texts. Later, they founded the first Buddhist monastery in Tibet at Samye near Lhasa in 767 AD. The King declared Buddhism as state religion in 762 AD. They must have passed through Kashmir during their sojourn in Tibet and influenced the local Kashmiri scholars. In fact, many of the translators in the team were Kashmiri *pandits*. Ananta was the interpreter for *Santarakshita* in Tibet. Kashmiri scholars like Dharmakaradatta, Jinamitra, Danasila, Sraddakaravarman, Ratnavajra, Lakshmi, Subhutisristani, Somanatha, Mahajana, Suksmajnana, Parahitabhadra, Parahita, Kumarsri, Trilakalasa, Kanakavarman were some of the well-known scholars and translators from Kashmir who were invited to preach or translate works in Tibet.

The Tibetan king organized a two-year dharma debate at Samye (792-794 AD) known as the 'Council of Lhasa'. A master of Ch'an Buddhism, Hva-shang Mo-ho-Yen was propagating the view of sudden enlightenment that could spring without much effort. Ch'an Buddhism had become popular in China after being introduced by Bodhidharma who hailed from Kanchipuram during the early 6th century. Ch'an Buddhism on its way to Japan evolved as 'Zen Buddhism' which outrightly rejects logic as a way to realize Truth. Kamalshila, the disciple of Santarakshita and a resident of Magadha, defeated the Ch'an master in the debate on the nature of 'emptiness'. Since then, the trajectory of Buddhism in Tibet followed the Indian path and the Chinese influence on religious evolution of Tibetan Buddhism was arrested. The victory of Kamalshila must be known to Kashmiri scholars who often accompanied Buddhist masters from India into Tibet.

Subsequent to Kamalshila's victory, Indian Buddhism emanating from the centre of Nalanda was officially declared as the state religion in Tibet. This is known as the 'First spreading'. But soon it suffered a serious setback at the hands of an unpopular king Langderma. He ascended the throne in Tibet in 836 AD and began a drive to cleanse Tibet from Buddhist influence. Monasteries were destroyed and monks were forced to convert to laymen or exiled. Though Langderma was assassinated in 842 AD, Tibet fell into a civil war, which lasted for more than a century.

The exile of Buddhist monks from Tibet and the revelation of *Shiva Sutra* to Vasugupta occurred at the same time. Therefore, there is a strong possibility that Buddhist monks fled to Kashmir, which was famously known as the abode of wisdom. This might have initiated a process of philosophical synthesis in Kashmir. The way the *Shiva Sutra* is stated to have been revealed to Vasugupta is reminiscent of the legend of revelation of *Prajnaparamita Sutras* to the great *Madhyamika* philosopher, Nagarjuna, in the land of *Nagas*.

In *Nyingma* tradition (the oldest school of Buddhism in Tibet founded by Padmasambhava during the 8th century), the concept of *'terton'* and *'terma'* was widely prevalent. Terma is the revealed teaching which the past masters hid for discovery by later tertons (discoverer) at appropriate time. Generally, the secret knowledge (terma) was physically discovered as engravings in rocks or caves or many a times in intuitive flash in the mind itself.

There is a preponderance of possibility of deep influence exerted by the exiled Buddhist masters upon discovery of the *Shiva Sutras* by Vasugupta. Kashmir was under the rule of Karkotas (626-855 AD). They followed the Vaishnava sect. Spread of religious ideas is inextricably linked to the proximity of a particular religious worldview with the political authority. Since major monasteries and institutions were funded by the imperial authorities, the sects vied with each other to mould the viewpoint of the kings and their ministers or else to modify their own teachings to accommodate the viewpoint of the king.

More than Two Centuries of Shaivism-Buddhism Fusion

Alexis Sanderson (2009) mentions how Shaivism was on ascendancy all across India and South-East Asia at this juncture. In Tungabhadra-Cauveri and Tungabhadra-Bhima zone of Karnataka, construction of new Shiva temples far outnumbered the temples and monasteries of other religious sects. A similar pattern was evident in Andhra Pradesh. Pala dynasty encouraged and supported the spread of Buddhism from Tibet to South-East Asia. Palas contributed significantly in building and maintaining major Buddhist centres like Nalanda, Vikramshila, Semapura, Trikatuka, Uddandapura, Jagaddala. Devpala had a son Mahendrapala (812-850 AD), who was strongly attracted towards Shaivism. Mahendrapala (850-865 AD) built two temples, one for Buddha and the other for Shiva. This suggests a fusion of Shaivite and Buddhist philosophies and practices since major centres for innovation of concepts in Buddhism were dependent on Pala's support.

During the same period, Shaivism was gaining pre-eminence in

Khmer kingdom and the fusion process of Shaivite-Buddhist texts and practices gained momentum. During the 9th and 10th century, the Shaivite idea of '*Lokeshwar*' was fully integrated by the tantric Mahayana Buddhists. Kings were portrayed as avatars of Shiva as in Angkor and even as *Bodhisattva* as in the temple at Bayon. The cult of *Heruka* emerged in Buddhism based upon iconography inspired by the imagery of Shiva. Since single donors supported both religions, both philosophies were vying with one another to win the support of the political authorities.

Buddhanirvana of Cham Kingdom in Indo-China records that his father Somnatha donated two viharas for Buddha and two temples to Shiva. Similar assimilation and appropriation is evident in eastern Java. George Coedes mentions in his work *The Indianized States of Southeast Asia* (1968) that a syncretic cult of Shiva-Buddha evolved both in Mataram (Central Java) and Angkor. Two great works appeared simultaneously under the patronage of the Mataram ruler Sindok (929-948 AD), the Javanese Ramayana and the Tantric Buddhist treatise *Sang Hyang Kamahayanikan.* Airlangga (1010-1050 AD), the founder of the Kahuripan kingdom, was consecrated as the King in 1019-20 AD by a Buddhist and a Shaiva priest in Mataram. During Singhasari and Majapahit period (1222-1292 and 1293-1500 AD, respectively), this syncretism continued to flourish. Imperial formations provided simultaneous support to both Shaivism as well as Buddhism.

Even in Kashmir, Lalitaditya (724-761 AD) gave equal patronage to both sects, Hindu or Buddhist. He constructed temples for Shiva as well as statues of Buddha. But, his successor Karkota kings were weak and unimaginative. Avantivarman (855-883 AD), who ascended the throne when Tibet was in the throes of a civil war causing a massive exodus of scholars to adjoining areas, founded the Utpala dynasty. He patronized Kallata, the pupil of Vasugupta who is credited with writing the *Spandakarika*. His reign is credited with effervescence in every aspect of life in Kashmir. It is debateable whether the impetus came from scholar-émigrés from Tibet or was it locally inspired?

Some conclusions for this fusion in a vast geo-cultural region can be drawn. The Siddha tradition gained prominence during the 9th century with the advent of Saraha. Saraha, too, was associated with the Nalanda tradition. The Siddha repudiated the use of language of metaphysics engaged by scholars and sang charyapadas in *apabhramsha,* the mother of modern day languages like Hindi, Bengali or Oriya. They were the pioneers of the fusion process. They were the great alchemist of ideas and took the best practices from the flourishing sects. They emphasized more on direct realization than contemplation over obtuse philosophy. Since, they wanted to take their teachings directly to the people and not to the imperial overlords, they introduced theistic elements in their teachings which could attract all and sundry. Siddhas accepted Shiva, Jina and Buddha to be one and the same from different views. The Tibetan teachings of Padmasambhava carried the stories about experiences of Siddhas to Tibet. It is this fusion which has left an indelible mark on history of various sects in India, Nepal, Bhutan and Tibet.

Kapalika, a fiery Shaivite sect that flourished in Kashmir during this period mentions Nagarjuna as one of the 12 pupils of the sect. In *Guhyasiddhi Sangraha,* it was stated that Vajrayana was inseparable from Shaiva and Pashupata system as basic practice for both was *Mahamudra.* Some consider *Kapalika* itself as a fragment of Niruttara tantra practices of *Nyingma* tradition. There is a strong overlap between *Natha, Siddhas* and *Kapalikas.* Name of Gorakhnath, Jalandhar Nath and Nagarjuna as lineage guru are common in all these sects.

Kumarila, a Buddhist monk, who later converted to Shaivism is a good example of fluid matrix. There is strong likelihood that Shaivism in new avatar sprouted in Kashmir upon the vehicle of Tibetan Buddhism following tumultuous affairs after Langderma's ascension.

In *Spandanirnaya,* the commentary on the Spandkarikas, Kshemraja emphasizes that *Spandakarika* is basically a presentation of *Mahamudra,* the cosmic gesture, which later became the foundation of Kagyu lineage in Tibetan Buddhism. The great transmission master of the Kagyu sect, Naropa (1016-1100 AD) though born in a royal family of Bengal, went for study in Kashmir at the tender age of 11, since at that time Kashmir had emerged as an important seat of Buddhist wisdom. In 1049 AD, Naropa went to Nalanda and was elected as an abbot. Naropa's name is mentioned in the list of 84 Siddhas along with familiar names like Gorakh, Saraha and Matsyendranath. Naropa epitomizes the close connection and free exchanges between Nalanda, Kashmir, Tibet and Bengal. Naropa received *Mahamudra* from his guru Tilopa, who had four transmission that included *mahamudra, tantra, bardo* and *candali* (correspondence with Kundalini, the Mother shakti contained within the human body) from different teachers. Now, *Mahamudra* is the ultimate goal not only in Kagyu sect and Kashmir Shaivism (it is epitomized in *tandava* dance of Shiva), but also found as an important aspect of teaching among Natha and Siddha sects.

Bodhibhadra, the disciple and successor of Naropa at Nalanda was a Kashmiri pandit. Bodhibhadra is credited with translating the texts of the *Kalachakra* tradition. He was also the teacher of Atisa Dipankar (982-1054 AD), who went to Tibet in 1040 AD upon the invitation of Tibetan king and is credited with reforming the excesses that had crept into Buddhist practices due to misinterpretation of texts. Abhinavagupta who synthesized various schools of Kashmir Shaivism in his magnum opus, *Tantraloka,* pay obeisance to Matsyendranath. The Kalachakra tradition considers *Tantraloka* as an authoritative text in their practices. There is so much similarity among various sects and emerging syncretism that sometimes the sense of distinction itself evaporates.

Take the case of Matsyendranath. *Tantraloka* begins with salutation to him. He is considered direct disciple of Shiva. His name is encrypted in Buddhist legends. He is identified with Avalokiteshvara in Buddhism. In Nepal, he is the patron saint. This concept of Ishwar/ Adinath/Svayambhu is common in every sect during this period. Probably, this kind of fusion took place in the centre of Nalanda and spread to the Himalayan region comprising Kashmir, Tibet, Nepal, Bhutan and Assam. The Himalayas seem to be a crossroad between

Kashmir and Buddhist as well as non-Buddhist tradition of Eastern India. What can be stated as the better synthesis and synchronous throb in the geo-cultural zone than the fact that the sacred mountain of Kailash and the pristine lake of Mansarovar are revered by both Hindus and Buddhists?

Shaivism cannot be viewed in isolation from the criss-crossing and fluid trajectories of dynamic religious ideas emanating from various centres across South and Southeast Asia. The evolution of these trajectories were often determined by the imperial formations as well as advent of creative genius like Gorakh, Saraha, Padmasambhava, Naropa, Matsyendranath, Vasugupta, Abhinavagupta. In all likelihood, the expulsion of Buddhist scholars during the first half of the ninth century to adjoining areas caused effervescence in Kashmir analogous to the process of renaissance created in Italy after the fall of Constantinople and exodus of the Arab scholars into Italy. Since most of the interpreters as well as translators in Tibet were Kashmiris, they would have returned to their native place and reinvigorated the debate, through fusion and assimilation with fresh ideas of synthesis, idea of theistic God in spite of a philosophy of 'vacuity' and Absolute monism carried in their mind through translation of great works of Buddhist tradition.

Sixteenth Karmapa often stated that Kashmir Shaivism is the 'southern lineage' while Karma-Kagyu's *Chakrasamvara tantra* is the 'northern tradition'. But, emergence of Kashmir Shaivism was determined by local dynamics of evolution of vedantic thought and phoneme-transcendentalism. A brief description of the main tenets of Spanda school of Kashmir Shaivism is necessary before charting out the influence of other thought trajectories.

Basic Tenets of Spanda School

There are four schools in Kashmir Shaivism namely—*Krama, Kula, Spanda* and *Pratyabhijna.* Each of these school has a common conceptual framework, like primacy of consciousness over material world, physicality of appearance, reality as manifestation of absolute consciousness, non-duality, and a close interconnection between phoneme and phenomena. The basic postulate of the Spanda School is the dynamic nature of the fundamental reality that the universe is the grosser manifestation of the vibration mediated through sound/ letters/phonemes. The vibration emanates from the 'ecstatic self-recurrent consciousness (Jaideva Singh, p. xvii). Everything in the Universe throbs, but the genesis of throb is a-temporal vibration of Supreme Consciousness. If a practitioner can learn to contemplate over the movement of the tiniest of entity or phenomena, the aspirant can reach the source, the Absolute consciousness. This brings the state of liberation and permanent bliss, and the Will of the realized person merges with the Will of the Supreme Shiva. He becomes one with Shiva.

Since *Shiva Sutra as* revealed to Vasugupta is an *agam shastra,* the first commentary, *Spandakarikas* being composed by his disciple Kallata, the main propositions of these two texts constitute the foundation of the Spanda School of Kashmir Shaivism.

The *Shiva Sutras* contain 77 verses in three parts which reflects the *Trika* philosophy, the unique feature of Kashmir Shaivism. The first part contains 22 aphorisms, second part contains 10, while the final contains 45. The very first aphorism, '*caitanyamatma*' (the creative state of the Highest consciousness is the Reality of everything) posits primacy of consciousness over matter. Thence follows the aphorism on recurrence of triad structure at various level of manifestation like three kinds of bondage, three kinds of knowledge, three states of consciousness (verse 1.7-1.10).

An authentic yogi enjoys the oneness of awareness in all the above mentioned state of consciousness and he gains Shiva's unlimited power of creativity. The second part begins with the aphorism, '*cittam mantrah*', mind is mantra (verse 2.1) Guru is the means i.e. one who guides towards the knowledge of the wheel of *Matrikachakra* (wheel of alphabets). The world is seen as manifestation of words. The universe is gross manifestation of *Shabda Brahma* (Highest sound-consciousness). At the highest level of *Paravak* (beyond speech), words (*shabda*) and the meaning (*artha*) are in a state of unity. It is only in the descent of manifestation that differentiation occurs. The world as well as the word are manifestation of *matraka* (phonemes), which emerge from the primordial 'supreme speech' or *Paravak*, the original spoken word of Shiva. *Paravak* is the creative power (*vimarsha*) of Param Shiva. Mind of a practitioner itself becomes 'mantra' by intense contemplation of the deity inherent in the mantra. Mantras as such, are not mere mumbo-jumbo, but a gradual ascent towards *paravak* and the Ultimate Reality.

Matrikachakra is the art to unite the subjective world and the objective world through phoneme-universe. There are two series of alphabets in Sanskrit: 16 vowels representing Shiva principle (subjective world) and 34 consonants for the Shakti principle (manifested, objective world). The Universe is a manifestation of the alphabetic soup. Shiva has five Shaktis—Cit Shakti (anuttara/ Highest consciousness), Ananda Shakti (bliss), Iccha Shakti (will), Jnana Shakti (knowledge) and Kriya Shakti (action). Shiva ceaselessly acts in the world through these five Shaktis in manifestation (srishti), maintenance (sthiti), withdrawal (samhara), concealment (trirodhana) and grace (anugraha) (Verse 3.30).

Based upon the works of earlier grammarians, the aphorisms presuppose three stages of manifested sound—*pashyanti, madhyama,* and *vaikhari.* Wherever there is motion, there is vibration and sound. *Spanda* is the throb of Param Shiva, a movement without succession. Thence arises the soundless sound, *nada* and *bindu* (light). Two aspects of creative *Shiva, prakasha* (manifestation) and *vimarsha* (concretization) are symbolized respectively by *bindu* and *nada.* Para-Vak or the supreme speech gradually materializes into physical universe as syllables and alphabets through three stages *pashyanti, madhyama* and *vaikhari.* Para-Vak is the vimarsha aspect of Param Shiva, the power of '*aham*' (self-awareness). *Pashyanti* is the visual sound, the image of idea before expression. *Madhyama* stands in the middle between ideal form of speech and spoken word, between visual speech and vocal speech. *Vaikhari* is the uttered sound. *Matrikas* are phonetic constituents of vaikhari, while vaikhari represents Kriya Shakti. Matrika are the seed of every language from which all kinds of words and sentences emerge. Since, there are three-fold energies of Shiva, i.e. *Para* (subjective), *Parapara* (cognitive) and *Apara* (objective), man can realize his identity with Shiva through cognitive path. That makes the world of *matrika* and *mantras* very important for the practice of an aspirant. Since mantras arise from the *spanda* principle, these contain the aspect of Shiva.

First verse of the Second Awakening of *Shiva Sutra* is *'cittam mantrah'* or `mind is mantra'. It is through the deep awareness of one's identity with the Supreme consciousness embodied in a mantra and becoming identical with that Supreme consciousness that the mind itself becomes mantra. Kshemaraja explains in the commentary, *Vimarsini* that the mind *(cittam)* is not merely a combination of letters, and that it itself is mantra.

The first vowel 'A' (अ) stands for the ultimate reality since there is nothing beyond this. It is the anuttara. When 'A' self-reflects, it duplicates and reunites with itself, creating A-A (अ + अ = आ). Aa represents *'ananda'* principle. Phoneme 'I' (इ) signify *iccha Shakti,* the desire for manifestation. 'U' (उ) connotes *unmesha* (manifestation of iccha in ideal state of jnana). A (अ) is the root of all creation and through 'I' (इ) (iccha) comes into manifestation 'u' (उ), unmesha. *Anuttara* manifests in infinite form through combination with iccha and this describes the *svachhanda* (freedom) aspect of Param Shiva.

In *Matrikachakra,* Panini's rule of grammar is followed to create a linguistic universe that corresponds with the physical reality. Panini's grammar had significant influence over scholars in Kashmir. Chandragomin founded the Chandra school of Sanskrit grammar in Kashmir. Lalitaditya's grandson Jayapida ruled Kashmir for 31 years (782-813 AD). He himself was a student of Sanskrit grammar and one of his ministers, Vamana, was the author of *Kashikavritti,* a commentary on Panini's work. It is the influence of Panini and Bhartrihari that shaped the esoteric ideas of *Matrikachakra.*

Structural resonance recurs all around. Panini divided his magnum opus, *Ashtadhyayi* into eight chapters. Patanjali, who wrote the *Mahabhashya,* a commentary on Panini, is known for his concept of *Ashtanga yoga.* In *Matrikachakra,* similar structure is reiterated. There are two garlands of letters containing vowels and consonants.

There are 16 vowels with 8 pairs like 'a', 'aa'. There are 8 vargas of consonants each governed by the great Mother Shakti. It is not a mere coincidence that Kalhana chronicled *Rajatarangini* in a similar structure with 8 chapters and used 'taranga' (etymologically related to *spanda*) in his historical narrative about this period in Kashmir.

By employing the technique of *pratyahara*, i.e. combining the beginning and the end, *udaya* and *pralaya*, the whole universe can be perceived. To master this *Matrikachakra* is a sure way to achieve one's identity with the Supreme consciousness. 'a' (अ) is the anuttara. 'Ha' (ह) is the anahata. 'A' is the para (highest in the hierarchy of vowels, the subjective world). 'Ha' is the lowest in the list of the consonants (objective world). Bindu is the consciousness of Shiva, the potential for manifestation. One can create a chakra (cycle) by uniting the supreme subjectivity (A) with supreme objectivity (ha). The word 'aham' is one of the most significant conceptual categories in the *Spanda Shastras. Aham* is 'self-awareness', the sense of self-awareness that pervades the whole universe.

Matrikas contains five great energies of Shiva. These energies are like chakras as they move in rhythmic cycles. An aspirant who realizes that these chakras are the same as Shiva, the knowledge of *Matrikachakra* dawns upon him.

In the verse 4 of the *Second Awakening* in the *Shiva Sutras,* the state of '*khechari*' as the stage of realization of Shivahood is mentioned. This is the stage of *ananda* (bliss) of vast expansion of spiritual consciousness. (*Khechari* is one that moves in 'kha' or the vast space.) This comes after realizing the infinite creative power inherent in the paravak and its manifestation, the *matrikachakra.*

The first verse of the Third Awakening in the *Shiva Sutras* mentions '*atma cittam*'. This verse itself is a combination of first verse of the First Awakening (*chaitanyamatma*) and first verse of the Second Awakening (*chittam mantrah*). If two verses are combined, the first verse of the Third Awakening (*atma chittam*) can be created. The full verse on combination will run as '*atma chittam, chaitanya mantrah*'. Since, Kashmir Shaivism followed trika structure to unravel the way to achieve liberation in this very life, the three Awakening and three verses are strung together in the same structure. It is stated by the commentators that the First Awakening describes the *Shambhopaya,* the Path of Shiva to achieve liberation. The second explains the *Shaktopaya,* the Path of Shakti and the third *Anavopaya*, the Path of the Senses. If the first path is the path of supreme Will (*iccha*), the second and third corresponds with the path of knowledge *(jnana)* and action *(kriya),* respectively.

But the *Trika* philosophy is not concerned with merely understanding triads. There is the *turiya,* the way to transcend the triads in the world of immanence. This was known as *'chatushkoti'* in the Vedas. *Om* has three phonemes: *a, u, m* and the fourth is the vibration. Similarly, speech is made up of three parts, *pashyanti, madhyama, vaikhari* and the fourth is the *paravak. Chatushapada* has been extensively used in Kashmiri literature. Therefore, I am of the view that the Kashmir Shaivists merely renamed the prevailing idea of *chatushkoti* (3+1) in Buddhist and *Vedic* philosophy as well as grammar (*Trika* +1). Even the trident (trishul) in Kashmir Shaivism represents '3+1' structure. The three prongs represent three Shaktis: *para* (supreme), *parapara* (supreme cum-non-supreme) and *apara* (non-supreme). But, the *'paratita'* is above the central prong of the trident that represents 'beyond', the Shakti embodying supreme beatitude. Cryptic text of *Shiva Sutra,* structured in *Trika* way contains the seed of the transcendence by an unnamed fourth. There is hierarchical nesting of the self-similar structure as found in the fractal paradigm of a dynamic universe. While combining the first verses of the First and Second Awakenings, one arrives at the fourth of this *chatushpada/chatushkoti* structure. In the combination, *'atma chittam, chaitanya mantrah'*, since *'atma chittam'* is the first verse of the Third Awakening, *'chaitanya mantrah'* is the fourth, *turiya,* the beyond. This sums up the emphasis and deep engagement with the sonic nature of the Universe, structure of the phoneme and the textuality of the phenomena.

The Third Awakening describes inferior ways to achieve realization, the way of *kriya* that includes various breathing techniques, visualization and yogic postures. This section expound on the eight shaktis of Shiva manifesting in the phonetic world. Eight vargas of consonants represented by different shaktis is visualized as surrounding the highest shakti sitting in the centre of brahmarandhra. These eight matrika mothers have been termed as the Mother of 'beast' in the Shiva Sutra since these shaktis govern all differentiated knowledge mediated through linguistic reality. Since the manifest universe has limitations and is bound by succession (karma), i.e. time as well as language, it is symbolically addressed as the beast. By the practice and constant japa, the mantras reveal as the deities themselves. The 43rd verse in this part reveals the technique of self-realization through breathing, while the 44th verse concerns with the Kundalini yoga. Mother Kundalini is termed as the prana (energy of life).

A yogi repeatedly experiences the revealing and concealing aspect of the objective universe. For him, the objective universe is visible as mere grosser manifestation of inner light of consciousness and is identical with it. *Spanda* in the form of *paravak* is the supreme consciousness which once realized fills the seeker with eternal delight. The three methods contained in the three parts of the *Shiva Sutra* for self-realization lead the *sadhak* to the state of *anuttara*. In this state, unity of the universe and the self is realized. The '*soham*' (I am That) state pervades consciousness in the three states of consciousness. There is experience of indivisibility inside and outside. One finds consciousness as the root of physical universe. Physicality is mere concretization of grosser state of consciousness. This causes dawn of the Highest Bliss *(jagdananda)*.

Spandakarika, contains 51 verses reflecting the manifestation of matrika (50 alphabets plus dot [*bindu*]) as the phenomenal universe. The first verse describes the *spanda-shakti* (*Shankari*) representing unmesha (emergence) and nimesha (absorption) of the Shakti of Shiva. *Spanda* is at the root of experience. Mantras derive their power from the *spanda*-principle and take individual to the state of identity with Shiva. The last verse states that when the aspirant realizes the spanda-principle, he can control the emergence and dissolution of the samskaras (mental impressions of one's action as stated in karma theory in Indian tradition). One can become the lord of each of the five group of shaktis i.e. iccha (will), kriya (action), jnana (knowledge), chitta (consciousness) and ananda (bliss). There is always a rhythmic oscillation in the existence due to the succession (krama). Unmesha and nimesha are the play of evolution (vikasa) and concealment (sankocha). One, who understands spanda-principle, realizes the Supreme Reality, the source of all powers of creation and dissolution of the world.

'*Aham*' and '*maha*' exist simultaneously. *Aham* is the perception of phenomenal universe, the first awareness. Its inverse is '*maha*', the principle of re-absorption or the dissolution. The *Spanda Shastras* present a view of existence where consciousness is primary and the objective universe is mere manifestation, a condensation of consciousness. The pulsation and rhythm is at the root of the existence. The words correspond to the world. Since the whole universe is always dynamic and in ceaseless motion, the sound-principle gets greater attention. Each motion produces sound, audible or inaudible for us. The sound-principle manifests in a hierarchical universe from subtle to gross and constitutes the world. The *paravak* is represented within human body in the *sushumna nadi* (central channel) as the Mother Kundalini and by comprehending *Matrikachakra*, the cycles of phonemes and their manifestation in the universe and aspirant can move from gross mantra to the source, *paravak*. *Paravak* is the succession less (*akramic*) soundless sound where words and meanings exist as an undifferentiated unity. Realization of that state fills the yogi with eternal delight. The yogi realizes that the world is not an illusion (*maya*), but real and manifestation of the spanda-principle. The world is a creative play of words. There is no extra-textual reality. The Highest Reality is dynamic, creative, free (*svachhanda*) and the cause of primordial vibration. Through mastery over sound (*mantra*), the highest principle can be realized and one can attain the creative and blissful *svachhanda* power of *Param Shiva*.

The *Spanda Shastras* are unique texts that combine the best principles of grammar, linguistics, subtle energies, subjective experiences, human anatomy, physiology, psychology, philosophy and traditions. The Spanda doctrine situates the individual in the cosmic hierarchy and delineates the way to realize the Supreme Consciousness. Retrieving the genealogy of certain elements of the *Spanda* doctrine is necessary to appreciate this jouissance (*rasa*) of multiple Indian and Asian traditions which were colliding, fusing and parting during this landmark period.

Rajovada of Vedas and Spanda

The *Nasadiya Sutra* of the *Rig Veda* describes the *Vedic* doctrine of cosmogony which contains the seeds of many of the ideas of the *Spanda* doctrine. '*Sat*' is the physical existence while '*asat*' is the *Prana*. The *sat* is born from the *asat* (Rig Veda. 10.72.2-3). *Asat* and *sat* have their existence in the Absolute Brahman called *Parama Vyoma* (RV 10.5.7). *Asat* and *sat* interact in mutual conjunction as Bull-Cow (Father and Mother Principles of Creativity). *Asat* is the feminine principle, *Aditi*. *Sat* is the male-principle. *Vak* (speech) is an attribute of *vyoma*. *Param Vyoma* is the *akshara* (alphabet), imperishable Absolute. One can notice the parallel thought in the *Spanda* principle where *Param Shiva* is the Absolute Consciousness. The dynamic vibration principle is the feminine Shakti and the existence principle is masculine Shiva. In the *matrikachakra* system, the two principles conjoin. This is the source of emergent creativity in the Universe.

The Vedas conceived '*rajas*' as the primordial movement of existence that is the source of creativity. It is visible to human beings in the form of the dust particle (*rajamsha*) which is always in vibratory motion and clearly visible in the light rays. *Rajas* is responsible for rhythmic movement in the Universe. When opposite poles of rajas (light/darkness; day/light) are created; an oscillatory movement ensues between the two poles. The *Pranapana Sutra* (Rig Veda, Sutra 6, 44-64,) mentions the twin forces of rajas as *prana* and *apana* (expansion and contraction), *vriddhi* and *hrasa* (growth and decay), *udaya* and *pralaya* (manifestation and dissolution), *udgrabha* and *nigrabha* (ascent and descent) of a chakra. The cosmic rhythm of *rajas* is manifested as in-breath and out-breath like the rays emitted from a pulsating centre. This underlying rhythm of life and cosmos is termed *udgitha* (*Udgitha Sutra,* Sutra 7, 65-75) which is a cyclic oscillatory movement (*praartate chakramidam sadaiva*). At every level of the universe, pranic vibration unfolds through this bifurcation and rhythmic motion in the universe. Chhandas, the rhythm, is omnipresent. The *unmesha* and *nimesha* (opening and closing of the eye-lids), *uchchavasa* and *nishsvasa* (in-breath/out-breath) in the two nostrils testify to the rhythmic structure of the universe.

It is apparent that the ideas of primordial a-temporal vibration, rhythm of *Spanda Shastras* have their earlier roots in the *rajovada* doctrine in the *Rig Veda.*

The *Shatpatha Brahman* proposes the doctrine of the five eggs, *panch-anda vidya.* Whenever there is a creative manifestation, there exists the *anda*-principle (egg-principle). The Five Eggs in the Vedic texts are named—*retanda, mukhyanda, yasanda, poshanda* and *praranda.* Prithvi corresponds to *mukhyanda* (material manifestation). Surya corresponds to *yasanda.* Out of the surya principle, *vijnana* (Higher) is created. Chandra corresponds to *retanda. Vayu* corresponds to *poshanda.* It is *vayu* that links earlier three, viz. earth, sun and lunar spheres. Higher than *vijnana* (surya) is '*ananda*' which is eternal and the ultimate end of all creation.

The Kashmir Shaivites modified the egg-principle of the *Vedas* to incorporate it in their own doctrine. Abhinavagupta discussed the *andachatushtaya,* four *andas,* in the cosmic scheme of evolution, viz. *shaktyanda, mayanda, prakrtyanda* and *prthvyanda. Shaktyanda* holds the other three in womb and the basis of all. Incorporation of four-egg principle in the doctrine might have been done as a correspondence to the *chatushyapad* structure (3+1) that recurs in each aspect and hierarchy of cosmic evolution in Kashmir Shaivism.

The *Spanda* doctrine itself seems to be an improvement over Vedic cosmogony. *Spanda* is higher than even *ananda. Spanda* contains the seeds of cosmic manifestation and holds all other eggs in its womb.

Gaudapada, Shankaracarya and Spanda doctrine

Natalia Isayeva has done an extremely interesting study on

influence of *Gaudapada* and *Bhartrihari* on Kashmir Shaivism in her book *From Early Vedanta to Kashmir Shaivism* (1995) and concluded that Gaudapada, the grand teacher of Shankaracarya should be regarded as "predecessor of certain schools of non-dualistic Kashmir Shaivism" (Isayeva, p. 2). Gaudapada upheld the creative and dynamic nature of the Reality that leads to the emergence of a structured universe. He even seems to be the link who adopted Buddhist ideas in the Vedanta and developed the doctrine of *'ajativada'* (no-origination). Gaudapada unified dynamic spanda doctrine found in the Vedas with Vijnana doctrine of Buddhism in his commentary on *Mandukya Upanishad*, the *Mandukya Karika*. It is plausible that many of the Buddhist ideas like apoha (discrimination), primacy of consciousness and shunyavada crept into the non-dual schools of Kashmir Shaivism through Gaudapada who had a substantial influence over Shankara's *Advaita* philosophy.

It is interesting to note that the terms 'spanda' recurs throughout in the *Mandukyakarika*. 48th, 49th, 51st and 72nd verse of IV Chapter (*Alatasanti-Prakerana*) discuss the *spanda* principle. Gaudapada describes the appearance of phenomena when *vijnana* (consciousness) is in *spanda*. The 72nd verse sums up the spanda-principle. The duality of subject and object is mere creation of spanda-principle in consciousness.

Gaudapada discussed elaborately on nature of consciousness in the first chapter, *Agama-Prakarana* and reiterates the four-pada principle in describing various avastha of consciousness that leads to ultimate liberation. The first three states are wakefulness, dreaming, and deep sleep while the fourth is unnamed, without attribute, mere number four, turiya. This fourth state is the state of *advaita*, the non-duality. It is symbolized by a dot or bindu, in the phonetic system. Gaudapada put Om as having four-fold structure (*chatushya-pada*) signifying Brahman. Since Shankaracarya (788-820 AD) visited Kashmir, and is credited with rolling back Buddhism in India by appropriating Buddhist categories in *Vedanta*, his influence over sprouting of non-Dual school of Shaivism in Kashmir is likely to be significant. Most of the writers try to show difference between

Shankara's *Vedanta* and non-Dual Kashmir Shaivism by pitting the highest principle, Brahman as inactive in *Advaita Vedanta* while *anuttara* as dynamic, *svatantra*, self-aware and creative. This is a misconception created by western commentators. We have seen how the root of dynamic and creative first principle can be traced as far as in the *Rajovada* doctrine of Vedas. Even the term '*spanda*' was liberally used by the founder of *Advaita Vedanta*, Gaudapada in his *Mandukya-karikas*.

Some try to drive a wedge between even Gaudapada and Shankara on the nature of Brahman. But, Shankara attributes vibration as well as light as the aspects of Brahman. The idea of *vimarsha* and *prakasha* in *Spanda* School reiterates Shankara's espousal. Verse 39 of the *Brahmasutra* mentions '*kampanat*' (vibration) as verily Brahman and verse 40 is devoted to the light aspect of Brahman (*jyotidarshanat*). Shankara has written extensive commentary on the *Brahmasutras* and it is in this very commentary that he propounds the concept of non-duality in *Vedanta* philosophy. Shankara frequently mentions that the way to liberation lies in meditating on 'Om' which *Mandukya Upanishad* states to be Brahman itself. Om is called *udgitha* in the Vedas and Brahman, the Highest non-dual Absolute is often eulogized as '*udgitha*'. *Udgitha* in the Vedas connote the underlying cosmic rhythm , the expansion and contraction, a chakra-movement.

The dynamic nature of Brahman and the ceaseless rhythmic and ordered creativity is ascribed as the nature of Brahman in the Advaita Vedanta as much as in non-dualist Kashmir Shaivism. It is not merely a coincidence that the very first verse of the Mandukya Upanishad mentions letter 'Om' as everything. Whatsoever exists in time (past, present, future) or beyond time is also verily Om. Both Gaudapada as well as Shankara wrote commentaries on this short *Upanishad*. What a better example to reveal the commonality of two traditions than the importance attached to Shri Vidya in both schools.

Science and Spanda: The Road Ahead

As discussed in the beginning of the chapter, there is a race for dominance of two paradigms. *Spanda* is a doctrine where the two conflicting paradigms can attain synthesis. The sonic nature of universe is getting unravelled at an amazing pace. There is sound in every motion at every scale. Our senses can hear only a short range of sound (between 20 Hz to 20,000 Hz). What is not audible to us is audible sound for other species. While elephant can hear more lower frequency sounds (below 20 Hz) than us, bats can hear ultra sounds. Dr. Valdimir Gavreau, a French military engineer, built a huge instrument during 1960s that emitted infrasound between 3 and 7 Hz. The whole building where the experiment was being conducted began to shake abruptly. He and his team experienced violent shaking of their body cavities and they felt ill for weeks afterward.

Infrasound can cause permanent damage to various organs of our bodies. Our organs have different resonant frequencies. Our eyes can vibrate at 16 Hz. That may cause inner visualization or seeing phantoms. The full body vibration can occur at 2 Hz. Japa of mantras does produce low frequency sounds causing physiological effect over body. Body organs can begin to tremble and shake if the resonant frequencies of organs are continually produced. A practitioner can vouchsafe efficacy of *Omkara japa* that may induce full body trembling. Words are, therefore, not merely sounds. Words and sounds affect our body and mind. The lower the vibration, lower is the frequency and greater is the intensity of effect over our physiology. One can imagine the effect of nada/paravak, which correspond to spanda, the a-temporal vibration over our body and mind. The growing field of bio-resonance will open up the vista to decipher the connections between *vak* and material world.

Scientists have found a correlation between warm touch and release of the hormone, oxytocin. Oxytocin is produced in body when a sucking toddler stimulates nipples that send signal to brain and muscles activate secreting breast milk. During labour pain, oxytocin is produced that induces rhythmic pulsation of muscles and parturition of the baby. During orgasm, the amount of oxytocin in blood is found to be higher. It can be seen that oxytocin induces rhythmic pulsation of muscles that causes thrust movement and helps in secretion. Soft kindling is responsible for production of oxytocin. Oxytocin is found to be the root hormone responsible for feeling of love and empathy.

Mantra recitation kindles the brain and may cause secretion of oxytocin. Expansion and contraction of muscles in forehead, *unmesha* and *nimesha* of eyelids during deep mantra recitation and contemplation may be caused by secretion of oxytocin. But, rhythmic pulsation of muscles always has a finale in secretion. It is possible that there may be certain internal secretions as described in yogic traditions. Secretions are the *rasa*. 'Shanta rasa' and delight is produced by prescribed methods of self-awareness which cause kindling and triggers bio-chemical cascade.

But most interesting developments are still to come. Science will soon be incorporating esoteric concept like *Kundalini* in mathematical formulations. *Kundalini* in the Spanda Shastra is the presence of *paravak* within human bodies and lies dormant like a snake with three and half-coils in the base of the spinal cord represented as mathematical triangle, again a triad. The *Shiva Sutras* exhort an aspirant to unfold the dormant *kundalini shakti* so that it reaches the highest point, *sahasrara,* in the cerebral region. The unfolding is done by either grace of God or guru and constant practice is required.

Now, a team of mathematicians has presented a two-dimensional geometry of biological time (Bailly, Longo et al., 2010). Time (*kala*) the signifier of the succession (*krama*) has always been represented in single dimension as linear time in physical process. But it is not sufficient to understand the key phenomena of biology since rhythm is ubiquitous in biology and there is no corresponding phenomena measured by physical clock that is based on frequencies along with the linear time.

By incorporating temporality associated with external as well as internal rhythm in biological beings, the team has suggested representation of biological time by a two-dimensional geometry. The rhythm in biological system leads to certain non-changing properties. Mean number of heartbeat or respiration during life time is invariant among mammals; whereas in pure physical system it should have been proportional to life-span. These rhythms are not temporal rhythm or cycle as they are self-recurring of which total number is fixed independently from temporally physical life span.

This fact correspond very closely to spanda as a-temporal vibration, as rhythm not governed by *krama* (succession), i.e. time. Surprisingly, the geometry of two dimensional biological times produces a 'second order helix'. But, there is another level of rhythmicity in existence that operates at the level of 'consciousness'. A three-dimensional time in a three-dimensional space will generate kundalini-like geometrical structure. A-temporal kundalini contains the power to govern three layers of existence-physical, biological and consciousness. Is it not possible to fuse spanda-principle with physics and mathematics using the tools at mankind's disposal?

Now that leading inter-disciplinary scientists like Stuart A Kauffman are propounding the idea of "ceaseless creativity in the natural Universe as God" (Kauffman, 2007), shouldn't we attempt to fuse the doctrine of ceaseless creativity in the Universe with the ideas of leading edge scientific thinkers of our times? *Spanda* that emanated from the concept of various schools of thought and practice in India holds a fusion of sacred and scientific knowledge in its womb!

References

1. Coedes, George (1968). *The Indianized States of Southeast Asia*, Honolulu: East-West Center Press.
2. Singh, Jaideva (2005). *Spanda-Karikas: The Divine Creative Pulsation*, Delhi: MLBD.
3. Singh, Jaideva (2000). *Śiva Sutras—The Yoga of Supreme Identity*, Delhi: Moltilal Banarsidass.
4. Isayeva, Natalia (1995). *From Early Vedanta to Kashmir Shaivism: Gaudapada, Bhartrihari and Abhinavagupta*, SUNY:Albany
5. Bailly, Francis; Giuseppe Longo and Mael Montevil(2010). *A 2-Dimensional Geometry of Biological Time*, National Centre for Scientific Research, Paris, April, 2010.
   Available online at http://www.researchgate.net/publication/49831528_A_2-dimensional_geometry_for_biological_time
6. Koffman, Stuart A (2008). *Reinventing the Sacred: A new view of Science, Reason and Religion*, New York: Basic Books
7. Dyczkowski, Mark SG (1987). *The Doctrine of Vibration: An Analysis*

of the Doctrines and Practices of Kashmir Shaivism, Albany, New York: State University of New York Press.

8. Lakshmanjoo, Swami (2003). *Kashmir Shaivism: The Secret Supreme,* 1st Books Library.
9. Mishra, Kamalakar (1999). *Kashmir Saivism: The Central Philosophy of Tantrism,* New Delhi : Sri Satguru Publications.
10. Sanderson, Alexis (2003-4). "The Saiva Religion Among the Khmers", Part I, *Bulletin de l'Ecole française d'Extrême-Orient*, 90-91 (2003-2004), pp. 349-463.
11. Sanderson, Alexis (1988). "Saivism and Tantric Tradition" in S Sutherland, L Houlden, P Clarke and F Hardy, eds; (1988). *The World's Religions*, London : Routledge and Kegan Paul, pp. 660-704. Available online at http://www.alexissanderson.com/uploads/6/2/7/6/6276908/sanderson_1988_saivism.pdf
12. Sanderson, Alexis(2009). *The Śaiva Age—The Rise and Dominance of Śaivism during the Early Medieval Period,* in Einoo, Shingo, ed., (2009). Genesis and Development of Tantrism, Tokyo: Institute of Oriental Culture, University of Tokyo Special Series, 23, pp. 41-350. Available at http://www.alexissanderson.com/uploads/6/2/7/6/6276908/sanderson_2009_the_saiva_age.pdf

Chapter 2

Shiva, Shivaratri and Hollowsophy

Shivaratri is celebrated across India and the world over with lots of enthusiasm. There are numerous stories that describe the origin of the festival. On the eve of Shivaratri, the devotees keep fast, visit Shiva temples and maintain a full night vigil. Shivaratri is the Night of Shiva. This is a dark and long night on the eve of the New Moon in the lunar month of *Magh*.

One of the legends is that this day Shiva married Parvati, the daughter of Daksha. Married women keep fast so that their husbands may attain immortality like Shiva. Unmarried girls have different objective—to marry a man who possess the virtues of Shiva. According to another legend, Shiva was born on this day. Some suggest that this was the night when Shiva realized his Shivahood. Yet another legend say that Parvati performed penances on this day to ward off any evil that might befall Shiva on this moonless night. Married women consider this day auspicious and pray for longevity of their husbands. Another legend associated with *Shivaratri* is that of *Samudra Manthan*, the churning of the Great Ocean with the *Mandar* mountain tied up with the *Vasuki* snake. The *asuras* (ogres) and the gods joined hands to churn out *amrit* (nectar of immortality).

While churning the ocean, as many things appeared including the pot of nectar along with various gems and snake spilled venom, *halahal.* Since, no one was willing to take the deadly poison, Shiva drank *halahal.* The poison turned the colour of Shiva's neck to blue. But, Shiva survived. *Shivaratri* is celebrated to commemorate the day of immortality of Shiva. Many believe that it was the night when Shiva performed *tandava* out of sheer joy and made Parvati believe that He could create, preserve and reabsorb the whole Universe.

Symbolic Offerings

Offerings made to *Shivalingam* on this day are rooted in various legends. Let us see what special offerings are made to Shiva. Flowers, incense, camphor, etc are used just as in any other worship by Hindus. Bilva leaves (bel patra), dhatura (thorn apple) fruits and *rudraksha* are three special offerings. Bilva leaves are considered manifest form of Shiva himself. Bilva leaves are found in bunch of three leaves, which is believed to represent three qualities (*sattva, rajas, tamas*), three *Nadis* (*ida, pingla, sushumna*) and which are like the three eyes of Shiva.

According to *Puranas,* Bilva is believed to be born of breast of Goddess Lakshmi herself and, hence, is special to Shiva. By touching the bilva leaves, one can be cleansed of sins of three lifetimes. *Shivapurana* mentions that those who meditate upon *Shivalinga* at the root of *Bilva* can obtain *Moksha* and become purified souls.

Dhatura is considered very dear to Shiva. Since Shiva performed *ananda tandava* (dance of joy) on *Shivaratri,* and *dhatura* is an intoxicant that with certain combination produce the effect of 'bee', the correlation seems to be built by the Shaiva followers upon this aspect. *Dhatura* finds mention in ancient Ayurvedic texts as well as Vatsyayan's *Kamasutra* as intoxicant. Various early Tibetan tantras like *Vajramahabhairava Tantra* and *Mahakala Tantra* mention the use of *dhatura* in rituals. It is because of its effect that *dhatura* is also known as *Unmatthadhatura,* since its consumption drives a man crazy (*unmattha*). In all probability, since *Shaivism* and *Buddhist*

Tantras shared common cultural matrix, *dhatura* impregnated the ritual use to placate fierce deities in both traditions.

Rudraksha is also offered to Shiva on this day. In many places, special *Shivalingam* made of *rudraksha* is worshipped. Etymologically, the word '*Rudraksha*' consist of two Sanskrit words, '*Rudra*' and '*Aksha*'. *Rudra* denotes Shiva. *Rudra* of the Vedas are considered to be proto-Shiva. *Aksha* means eyes. It also means non-dissoluble, a-ksha. Ksha (क्ष) is the dissolution of material universe and *aksha* denotes the eternal. Thus, *Rudraksha* denotes eternal Shiva. Since *rudraksha* beads appear like tear drops, the Shaivist thinkers correlated *rudraksha* with tear of Shiva. Shiva cannot cry in despair, the legend makers put up different version to explain the same. Tears of joy flew from Shiva's eyes after Shiva meditated on *Shivaratri*. Thus, *rudraksha* is considered as index of Shiva himself.

Shiva Worship in Retrospect

Though many commentators trace the origin of Shiva worship as far as Indus Valley civilization citing the *Pashupat* seal as evidence, it is unlikely. A single seal cannot be interpreted as *Pashupat*. Shiva is not the god of animals (*Pashu*), but *pashu* denotes the human-self in bondage. Such a complex trika philosophy (*shiva, jiva, pashu*) could have originated only after sophistication in different knowledge traditions. Many have tried to discover the worship of Shiva during the Vedic period by relating *Vedic Rudra* as the proto-Shiva. There has been hardly any mention about Shiva in the etymological study of the *Vedas* by *Yaska* in pre-Panini period. The first evidence of Shiva worship comes from the Gudimallam Shivalinga which is placed in a Shiva temple, locally known as Parsurameshwara Temple in a small village of the Chittoor district in Andhra Pradesh. Here the *Linga* placed in the *garbhagriha* is the earliest *Linga* discovered so far and estimated to belong to the 2nd or 1st century BC. The presence of *yaksha* and the semi-circular shrine clearly points to Buddhist influences. In Buddhism, stupas were built as indicative (linga) for the fomless Absolute. Shiva Linga appears as miniaturized domes of stupa and indicative of divine presence of the power of dissolution.

The first organized sect is that of *Pashupat Shaivism.* Then came the *Lakulish* sect. During the Gupta Period, the *Puranic* literature developed (c 320-500 AD). This is the period when the sect grew manifold. It was at this time that Nayannar saints emerged in South India with emphasis on devotion for Shiva. By the early seventh century, Shaivism developed a great religious literature with compilation of verses as *Tirumantiram* authored by the great Shaiva saint, *Tirumular.* When the Palas rose in Bengal, they supported both Shaivism as well as Buddhism. It was under their tutelage and later under the Cholas that Shaivism also moved beyond India's territorial water. It is at this juncture that tumultuous changes occurred in the northern corner of India.

Vasugupta (860-925 AD) discovered *Shiva Sutra* after guidance in dream. *Shiva Sutra* became a light house for emergence of Kashmir *Shaivism.* Vasugupta or his disciple composed *Spandakarika* as a commentary over *Shiva Sutra.* Shiva was now elevated as the cosmic principle of *spandan,* the sequential creation and dissolution, *srishti* and *samhara.* The *spandana* principle (vibration) signified Shiva. The *Shivatattva* is said to have existed in the *prana-apana* (exhalation-inhalation of breath), *unmesha-nimesha* (closing and opening of eyelids), *srishti* and *pralaya* (manifestation-dissolution). Shiva became an all-pervasive primordial vibration.

Om Namo Shivaya

Shiva sect developed detailed rituals. But the most famous *mantra* that became popular subsequently is the *Panchakshari—Om Namo Shivaya.* This is one of the most ancient mantras. But a systematic philosophy was developed as far back as 6th century. *Tirumular* composed 3,333 verses of the *Tirumantiram* which is the basis of Shaiva-Siddhanta System in South India. *Tirumular* devotes a full section on elaborately discussing the linguistic root of the *mantra* just as in great *tantra* tradition which flourished subsequently.

Tirumantiram: 2698

Fifty Letters Become Five
The letters Fifty are Vedas all;
The letters Fifty are Agamas all;
When the secret of letters Fifty is known,
The Fifty letters, Five Letters Became.

Since Indic civilization has this common belief in the world as mere grosser manifestation of word, the study of phoneme, their structure and their intonation became an important aspect of religious tradition. The whole Sanskrit alphabet consists of fifty letters: 16 vowels and 34 consonants. When the sum of all consonants as per Paninian *pratyahara* technique is done, the phoneme '*ksha*' ('क्ष') is created. There is nothing beyond the phoneme-universe which can be found in the *Vedas* or the *Agamas.* Just like *sutra* tradition in which the gist of an idea is miniaturized, the fifty letter universe can be reduced into a five-lettered universe of '*Namah Shivaya*' (नमः शिवाय). *Om* is the auspicious *sampoot,* prefixed with mantras as done in practice of *chikitsa shastra* (medicines). *Tirumular* further distributes the mantra inside human body:

Tirumantiram: 2701

How Aum and the Five Letters are Distributed in the Six Centres:

In the six Adharas (centres) within
Are distributed the Five Letters and Aum;
That comprise Aum Nama Shivaya (Na, Ma, Si, Va, Ya);
In the Muladhara is Na
In the Svadhishtana is Ma
In the Navel Centre is Si
In the Heart Centre is Va
In the Throat Centre is Ya
In the Eye-brow Centre is Aum.

Thus, the mantra *Om Nama Shivaya* is not verily Shiva, it also represents Kundalini Shakti. This mantra is also the path to salvation from the cycle of rebirth.

Tirumantiram: 2707

Shiva's Five Letter Mantra is the Final Refuge
Think of Him in your heart,
Praise Him as 'My Lord'
When Death approaches you, say:
"Lord, You alone are my Refuge;"
Then will you receive
The Grace of Lord in Letters Five seated,
The Lord who resides
In the snow-clad mountain of North (Kailash).

In the same text, the subtle linguistic discussion has been made. *Shi* denotes Shiva. *Va* is the Shakti. *Ya* is the Jiva. *Na* is the impurity, *mala* and *Ma* is the Maya (illusion). By enchanting the mantras, one can remove the impurity of sin and verily break the bondage of illusion.

Tirumantiram: 2710

Si-Va-Ya-Na-Ma Brings Union of Jiva With Shiva-Shakti
The Letters Si Va Ya Na Ma denote
Shiva, Shakti, Jiva, Mala and Maya respective;
Chant it, for the five Pasas—Mala to disappear;
When with Shiva and Shakti, Jiva unites
(That is when you say Si Va Ya)
The harassing Pasas flee away.

But what happens when one attains the supreme state through devotion of Shiva? One verily becomes Shiva by attaining the state of *Sat-Chit-ananda* or *Satchidananda* (Truth-Consciousness-Bliss). Again *Tirumantiram* desribes wonderfully the highest state of realization in the following verse:

Tirumantiram: 2825

In the Seventh Void is Shiva-Knowledge-Bliss
All voids as void

As all and nothing,
The three Voids below,
And the three Voids above,
Seeking them,
And knowing not what this Void is like,
In that Supreme Bliss
Is the Tat-Para Jnanananda;
Shiva-Knowledge-Bliss
In that He and I one become.

In Indian tradition, reality is analogous to onion peels or lotus petals. It's concentric and hierarchic. Every flow has seven ways. Since Reality is not only a sheathed reality (concentric) but also an incessant flow, there are seven layers of reality. Upon realization of the highest seventh sheath of sat-chit-ananda, the devotee finds everything is void. In fact, all other layers appear as void.

In the next verse, Tirumular narrates the state beyond the beyond—beyond the Pure State, *Turiya* is the Fourth state, but beyond it is the *turiyatita*. This *turiyatita* itself is void.

Tirumantiram: 2863

Ariya-Turiyatita Beyond; Turiyatita Beyond is Svarupa
Turiyatita is Void
That is beyond words;
When Ariya Turiyatita state still above is reached,
Jiva blossoms shimmering;
Neither folding, nor unfolding;
The Form too is altered;
How to describe it!

The ultimate State of realization is the state of Void. It is like Buddha's dependent co-arising, *pratityasamutyapada*. Nothing is independent. Nothing has *svarupa*. Everything is empty of own self-nature. *Sunyata* in Buddhism and the state of void as the state of liberation among a Shaiva devotee seems to point to similar state.

Is Shivahood the State of Void?

In recent months, I came across a marvellous work of philosophy disguised as a fiction, *Cyclonopedia* (2008) by Reza Negarestani. He has done different reading of the terrestrial history. He writes about the holes, the holey spaces underneath the surface where nematodes, vermins and rats live. He writes about the minerals and oil, pipelines and urban sewage system, tube trains and the underground Mesopotamian warriors. Reza explores the under-ground universe:

> "Holey Space, or more accurately hole complex (connoting a degenerate wholeness), speeds up and triggers a particular subversion in solid bodies such as earth. It unfolds holes as ambiguous entities—oscillating between surface and depth—within solid matrices, fundamentally corrupting the latter's consolidation and wholeness through perforations and terminal porosities. For a solid body, the vermiculation of holes undermines the coherency between the circumferential surfaces and its solidity. The process of degenerating a solid body by corrupting the coherency of its surfaces is called ungrounding. In other words, the process of ungrounding degenerates the whole into an endless hollow body—irreducible to nothingness—and damages the coherency between the surfaces and the solid body in itself." (*Negarestani*, p. 43)

He also exclaims that there is no chronology in the holey space or the hollow space. "For the Unground is a shadow outside of time and space." (*Negarestani*, p. 43)

He further develops a hollowsophy and shows how solid must include void to architectonically survive. Solid needs void "to engineer its composition; even the most despotic and survivalist solids are compositional solids, infected by the void." (*Negarestani*, p. 47)

And he puts forward a unique dynamics between void and solid, "The dynamic traits of solid can only be actuated when solid is eaten, convoluted and messed up by the void." (*Negarestani*, pp. 49-50)

These utterances catch the Shiva-principle in a clear manner. Shiva is the great destroyer and decomposer. Shiva is also the void within each phenomena. The *Shivahood* is the state of void that permeates every substance, and the Void is also the swallower of the universe. It is unto void that things dissipate. It is the void which causes pralaya for any existence.

The void not only permeates the surfaces as holes, but the Void is at the very core of our Existence. If one tries to look at the universe in concentric way, what is here is correlated and merely reiterate analogous structure in the other layer. Thus, it is not only a coincidence that Buddha discovered Noble eight path for the human beings in this world which is bound in an eight-planet system and where atoms have propensity to keep 8 electrons in last orbit. If one looks at the thing from scientific perspective, the large scale structure of the universe is fractal and there is self-replication of forms at different levels.

Let us see at our very universe from another perspective. For sure, the Universe does have a centre, but the centre holds nothing, else it would not be the centre. Our own galaxy, *Milky Way* has massive black hole at the centre. It is now assumed that each galactic centre may be a massive black hole. What is the black hole? It's the holey space of the Universe, it is the ultimate physical void, and it is the presence of the Shiva which dissolves matter. Human Being is void at the centre. It was this realization that Buddha posited for no-soul idea. The same thing was experienced by the spiritual luminaries who began to work out the holey connections inside body underneath grosser anatomy. The heart space is believed to be void and various rituals were created to experience the state. Similarly, the highest hole inside body was discovered at the cranial top, sahasrar that correlates with the realization of Shiva. A yogi who could learn to move in and out of the cranial hole at will becomes a Param Yogi, freed from the cycle of birth and death.

Ancient men and sages learnt from the discovery of spoked wheel, how it is the void that moves the world. There is a central hole inside nave of the spoked wheel which was known as Pavi by the Vedic people. The sages were amazed as to how the central void moved the rim, the rim moved the wheel and the wheel moved the chariot. This is how they realized that the whole movement in the universe might be propelled by a central void.

The void as the source of movement became inspiration for the modern physicists also who worked on the idea of ether till Einstein came into the picture. The void is once more into focus, since the energy of the whole universe comes out to be exactly zero. The universe, thus, if it is expanding from a minimal state must have cropped out of nothing. The dilemma is being addressed by taking recourse to the multi-verse theory, but it becomes a paradox *ad infinitum.*

If the universe emerged from the void or nothingness, it is again the void in the form of the black holes which is hollowing the universe. The void is the source of the srishti as well as the pralaya. The Eastern sages built up elaborate descriptions about the movement of energy beneath the grosser surface of human body through various holes, which have to be pierced sequentially before reaching the cranial space and piercing the highest hole at the top of the crown.

I am optimistic that in the coming decades astrophysicists and astronomers would draw a map of the universe and discover interesting pattern in the flow of matter, the porodynamics across various holes(black/white/worm). They may find nematodes in the cosmic space just as they have begun to observe blooming rose, crabs, hearts, spider, cat's eye in form of various nebula in the vast cosmos. Similarly, there is porodynamics at the quantum level which causes the phenomena of quantum tunnelling, entanglement and observable phenomena of release of radiation like gamma rays, beta rays, alpha rays, X-rays. Once the mapping of the holey cosmos gets complete, mankind would be in a better position to correlate the different layers of void's existence. It will be a leap towards understanding the nature of Shiva.

Shiva is the principle of spandan as discovered by Vasugupta. On the other hand, Shiva is also the principle of void that threatens our very Existence. To overcome the existential anxiety, mankind began to worship the generative structure. And in an endless imitation, the most advanced Shaiva sadhaks of Kashmir have learnt to propitiate Shiva with walnut (akhrot). The Shiva Lingam is elliptical since the first available record in Gudimallam. No doubt the elliptic form (egg-shape) has gained primacy in the world of moving phenomena. It may be the planet's orbit or atomic orbits, all such orbits are elliptical. Wheresoever, there is movement, there is generation of phenomena, and the manifestation, srishti.

Human generative organ too replicates similar form which became the inspiration to depict the generative power of immortal Shiva. With time, like the evolution of the symbols, the *Linga* itself became Shiva in an indexical transformation of signifier. Kashmiri Shaivites found walnut to be of two varieties, circular and elliptical. The elliptical walnut correlates well with the elliptical Lingam. Thus, Herat (Har-Ratri or Shiva Ratri) which Kashmiri pandits celebrate hinges around walnut. If walnut too is Shiva, can a more fascinating exposition of *advaita* be possible?

References

1. Tirumular (1991). *Tirumantiram*—Tamil Text with English translation by Dr B Natarajan, Mysore : Sri Ramakrishna Math.
2. Negarestani, Reza (2008). *Cyclonopedia: Complicity with Anonymous Materials*, Melbourne : Repress.
3. Farmer, Steve, John B Henderson and Michael Witzel (2002). "Neurobiology, Layered Text, and Correlative Cosmologies: A Cross-Cultural Framework for Premodern History", *Bulletin of the Museum of Far Eastern Antiquities*, 72, 2000 (2002), pp 48-90.
4. Sanderson, Alexis (1988). "Saivism and the Tantric Traditions", in S. Sutherland et al. eds., (1988). *The World's Religions*, London : Routledge and Kegan Paul.
5. Doniger, Wendy (2009). *The Hindus*. An Alternative History, New Delhi : Penguin.

Chapter 3

Discovering Shiva's Cave in Europe

Every year in the holy month of *Shravan,* the pilgrimage to the holy shrines gets into full swing. The ice *lingam* sometimes measure 16 feet. But the news of melting *lingam* during the very first fortnight of the pilgrimage has left the devotees as well as the governments in worry.

Now the State government has blamed that the heat from the presence of large crowd of pilgrims causes the melting of *lingam.* Scientific studies over longer period in ice caves of Europe have clearly ruled out any connection of variance in the size of ice shapes and the visiting crowd. What can be the reason? Can we relate the truant nature of *Amarnath Shiva lingam* post-2005 with the major Hindukush-Karakoram earthquake?

Amarnath cave is 130 feet high in the Kashmir valley near Pahalgam. It is situated at a height of 4,000 metres and 140 km away from Srinagar. The ice *lingam* is observed to grow from May to August and gradually dwindles after that. Some also point out how it waxes and wanes with the phases of the moon. Interestingly, its full appearance coincides with the month of July-August, *Shravan,* the holy month of Shiva when pilgrims carry across India water from sacred rivers to worship Shiva in their village temples. The mythology of the cave revolves around Shiva and his family. The two smaller ice formations are linked with Parvati, Shiva's wife and their son, Ganesha. The *Mahatamyas* describe how Shiva was explaining the secret of immortality to Parvati and it was overheard by a pair of pigeons, who also attained immortality. In fact, a pair of pigeons are often sighted inside the cave.

It is believed that the cave was a famous holy shrine till the time Hindu rulers were in ascendance in Kashmir. But, with the commencement of the Afghan-Turk rule, Hindu-Buddhism pilgrimage systems got disrupted. The believers kept religion within home and communities. During 15th century, the cave was accidentally discovered by a shepherd Buta Malik. Even now his descendants carry the *chhadi-mubarak*.

Figure 3.1

(Eisriesenwelt Cave in Austria)

Figure 3.2

(View of the holy Shivalinga, Amarnath)

The ice-formation in Amarnath cave is worshipped by believers to be the manifestation of Shiva in lingam form. Though this is not unique, the ice formation in caves is found across the world. The phenomena have been documented by the scientists. But everyone admits that it is rarest of the rare phenomena and it is also a very recent phenomenon if one compares the geological formation of caves with the appearance of ice formation.

Only two other places, both in Europe, have ice formation very similar to that of Amarnath. These are the Eisriesenwelt ice caves in Austria and Demänovská Cave in Slovakia. Eisriesenwelt ice caves is the biggest and the ice formation here resembles in greater degree with a lingam in comparison with even Amarnath Ice-lingam.

Figure 3.3

(Eisriesenwelt ice caves in Austria)

The Eisriesenwelt is a labyrinth of caves with a total length of over 40 km in the Salzburg area of Austria. The cave remains open till last week of October. The discovery of the cave is very akin to Amarnath caves. At the end of the nineteenth century, the caves were known to hunters only. It was only in 1879 that Anton Posselt, a natural scientist from Salzburg, went 200 metres into the caves and officially discovered 'the Eisriesenwelt'. A year later he published a detailed report of his discovery in a mountaineering magazine but it was not taken notice by his contemporaries. Alexander von Mörk, a pioneer of cave exploration in the Salzburg area, discovered Posselt's report. Fresh expeditions were made and by 1920's tourists began to throng the caves. Data from geological and scientific tests on deposits taken from the ice show that the oldest layers of ice in the Eisriesenwelt are approximately 1,000 years old. Thus, it is a very recent cave.

The cracks and crevices in the limestone appeared during the early elevation of the mountains millions of years ago. But those fissures became more developed and extended due to chemical reactions and water erosion. Limestone is water-soluble. The limestone breaks down and dissolves and hollow areas are formed underground. It is accentuated by corrosion. Carbon dioxide (CO_2) and water (H_2O) form an acidic compound known as carbonic acid (H_2CO_3). When this acid permeates the cracks in the limestone, it dissolves the limestone further to form calcium bicarbonate:

$CaCO_3+H_2O+CO_2=Ca(HCO_3)_2$ (Calcium bicarbonate)

Once this becomes cyclic, the cracks get wider and the crevices allow greater volume of water to pass through, which, in turn, causes greater erosion.

How does Ice form in the Cave?

The Amarnath and Eisriesenwelt are dynamic caves as the crevices connect lower lying entrances to higher openings, making it possible for draughts of air to circulate. Geologists equate the phenomena with the effect in a chimney. Depending upon the outside temperature, it is either warmer or cooler inside the mountain and this causes the air to circulate upwards or downwards. In winter, when the air inside the mountain is warmer than outside, cold air streams into the mountain and reduces the temperature of the lower areas of the caves to below freezing point. In summer, the ice melts and water seeps through the cracks in the rock and when it reaches the colder lower areas of the caves it freezes and turns slowly into sublime ice-formation.

For ice *lingam* to form, there must be sufficient quantity of water. It must seep through the crevices for a certain period of time. The source of water here is not rain water but the melting snow outside. This entails a period of sufficient warm temperature outside. Geologists sum up the principle in following words:

> "In winter the climate must be such that the mountains are sufficiently covered in snow, and that in summer the temperature should be high enough to melt the snow but without significant warmth in the air which streams into the caves."

Figure 3.4

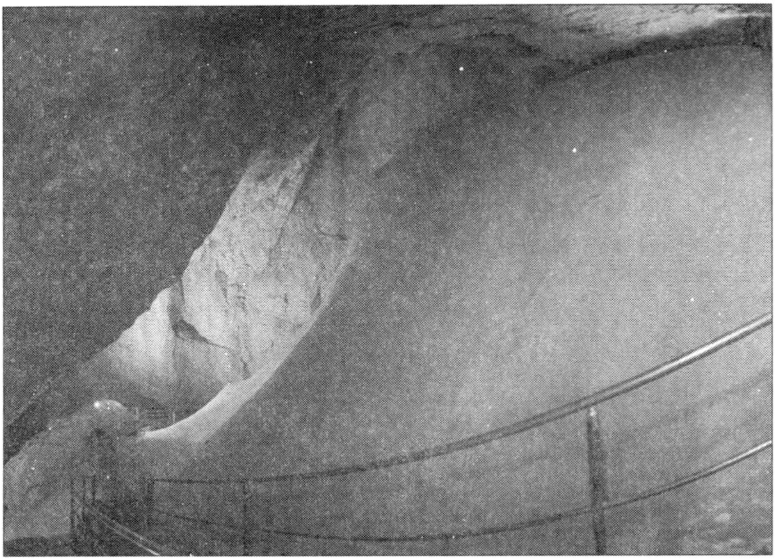

(Demänovská Cave in Slovakia)

Now, we can guess what is causing the disturbance in the formation of ice lingam in Amarnath. After the 2005 earthquake, the crevices did suffer/damage and this caused the poor formation of ice-*lingam* in 2006. To maintain the visit of pilgrims, the Amarnath Shrine Board had to create an artificial *lingam,* attracting lot of flak from both media and pilgrims. But with the corrosion, it appears that the fissures have regained the original position. This year the ice formation was timely as well as grand. But it began to melt and lose its size within 2 weeks. It was not because of the arrival of large number of pilgrims there. It was because of the outside temperature that conditions the formation of ice. It has been widely reported that the glaciers in the Karakoram range has grown in thickness and spread. The impact has been severe for the Amarnath region which has witnessed very cold conditions in recent years. If there is not enough warm temperature outside to melt the snow, the ice-formation would disappear. This is what is happening now, but the State government is blaming the poor pilgrims for ecological problems in the region.

One thing is clear that like the other two ice caves, even Amarnath ice formation is a recent phenomenon and would not be more than 500 years old. Buta Malik was led to discover it almost at the same time when it began to form during the 15th century. If it had pre-existed the period, surely the Kashmiri Shaivites like Vasugupta, Abhinavagupta, Kallata, Utpalacharya would have discovered and mentioned about the gigantic caves. Kashmir was also a famous centre for Buddhists. The Buddhists explored far-flung caves like Dunhuang, Karle, Ajanta to build magnificent monuments. It is surprising that the huge Amarnath cave escaped their attention.

Many secularist would jump at the scientific explanation to demolish the myth behind the ice formation in Amarnath. But one must ponder that the world has only two such dynamic ice-cave formations. Is it not better to appropriate the Eisriesenwelt caves in Austria for Shaivite pilgrims from India? Austrian government should promote the pilgrimage to Eisriesenwelt caves for Indians, which can boost local economy. The growing Indian middle class list Switzerland on top of their foreign itinerary. For them, Austria's ice-caves would offer an opportunity to be at home away from home. This will build a Eurasian bridge for people. Who knows Austria might become a receptacle for *Shaiva Agama* in the coming days?

RAMA

Chapter 4

Buddhist Origin of Rama?

Though a section of intelligentsia is trying hard to pit Rama as a historical figure pre-dating Indus Valley Civilization, it is surprising to find the absence of his name in the earliest Vedas or Vedic works of serious import. *Valmiki Ramayana* is a great Sanskrit classic. The fact that the entire *Ramayana* has been composed in anustabh metre is a stupendous feat of creativity. It, however, has escaped the attention of Vedic grammarians like *Yaska* in his *Nirukta*. Yaska pre-dates the great grammarian Panini. Panini devised rules of grammar in his famous *Ashtadhyayi* during 4th Century BC, and seems to be acquainted with themes of *Mahabharata*. Panini had discussed the formations of words like *Mahabharata, Vasudevaka* and *Arjunaka*. Patanjali wrote a commentary *Mahabhashya* on Panini's work during 2nd century BC. Patanjali not only discussed the romances of Vasavadatta but also refer to the killing of Kansa (Kansavadha). This postulates emergence of *Valmiki Ramayana* only after Patanjali's classic works.

Earliest References to Ramayana

It is increasingly accepted that the *Dasaratha Jataka*, a Buddhist tale is the earliest source of Rama story. This was composed during the third century BC. Weber, DC Sen and contemporary historians believe that the Ramayana has its roots in *Dasaratha Jataka* (400-300 BC). This has some inscriptional records. The earliest visual imagery of Rama story is found in the stone engravings of Bharhut (2nd century BC) depicting themes from *Dasaratha Jataka. Dasaratha Jataka* was found in Chinese sources of 2nd century AD.

Most of the historians pit *Valmiki Ramayana* to a later date (~300 BC). Some historians claim that the earliest influence of *Ramayana* can be noticed in Ashvaghosha's work (1st Century AD), a contemporary of Kushana Kings. He is famous for composing *Buddhacharita*, the biography of Buddha in Sanskrit. Many a poetic imagery and even the style and diction seems to be borrowed from *Valmiki Ramayana*. It is only during the late 5th century that the story of Rama finds mention again in literature. Kalidasa wrote *Raghuvansham* in a perfect literary style. Bhatti (6th Century AD), a poet from Gujarat, used the story of the *Ramayana* in his *Ravana-Vadha* (*Bhatti-Kavya*) to explain the workings of Sanskrit grammar. It was Bhatti's work which moved along with the merchant class to South East Asia and influenced the composition of Javanese *Ramayana*.

Rajshekhar, a 9th century philosopher-poet, famous for his *Kavya Mimamsa* composed a poem *Janaki-harana* as the Ramayana theme. During the reign of King Pravarasena of Kashmir (5th century AD), an epic *Setubandha* (*Ravan-vadha*) was composed in Prakrit to commemorate the building of a bridge across the river Vitasta (presently Jhelum).

The theme of *Ramayana* influenced Sanskrit dramas to a large extent. Bhasa, a predecessor of Kalidasa, composed *Pratima-Nataka* and *Abhisekanataka* narrating Ramayana story. Bhavabhuti, the successor of Kalidasa (8th century AD) wrote *Mahavira-Charita* and the *Uttara Rama Charita* narrating Rama story. Rajshekhara wrote the drama form of *Ramayana* in his *Bala-Ramayana* with the objective to popularize the story among children. Kamban wrote the *Ramayana* in Tamil during 12th century and elaborated the concept of *Avatar.*

It is pertinent to note that in extant form, the oldest surviving manuscript of *Valmiki Ramayana* dates back to 11th century.

Earliest Inscriptions on Rama

The earliest inscriptions depicting the Ramayana theme can be found in the Girnar inscriptions (130 AD). King Rudradaman paid his tribute to Valmiki.[1] Kapila Vatsyayan has summarized the inscriptional evidences in a brilliantly written essay, *The Ramayana theme in the Visual Art of South and Southeast Asia.*[2] She adds that other inscriptions on Girnar rocks dating back to 457 AD does depict the theme of Ramayana. Champa inscriptions from the same period also have engravings from Ramayana theme.

Vatsyayan extols how the sculpture was the richest medium through which the *Ramayana* was propagated. The earliest sculptural evidence of the Rama theme is found in the relief of Bharhut (2nd century BC) depicting scenes from *Dasaratha Jataka;* then again at Nagarjunakonda and Sanchi (1st century BC-1st century AD). But it is only during the later Gupta that detailed visual narrative appeared in the Vishnu temple in Deogarh (425 AD). In Deogarh, though Vishnu is represented as God, Rama is treated like a human being without any divine aura, claims Vatsyayan.

The visual representation became popular only during early eighth century. Pallava kings erected marvellous temples at Kanchipuram with panels depicting scenes from the *Ramayana*. The Kailash Temple in Ellora Caves (late 8th century) has huge number of illustrations from Rama story. It is to note that Ellora paintings are the high marks of Buddhist art. By the end of the first millennium, the Ramayana story moved offshore towards the Southeast Asia. At the temples at Angkor Vat, Banteay Srei, Prambanan, Panataram, the Ramayana story finds prominent depiction.

Vedas and Valmiki Ramayana

There is an excellent work on the Ramayana edited by Jaydip Singh Dodiya.[3] Dr Didhiti Biswas has shown in his chapter how the Vedic gods like Indra, Agni, Varuna, Prajapati and Visvakarma became subordinates to Vishnu. In particular, Indra whom Rishis invoke in Vedas is shown to be cursed by a Rishi in *Valmiki Ramayana*. In *Ramayana*, Indra is mentioned as the son of Kashyap and Aditi, while in Vedas, Indra's parentage is attributed to cow (grsti) (Rigveda IV Hymn 18.10, X.111.2) and Dyaus (RV 6.59.2).

There is no reference of Rama but the founder of his dynasty Iksavaku did find mention in Rigveda (X.60-4). But the term Iksavaku doesn't occur in the same meaning as it is narrated in *Valmiki Ramayana*. The word 'Sita' is found in Vedic texts and it refers to a furrow *(Rigveda IV.57.6)*. Sita in *Ramayana* carries similar meaning of her name as Janaka found her while ploughing with a hoe.[4]

In *Vedas*, there are 10 families of Rishis—Angira, Kanva, Vasishtha, Vishwamitra, Atri, Bhrigu, Kashyapa, Grtsamada, Agastya, Bharata. Though in *Ramayana*, Vasishtha and Vishwamitra find important roles, it is interesting that Valmiki himself has not traced his lineage to any of these 10 families. Valmiki is supposed to have met Rama and taught *Ramayana* to Luv and Kush, Rama's sons.

Valmiki projects himself as a contemporary of Vashishtha and Vishwamitra. But there is no mention of Valmiki as a sage in the Vedas, though 'Valmikam' is a term used to denote ant-hills. It is interesting to observe that the composer of *Ramayana,* Valmiki has the name beginning with '*Va*'. This is the only characteristics that link him to the two Vedic rishis whose name begin with '*va*', Vasishtha and Vishwamitra.

In all probability, the composer of this epic drama took many of the words and ideas from the Vedas and embellished the character 'Rama' from *Dasaratha Jatak*.

Valmiki or Ashvaghosha—Who Imitated Whom?

Ashvaghosha (1st century AD), the great Buddhist scholar and *Mahayana* preacher, wrote the biography of Buddha in classical Sanskrit unlike other Buddhist writers. His *Buddhacharita* was translated into Chinese by Kumarjiva. The famous Chinese traveller Xuanzang called Ashvaghosha as one of the four suns which illuminated the world. Yijing mentioned that *Buddhacharita* was very popular in all the five parts of India and in the countries of the South Sea (Sumatra, Java and other islands). Thus, there is no doubt about historicity of Ashvaghosha and his being the composer of *Buddhacharita* unlike that of sage Valmiki.

Ashvaghosha made a reference to the first verse of Valmiki in his *Buddhacharita.* He wrote, "The voice of Valmiki uttered its poetry which the great seer Chyavana could not compose; and that medicine which Atri never invented the wise son of Atri proclaimed after him."[5] (Verse 48, *Buddhacharita*) From the verse, it is clear that Chyavana was the father of Valmiki, since the verse 46-50 of the first chapter, Bhagvataprasooti of *Buddhacharita* pertains to what sons have achieved which fathers could not accomplish. In this context example of Bhrigu and Shukra, Angira and Brihaspati, Saraswata and his sons have been discussed. It is interesting that there is no mention in other texts about some great epic poet with the name of Chyavana in Indian literature.

The fact that Ashvaghosha was a historical figure and he made reference to the poetic ability of Valmiki in comparison with another poet, puts the record straight. Valmiki must have preceded or be his contemporary. The first inscription pertaining to Valmiki is Girnar inscriptions under King Rudradaman (130 AD).[6] Since there is no mention of Valmiki and his composition in Patanjali's *Mahabhashya* (2nd century BC), it is possible to put Valmiki between these two periods. Valmiki and Ashvaghosha were almost contemporary writers.

The impact of Valmiki's composition must be immense, since *Buddhacharita* composed in classical Sanskrit employed various poetic imageries and even style and diction of *Valmiki Ramayana.* While *Valmiki Ramayana* was composed in *anustabh* metre with 32 letters, Ashvaghosha surpassed this feat by composing *Buddhacharita* in 48-letter metre. Surprisingly, Ashvaghosha did not adopt any theme from *Valmiki Ramayana.* Though, EB Cowell, who translated *Buddhacharita* into English has rightly observed similar resemblances between the description in the fifth book of the *Valmiki Ramayan,* where Hanuman enters Ravana's palace by night, and sees his wives asleep in their various unconscious states, and in the description in the fifth book of the *Buddhacharita* where Buddha on the night of his leaving his home in quest of Enlightenment witnessed the same unconscious sight in his own palace.

Valmiki Ramayana was also known as *Ramcharita,* just like Ashvaghosha's *Buddhacharita.* Both works spread Indian culture across Asia. While *Buddhacharita* helped popularize Buddhism northwards, *Valmiki Ramayana* took Rama's story southward in later centuries. But there appears to be an intriguing link between the composer of these two great epics.

Ashvaghosha was born of a Brahmin family in Saketa (Ayodhya). He was an erudite scholar. In debates, he defeated Buddhist monks. Buddhist rank and file was disturbed by the rising popularity of Ashvaghosha. Buddhist hagiographers narrate the story of Ashvaghosha's conversion from Hinduism into Buddhism. An elder Buddhist monk Parsva decided to use him for the propagation of Buddhist dharma. Parsva challenged him in a debate with condition that the loser would become the disciple of the winner. Being an old man, Parsva was given first opportunity to start the debate. Parsva said, 'The world should be made peaceable with a long-lived King, plentiful harvest and joy throughout the land." Ashvaghosha could not negate or contradict him. He became a disciple of Parsva, but he was not convinced of Prasva's virtues. Later, when Kushana King defeated the Central Kingdom, the losing King agreed to give Ashvaghosha in lieu of 100,000 gold pieces as tributes. The ministers were not convinced. But the King was confident of the monk's virtue. The King ordered that seven horses be starved for six days and then the converted monk be invited to preach the assembly. The horses, though having had their favourite food, plavana grass placed in front of them, listened aptly to the discourse and tears came down from horses' eyes. It was how the monk from Saket gained the title Ashvaghosha, one to whom even horses could listen.

Buddhacharita is an epic similar to *Valmiki Ramayana*. Both compositions are rich in *alankara* (metaphors). Ashvaghosha was also a poet. He was a popular musician who roamed the market towns just the way Luv and Kush are depicted singing the *Ramayana* in the town of Saket, a city where Ashvaghosha was born. It is the power of poetic image in Ashvaghosha's writings which inspired Kalidasa's *Raghuvansham*. Valmiki, Ashvaghosha and Kalidasa are the three gems who composed *mahakavyas* in Sanskrit. Though historical facts of Ashvaghosha and Kalidasa are beyond doubt, the same is inconspicuous in the case of Valmiki.

I would put forward a conjecture after examining similarities in the work and the fact that it was only Ashvaghosha, a Buddhist monk, who had made the first ever reference to Valmiki that Ashvaghosha and Valmiki were same historical figure. There are many pointers in this direction:

(i) Ashvaghosha and Valmiki were dramatist poets. They wrote mahakavya almost at same time in classical Sanskrit with similar imagery, style and diction.

(ii) Ashvaghosha was a Hindu ascetic from Saket (Ayodhya), the centre of *Valmiki Ramayana*.

(iii) Ashvaghosha was aware of Valmiki's Ramayana but he paid tribute to Valmiki's poetic ability and not to Rama. There are many references to the stories about Vedic seers and themes from Mahabharata, which was composed at an earlier date, but rare reference to Ramayana theme (See, reference at Verse 9, Chapter 9 of the *Buddhacharita*).

(iv) Dasarath Jatak was a popular Buddhist tale at the time of advent of Ashvaghosha. In all probability, Ashvaghosha composed Valmiki Ramayana by using the tale of Rama from the tale of Dasarath Jatak as a counter work to Buddhist works, before his conversion. Ashvaghosha believed in the concept of bhakti and salvation and it was he who was instrumental in introduction of Mahayana Buddhism with emphasis on love, salvation and divinity of Buddha. Ashvaghosha is credited with writing hymns for Amitabh and Avalokiteshvara. It was during his time that the concept of Maitreya Buddha sneaked into Buddhism. In all likelihood, Ashvaghosha might have carried the trace of his earlier belief in Avatar and contributed the same to Mahayana Buddhism.

(v) Being a great dramatist poet, musician, philosopher and debater, it is most likely that he wrote the two mahakavyas at different times, one before conversion for eulogizing Rama and another after conversion eulogizing Buddha.

Apart from the style, language, imagery, there are many similarities in the story of Rama in *Valmiki Ramayana* and biography of Buddha. Some of those congruencies are as follow:

(a) Both, Rama and Buddha belong to Kshatriya families. Both trace lineage to solar dynasty founded by Iksavaku. Ambattha Sutta (1.15-16) of Dighnikaya mentions Buddha's descent from Iksavaku (Pali: Okkaka). One can see the story as struggle of two Kshatriya heroes against evils named Ravana/Mara.

(b) The astrological chart of both Rama and Buddha are similar with cancer as ascendant and sun exalted in Aries. While Buddha was born in Pushya nakshatra. Rama was to be crowned in the same nakshatra.

(c) Both, Rama and Buddha had to leave the throne in pursuit of Maryada/Truth.

(d) Full moon is a significant marker in unfoldment of Buddha's life. Surprisingly, Rama's another nomenclature is Ramachandra depicting his relationship with the Moon.

(e) Buddha told his disciples about his two gurus Alaara

Kaalaam and Uddaka Raamaputta. (*Maha-Saccaka Sutta*, Majjhima Nikaya, 36) In Sanskrit, Raamaputta will be written as Ramputra (son of Rama). This name might have been appropriated by Valmiki/pre-conversion Ashvaghosha to declare superiority of Orthodox Hinduism.

(f) The kusa grass has prominent significance in both Ramayana and Buddhacharita. While kusa grass is the seat of Buddha's enlightenment, kusa is the source of Rama's son. Buddha entered mahaparinirvana at Kushinagar, a city named after kusa grass.

(g) In *Valmiki Ramayana*, there is a narrative about Gautama Rishi. Indra, the Vedic god is depicted as having amorous adventure into Gautama's ashrama. Gautama Rishi had gone for a bath in the Ganges. Indra was very fascinated with Ahilya, Rishi's wife. He took the form of the Rishi and made love with Ahilya. While escaping, he was caught by the Rishi who cursed both of them. Indra was cursed that he would possess thousand bhagas (female organ) (sahastrayoni), while Ahilya was cursed to turn into stone. Later, the Rishi had pity and he turned those curses into boon. In Indra's case, the yonis became eyes (sahastrachakshu) and Ahilya would come to life and blessed after the touch of Rama. Indra has been referred as sahastrachakshu in both Valmiki Ramayana and Buddhacharita. (Chapter 2, Verse 27)

It is important to note that Siddharth Buddha was known as Gautama Buddha. The Buddhist tales mention the close relationship of Indra with Buddha. Indra appeared as the grass-cutter Sotthiya (Sanskrit-Svastika), and offered him eight handfuls of kusa grass which Siddhartha took and spread out under the Bodhi tree. (Abhiniskramana Sutra, Abhidhammapitaka: 96) while sitting with a vow to attain enlightenment. This scene of Indra offering Kusa grass is inscribed as early as 1st century AD, and preserved in Peshawar museum.[7] Again, when Buddha was hesitant to preach, it was two most important Vedic deities, Brahma and Indra who appeared and requested Buddha to go to the Deer Park

(Skt. Mrgadava), Sarnath and teach the Four Noble Truths to his five former companions.

Thus, in all likelihood, the Buddhist eulogy of Indra-Gautama relationship seems to be downsized and demeaned in the *Valmiki Ramayana* by invoking the worst scandalous relationship, in what seems to be competitive humiliation of each other's heros/legends.

(h) Though, *Valmiki Ramayana* mentions Saket (Ayodhya) as the birth place of Rama, Ayodhya doesn't find mention in later texts like *Vishnusmriti* or *Ramacharitmanas* of Tulsidas. It is not in the list of 52 places of pilgrimage in the Chapter 82 of *Vishnusmriti* as per the research of RS Sharma, an eminent historian on ancient India. It must be mentioned that Ashvaghosha was born in Ayodhya.

(i) The origin of the story of sage Valmiki itself seems to be shrouded in mystery and herein lies the interface of *Buddhacharita and Ramacharita.* It is to be pointed out that there was no mention of Valmiki in any *Upanishad* or *Puranas* or any classic work before Ashvaghosha. Hagiographers claim that Valmiki emerged as a sage after transformation from being a forest robber, Ratnakar. The story goes like this. Once he tried to rob Narada Muni and being shown the right path, he sought guidance for penance. Since Ratnakar was a robber, Narada asked him to recite 'mara' (dead). He meditated for years. Ant-hills (valmikam) grew around his body. His tapasya was successful. Now, this story echoes the story of conversion of robber Angulimal by Buddha into a nobleman.

Valmiki had Sita in his ashram where Rama's two sons, Luv and Kush were born. Valmiki taught Ramayana to both children who later went to Ayodhya and sang the verses.

Ashvaghosha does mention the name of Valmiki and his father, Chyavana at verse 48 of the *Bhagvataprasooti.* Since this verse is devoted to the birth of the *Bodhisattva,* I am drawn to speculate that Ashvaghosha might have inserted his autobiographical element, including his own lineage in the *mahakavya* as was the prevalent custom of writing colophons during that period. It is interesting to observe that Ashvaghosha never refers to the *Ramayana* in the *Buddhacharita,* even though the opening verses do mention about Indra and Lakshmi. Though Ashvaghosha has used stories about many Vedic seers like Agastya, Vasishtha, Vishwamitra, Angira, Atri, there is no mention about Valmiki's conversion or his involvement as a character in the Ramayana.

The conversion story of Valmiki is a mere emulation of Angulimal incident in Buddha's life. But more important is to trace the emergence of Rama from this oft-mentioned episode. By the time, Valmiki/Ashvaghosha composed their *mahakavyas,* Panini grammar had become the standard for literary composition. The phoneme were variously joined and manifold rules of operations were employed to create new interpretations or even vocabulary.

We know how in later centuries Vasi/Hamsa yoga emerged in breathing meditation. In South Indian tradition, by observing the breath movement accompanied by sound vashi, one can meditate on Shiva (Shiva-Vashi). Similarly, Hamsa (swan) contains the seed mantra *Soham* (I am He). The Kashmir grammarians employed it extensively to create concepts like '*maha*' from '*aham*'. The same tradition continued in the medieval Bhakti poetries when dohas were composed with metric inversion. The expansion-contraction movement of Existence is thought to be comprehended in this operation. It also denotes chakra movement, a *parikrama*, a *kora*.

One can see the word 'Rama' as inversion of 'mara' (dead). If mara is death, then its inversion, Rama is life. Robber Ratnakar recited 'mara' and yet was meditating on the power of 'Rama'. This is the context of anadrome in which Indian culture is enmeshed deeply.

Let us trace the equivalence in *Buddhacharita.* Buddha was tormented by the demon '*Mara*' who created nine storms to distract Buddha from attaining enlightenment. Buddha's struggle against Mara echoes Rama's struggle against Ravana. Only by defeating Mara, Buddha could attain the Highest Truth.

One can tie up the loose ends. Mara, Ramaputra, Kusha, Indra, Angulimal have important roles in the narrative of Buddha's legend. Surprisingly, *Valmiki Ramayan* employs most of the imagery from Buddha's life in exaggerated version.

The surmises do point to the possibility of a common composer for two mahakavyas, *Valmiki Ramayana* and *Buddhacharita*. Ashvaghosha composed Ramayana before his conversion. Being a musician who performed in towns; he popularized the story of Rama and made it more attractive compared to Jatak tales and Buddha's stories. He, being a staunch critic of Buddhist sects, used scenes from Buddha's existing biography in derogatory manner. This caused consternation in Buddhist ranks. Ashvaghosha was converted to Buddhism by employing trickery. He was so popular by that time that Kushana King got him in lieu of 1,00,000 gold pieces. Ashvaghosha later used his knowledge to craft as good a mahakavya as his earlier work, *Ramacharita*. Therefore, we find that the Buddhacharita is composed in 48 syllable metre surpassing 32-syllable metre in *Valmiki Ramayana*. The common authorship might be the reason for similarities in two Sanskrit mahakavyas. For a pre-conversion *Ramacharita*, Ashvaghosha composed a post-conversion *Buddhacharita*. Some may try to postulate a father-son relationship between Valmiki and Ashvaghosha. This is not possible. In the Buddhacharita, where name Valmiki has been mentioned, the other names mentioned are Vedic seers of antiquity. It is only Valmiki and his father Chyavana who does not belong to antiquity and wherein lies the code to trace the autobiographical element of Ashvaghosha. If Valmiki's mahakavya would have been composed by any other person, the work would have been referred by other contemporary commentators. Moreover, Buddhist sources must have stated Ashvaghosha's great lineage from a great poet as he was one of the greatest luminaries in Buddhist history. It is to further note that Ashvaghosha was instrumental in convening Fourth Buddhist Council in Kashmir where the Mahayana sect finally emerged. It was in this gathering that decision to translate Buddhist texts from Prakrit into Sanskrit was taken under the influence of Ashvaghosha, the greatest Sanskrit composer of his times. Ashvaghosha wrote devotional hymns for Mahayana divinities and this shows the devotional side of the Buddhist monk, just like Valmiki of Valmiki Ramayana.

Another parallel must be seen. Valmiki Ramayana ends with the scene of Rama's two sons Luv and Kush interrupting Ashvamedha sacrifice organized by Rama. The two brothers visit the city of Ayodhya where they sing the Valmiki Ramayan. One may relate the story of Ashvamedha sacrifice by seeing the common nomenclature with Ashvaghosha. The fact that Ashvaghosha sang in the town of Ayodhya before his conversion might be the source of inspiration for this scene for the composer of Valmiki Ramayan. The long list of similarities and historical coincidences add twist to this intriguing aspect of Indian civilization.

References

1. Epigraphia Indica, Volume 8, p 42.
2. Vatsyayan, Kapila, "The Ramayana Theme in the Visual Art of South and Southeast Asia" in Mandakranta Bose (ed), *Ramayana Revisited*, New Delhi: OUP, 2004.
3. Dodiya, Jaydip Singh, ed., (2001). *Critical Perspectives on the Ramayana*, New Delhi: Sarup Sons.
4. Biswas, Dr Didhiti, "A Few Reflection of the Vedas as Observed in the Ramayana", in Jaydip Singh Dodiya ed., *Critical Perspectives on the Ramayana, 2001.*
5. Ashvaghosha (1894), *Buddhacharita*, ed. and translated by Edward B. Cowell, Book I, Verse 48, Oxford: Clarendon Press.
6. Vatsyayan, Kapila in *Ramayana Revisited*, Mandakranta Bose, ed., p. 336.
7. Samuel, Geoffrey (2009). *The Origin of Yoga and Tantra*, Cambridge University Press, p 105.

Chapter 5

Rama as Avatar and the Millennium Shift!

Number one thousand has extraordinary significance in Indian culture. It is the most powerful number in India's worldly affairs. Valmiki writes in *Ramayana* that he did penances for a sahasrar year (1,000 years). Buddha narrates one of the 32 marks of a great man as to possess a wheel with 1,000 spokes on one's feet. Sheshnag who holds the Universe in balance in Vishnu mythology, has 1,000 hoods. The highest esoteric chakra, Sahastrar has 1,000 petals of lotus. In *Valmiki Ramayana*, Gautama Rishi cursed Indra with 1,000 yonis for having seduced his wife. Mara raised 1,000 arms to frighten Siddhartha. Thus, this number was thought to be the maximum for even worst side of the life.

When Buddhism was the dominant thought in Indian history, the Buddha Nirvana calendar was in vogue for religious ceremonies, while Kushan-promoted Saka calendar (78 AD) was in use for civil administration. There were other prominent calendars like Mahavir Nirvana calendar and Vikram Samvat calendar with zero point in 57 BC. In Buddha Nirvana calendar (zero point is 544 BC), the advent of millennium (sahasrar years) occurs in the year 456 AD.

Since such an event of highest magnitude occurred for the first time in Indian civilization (there is little chance of existence of earlier calendar which requires a refinement of civilization and knowledge of astronomical phenomena), it would have caused lot of excitement and fear among the laity as well as the rulers. The question would have emerged whether the Age of Buddha was paving the way for another new Age? The calendrical time does introduce the simultaneity of experience, in particular when the society is ritual-based and rituals are calendar-based. Such circumstance is ripe for strong socio-political movement. Benedict Anderson pits the emergence of 'nationalism' and the 'imagined communities' merely on these two factors-simultaneity of experience due to emergence of newspapers after spread of printing technology and enumeration. Interestingly, Indian society was poised for a great change at this first millennium moment due to these two factors—high degree of enumeration that encompassed ritual universe and the simultaneity of experience due to the prevalent usage of calendars based on astronomical events.

I am certain that the emergence of *Puranas* at this juncture of time was a kind of millenarian movement across Indian geography. *Shaiva* and *Vaishnava bhakti* movements arose first and the idea of *Avatar* and salvation spread like wildfire. This calendrical moment might be the source of inspiration for the revival of sagging Hinduism during Gupta period. Re-emergence of Hindu sects and multiplication of divine figures as the source of salvation in the coming new age was the characteristics of this period.

It is not a pure coincidence that Kalidasa composed *Raghuvansham* at this juncture reviving the theme of *Ramayana*. *Raghuvansham* is inspired by two *mahakavyas*, Ashvaghosha's *Buddhacharita* and Valmiki's *Ramayana*. There is a possibility that *Valmiki Ramayana* which was almost unknown by this time was discovered or Kalidasa came to the knowledge from the continuing oral tradition among a small group of Hindu scholars based in around Kannauj/Saket. The legendary Rama of the *mahakavya* was still a human and had not obtained the divine status in the *Deogarh* inscriptions of the same period. Without Kalidasa, *Valmiki Ramayana* might have been lost forever. It took another millennium for Rama to be clothed in divine aura when the next millennial moment came and the *Bhakti* saint Ramananda emerged.

The end of the millennium led astronomers to rework calculations. Aryabhata put 499 AD (421st years of the Saka calendar) as the date of zero *ayanamsha.* This became the reference point for preparation of subsequent *panchangs* which were necessary for any ritual. Thus, 499 AD became the zero point for new astronomical as well as astrological calculations. This enhanced the sense of the coming of new age among the laity. The end of first millennium and reconstitution of zero *ayanamsha* coincide too closely and there is a possibility of former's influence over the latter event. It is pertinent to mention that Aryabhata was a teacher in famous Nalanda University, where the best of Buddhist works were composed and compiled attracting scholars from far and wide. The first millennium would have ignited debates in the Nalanda premises and Aryabhata, being a genius mathematician reworked the *nakshatrachakra* and fixed the zero date of cyclic motion of nakshatra orbits in the year 499 AD as per the requirements of his times. In later centuries, group of Buddhist believers overcame this crisis by claiming Padmasambhava (8th century) as the Second Buddha, but this school remained limited to the northern high altitudes.

The fascination with calendars has continued even to our times. Remember the buzz around the new millennium in the year 1999-2000. Similarly, Akbar was perplexed on the eve of completion of the first millennium in the Muslim Hijri calendar (1591 AD was the millennial year in Hijri calendar). Akbar made an attempt to create a new calendar. Finally, Akbar did propose a synthetic calendar, Tarikh-Ilahi in 1584 AD. In my view, Akbar's attempt of establishing a new calendar and a new synthetic religion, Din-i-Ilahi went side by side and possibly Akbar might be eyeing himself in the role of new Prophet/Avatar for new Age.

It is fascinating to rework Indian history through its calendars and the impact over emergence of many beliefs and their criss-crossing trajectories.

It must be kept in mind that only at the end of the first calendrical millennium, references about *Ramayana* began to appear (Girnar 457 AD, Deogarh 425 AD) along with various *Puranas*. If Buddha's time was coming to an end, was this not an opportunity to bring back another legendary Kshatriya Iksavaku hero, Rama from another Sanskrit *mahakavya*?

Chakra, Kalachakra Tantra, Kalki and Rama

After the beginning of the new *nakshatra-chakra* in the year 499 AD, there was a marked proliferation of the concept of *chakra* in rituals. One must keep in mind the operation of Saka as well as Vikrama calendar which was slowly gaining prominence now due to the ascendance of Hindu sects. In the Vikram calendar, the first millennium occurs in 943 AD. It is the time when Rajshekhar, another great Sanskrit writer propagated the theme of *Ramayana*. He even wrote *Bala Ramayana* to popularize story of Rama among children. At this time, the story of Rama began to sail across the seas to Southeast Asia pointing to the popularity of Rama theme in the Vikram calendar.

The idea of avatar (incarnation of God) was already a norm. But the Kalki idea was being shaped. Kalki was to be the *avatar* of *Kaliyuga* who would take mankind to the next age of righteousness. *Kalki Purana* was composed during this period. In Buddhism, there was growing emphasis on Chakra rituals to stem the crisis. The highest *anuttara tantra, Kalachakra Tantra* emerged in 966 AD. In *Kalachakra Tantra,* there are 25 legendary Shambala rulers with Kalkin in their title. *Kalachakra Tantra* mentions about the end of Age and the emergence of a Chakravartin King Kalki, who would spread righteousness.

It is interesting to relate these ideas with the coinciding historical events. At the same time, Mahmud of Ghazani began his foray into India. Peshawar was captured in 990 AD. From 1000-1025 AD, he looted the rich Hindu temples including one at Somnath. This was repeated by his successors on Buddhist monasteries until Buddhism was uprooted from its soil with the collapse of institutions. This might have made the idea of end of time-cycle very real. The avatar had to appear to save the Hindus. Buddhists were facing a common enemy. The two competing thought streams learnt to engage with each other and made heavy compromises. Kaliyuga idea that seized the best minds from Kalhana in north to Kamban in south had paved the way for this compromise.

In my opinion, the idea of Kaliyuga and Kalki necessitated the reworking of astronomical calculations. Four-part structure is ubiquitous in the Indian thought process. Thus, the idea of four *yuga* was worked out. If Kalki was to be the avatar for the *Kaliyuga,* there must have been avataras for each preceding age. Thus, a Rama and a Krishna for *Treta* and *Dwapar* yuga fitted in the pattern. This is to point out that the idea of yugas is a medieval development between the end of the first millennium in Buddha Nirvana calendar and Vikrama Samvat calendar.

The four-part structure of *yugas* has inherent fractional relationship. Thus, span of *Kaliyuga* is calculated to be 4,32,000 years, the *Satyayuga* is four times longer. Interestingly, the number of years in the *Kaliyuga* is same as the verses in the Vedas as per the *Shatpatha Brahman.* One can see the connection between the breath cycle of 21,600 per day and the Kaliyuga years. One can also see the similarities in multiplication of 27 nakshatras each with four padas and multiplied with a *sahasrar* year and the years of *Kaliyuga.* Thus, this calculation of *Yugas* was a highly sophisticated mathematical exercise that had to reiterate various prevalent concepts. If one can notice that the concept of zero itself was a late development during 6th century and without zero, such astronomical calculations were not possible, one can vouchsafe for the period when the *Yuga* idea took root in Indian civilization.

It must be borne in mind that the timings of yugas are mere mathematical calculations to be fitted in a particular pattern of thought. Therefore, when proponents of historical Ram use the astronomical figures as evidence, it is misguided historicization.

Hindu-Buddhist Compromises: Agni Purana and Ellora

With the new fervour, Hinduism began to spread during the fifth century. But it was a new form of theistic Hinduism far away from the fire-sacrifice based Vedic Hinduism. New form of Hinduism was propelled by massive literary activity. There was a plethora of composers of *Puranas* as devotional scriptures for multitude of Gods. Similarly, there was a spurt in making sculptures, inscriptions, paintings, drama, and dance forms. The accusation and counter-accusation began to wane. There was emergence of new fusion led by the Siddhas.

Esoteric sects emerged under both stream with common idioms and rituals. Kashmir Shaivism, Kapalika, Vajrayana Buddhism and Vaishnavism began to mingle. The major highlight of this phase of synthesis is the *Advaita Vedanta* propagated by Shankaracharya. Shankara appropriated *madhyamaka* philosophy of Buddhism, substituted '*Maya*' for *sunyata* and revived Hinduism by moulding it on the pattern of *Buddhism sangha*. Hinduism began to develop pan-Indian institutionalization. It is interesting to observe that majority of the new institutions cropped in hilly terrains unlike Buddhist institutions which were established within the centres of commerce. This helped Hindu institutions to survive the initial onslaught by the religiously-inspired western invaders, while every Buddhist institution in the mainland was obliterated. Only the Buddhist centres of the Himalayas survived, but their networks within commercial cities were completely dismantled causing disappearance of Buddhism from the mainland.

The fusion process of the two streams was inevitable in the new circumstances. Apart from the millennium moment/crisis, the impetus might have come from the news of advent of new religion in the West Asia, *Islam* which had begun to knock at India's doors as early as eighth century. Now Buddha-Rama debate was being buried. Mutual animosities seem to have been resolved by 8th-9th century when *Agni Purana* was composed. *Agni Purana* declared Buddha himself as the incarnation of Vishnu. This was an abrupt shift in contrast with depiction of Rama in *Dasaratha Jataka* where Rama and Sita were represented as brother and sister having incestuous relationship or in *Valmiki Ramayana*, where Indra seduced Gautama's wife in broad daylight. The competition to appropriate each other's belief and to devalue was finally over. This compromise was inscribed during this period.

The famous Kailash temple in Ellora caves was built by the Buddhists with detailed narrative of *Ramayana*. Ashvaghosha was forgotten and another avatar *Hayagriva* (horse-like neck) was postulated among both Hindus and Buddhists. Again, when the first millennium from Aryabhata's zero *ayanamsha* approached in 1499 AD, Ramananda emerged to propagate Rama's faith. The climax was the composition of another *mahakavya* in popular language by Tulsi Das *(Ramcharitmanas)*. Rama and Ayodhya became defining characteristic of Indian psyche. It is not only a pure coincidence that Rama movement peaked in last few decades at the juncture of another millennium from the Hindu calendar (Vikram samvat) under the banner of a party with symbol Lotus, signifying Buddha. Sahasrar-cyclicity is yet to be explored by the institutional historians.

Chapter 6

Anagrams and other Literary Devices in Ramayana

One can discover parallels in Buddha'a life and that of Rama. It is surprising to find that Buddha's companion, '*Mara*' (मार) is a term constituted as anagram of '*Rama*' (राम). It is often mentioned how *Valmiki Ramayana* was composed after Ratnakar learnt to enchant "Mara...Mara...Mara..." for eons, finally earning the merit of enchanting Rama's name. That was the power of anadrome.

One can discover various other literary instances in the Ramayana and reinterpret the *magnum opus* from a different perspective.

Ravana (रावण) and *Vanara* (वानर) constitute an anagram pair. Rama and Mara are anadromes. Lanka (लंका) and Kalam (कालं) are anadromes. Lanka is also the zero degree latitude and zero degree longitude in ancient Indian astronomy, and thereby, can be seen as transcending Time (Kala). Lanka becomes the timeless place. Thus, Lanka is nothing but the inverse of Kalam, the flow of time. It's how in the Ramayana, Lanka is described as the city of opulence, beyond the vagaries of *Kala,* Time. Ravana had also defeated Yama, the record-keeper of Time. The city is made of gold where the golden bird lives. In the *Aranyaka Kanda*, there is description of Ravana as seen by his sister Meenakshi (Surpanakha).

> Book III: *Aranya Kanda* (The Forest Trek, Chapter [Sarga] 32)Seated similar to the Sun in the firmament on a supreme golden throne, which resembles a golden Altar of Fire, and he himself resembling the blazing ritual-fire spurting out of it when that Golden-Fire-Altar is drenched with plentiful ghee, she saw such a Ravana. [3-32-5]

The city is beyond the movement of the Sun, the chariot of time as Ravana himself appears as the Sun for the opulent city of Lanka.

Now, I will try to locate the structural relationship and parallelism between Rama and Ravana legends through examination of the nomenclatures. *Rama* (राम) and *Ravana* (रावण), both are etymologically derived from same root—'*Ra*' (रा). *Ra* means to give, to bestow, to yield. Ra is the growth. Ra also signifies the Sun and Ra as a phoneme stand for the fire element. Just as fire grows, the sun bestows light, the two personalities of the *Ramayana* yield many things to mankind. Interestingly, if *Ra* stands for the Sun, *Ra-ma* (राम) comes from the *Suryavansha* (Solar Dynasty). Ravana, as discussed above, appears as the Sun and has the *jvala* (fire) principle. *Ra* and *Ma* combines to form Rama. Thereby, Rama can signify bestower of *Ma*, where Ma stands for Moksha (salvation). Rama is the eternal principle of salvation.

If one follows Panini's *pratyahara* principle, '*Ma*' stands for all the phonemes from '*ka*' to '*ma*'. It is the manifest universe, the grosser matter. With that principle in mind, one can postulate Rama as a semantic principle for the growth of grosser universe. Rama bestows prosperity, immortality; Rama bestows light. But his archetypal foe, *Ra-vana* shares the etymological half of Rama. Ravana is Rama's fractymological self. Ravana is a fractional foe of Rama.

Vana (वण) in the name, Ravana, means noise or sound. *Vana* (वण) is the village. Vanathalgrama is a village. It is from the root '*Vana*' (वण) that the terms like *Vanika, Vanijya, Vanijaka*—all related to trade and merchandise is derived. Vana, in that sense, is the commerce. *Vana* is also at the root of *Varna* (alphabet), *varnana* (description). Here, *Vana* represents the noise-principle. Though, its homophone, *Vana* (वन) is the forest and represents the serenity, peace, abdication of responsibilities; the *Vana* in Ravana stands for the commerce, activity, noise. Ravana had to enter *Vana* (forest) (वन) to bring back Rama from the world of inactivity into the world of activity, the *Vana* (वण) full of noise. Ravana, for me, signifies the merchandise principle and the noisy settlement. The Ramayana can be seen as the clash of two principles contained in homophone, *Vana*—the gift principle of the forest and the commerce/market principle of the city/settlements. But, it is finally the settlement *Vana* (वण) which wins over the forest principle and leads Rama back to the settled Kingdom.

Similarly, Rama (राम) is the anadrome of *Mara* (death) (मार). That way, Rama signifies immortality, the *amrita* (nectar). It is how Ramnama has become the vehicle of salvation for the Hindu mind. One can retrieve many more interesting literary features. *Vanara* (वानर) was friend of Rama and the anagram Ravana, his foe. Ayodhya (अयोध्या) is a palindrome. One can write it in both directions and find the same name of the city.

Ravana is also known as *Dashanana* (दशानन), the Ten-headed and Rama's father was Dasharatha (दशरथ), one who had control over ten senses. Here also, we see how etymological half replicates. Rama went into exile after his step mother Kaikeyi made a game plan to grab the Kingdom from Rama. Ravana who snatched Rama's wife Sita was born of mother Kaikesi. Ravana's grandfather was sage Pulastya and Rama sought refuge in the ashram of sage Agastya as narrated in the *Aranya Kanda*. The replication of etymological half is a persistent theme.

Now let us examine the numbers and the analogous character of personalities. It is the tale of parallelism. Rama had four brothers (fractional)—Rama, Bharata, Lakshmana, Shatrughna; as against Ravana who too had four brothers—Ravana (रावण) himself, Ahirava'na' (अहिरावण), Vibhisha'na' (विभीषण), Kumbhakara'na' (कुंभकरण). But, like Rama's one brother Bharat, who is seen as the cause for Rama's exodus from Ayodhya, Vibhisha'na' is seen as the brother responsible for Ravana's downfall. For an inactive Shatrughna, there is inactive Kumbhakara'na'. For a dynamic and angry Lakshma'na', there is complimentary demon brother, Ahirava'na'. The Ramayana appears to be structurally harmonious narrative. An interesting part is that all four brothers of Rava'*na*' share the phoneme 'na' (ण). Among the Rama's brother, only Lakshma'*na*' share the same 'na' (ण). Lakshmana is depicted as impatient, angry and hot-headed like the demon brothers of Ravana.

It will be interesting to see how Lakshmana's characterization is very similar to the opposite camp whereby the demons are always eager to destroy peace. The phonemic similarity of the last phoneme connects Lakshmana to his demon opponents.

Now, one can see other characteristics, too. The story of Ramayana is supposed to have occurred in the *Tretayuga* (Third Yuga). The King Dasharatha has three wives—Kaushalya, Kaikeyi and Sumitra. It is interesting to discover the passing over of the phoneme 'tra' (त्र) from the third wife. Only Shatrughna (शत्रुघन) born of Sumitra (सुमित्रा) has 'tra' in his name. It will be discussed in Tantra secon how tra/tri signifies the crossing over, the salvation.

Tran (त्राण), with the '*na*' (ण) as in name Rava'*na*' (रावण) signifies salvation. The usage of "na" was popular in even Buddhist term for salvation, Nirvana (निर्वाण).

Similarly, we can decode the etymology of *Rakshasa* (राक्षस) (demon). The term can be broken into ra+aksha+sa. *Ra* is fire, *aksha* is eye and *sa* signifies satisfaction. *Rakshasa* or demon is one who derives satisfaction by burning prosperity through greedy gaze. Interestingly, the characterization of *Rakshasas* in the *Ramayana* or other *Puranas* have been done in similar way. They always burn down any setting for ritual sacrifice to attain prosperity.

Most amazing has been the characterization of Mandodari and Sita. Mandodari is Ravana's wife. She is said to have a *mand+udar* (slow gestation), therefore, she gave birth to a single son, Meghnada or Indrajeet. If she would have had a normal gestation, it might have taken scores of *Ramayana* tales. Sita is the krishodari. She has a feeble or famished womb. Thus, the wives of two warriors share same problem with their wombs. Both were not born of womb, *ayonijasambhava*. Sita was discovered by the King of Mithila, Janaka while ploughing the field. The name Sita itself is derived from the word, *sita*, the furrow. Sita was born of the soil. Now, one can find similar tales about Mandodari. Most of the versions have stories that Mandodari transformed from a frog into a human.

Ranganath Ramayana gives a detailed account. Parvati makes the doll and Shiva breathes life into it. This doll is Mandodari. Thus, Mandodari also emerges from soil. But, her beauty made Parvati envious. She sought Shiva's intervention to turn Mandodari into a frog. But, when her mother Maya again sought Shiva's boon, the frog was given human form. This was Mandodari. Ravana married Mandodari.

Now, Mandodari is the Frog Princess of lore. Interestingly, the Han Chinese believe in having descended from the Frog Mother—Nuwa. Nuwa also makes doll from the mud and puts life into it that becomes human. Frog symbolizes the lives and multiplication of life in the Chinese civilization, as a frog has a strong ability to reproduce. But, in Indian tale, Frog Princess, Mandodari, is a contrast with slow capacity to reproduce. Why does two civilizations have similar tales with opposite characteristics? In 2012, Nobel Prize for Literature was won by Mo Yan of China, whose most popular work has been the '*Wa*' (Frogs) centred around the homophones of wa meaning differently as child, frog or the great Ancestral Mother.

'Mo Yan' himself shares other half of the term 'Ramayana'.

The literary play appears to transcend time and space, language and genre.

Let us cast a glance to examine the celebration of the Vijayadashami. On this day, the mood is boisterous. All of us eagerly await the ritual burning of effigy of Ravana. The effigy is fitted with fire cracker. What gives us joy is the simultaneous noise of crackers and the burning of the effigy. It is interesting to find that the Chinese also indulge in ritual burning of effigy during the New Year. But it is for the Kitchen God, Zhang and not the demon, Nian. 'Ravana' consist of two parts: *ra+vana*. Ra is fire and vana is noise. Thus, by burning the effigy of Ravana accompanied with sounds of fire crackers, we bring Ravana to life. Ravana is the commerce principle that renews each *Dushehra*. Therefore, for Indians, Dushehra is the best time for celebration, spending and indulging in the market-mania.

When character of Rama undertakes two devices of fire and sound to destroy Ravana, in fact, he succumbs to the principle of Ravana. It is the ultimate irony just like the depiction of Sita living under the Ashoka tree (Tree of No-sorrow), in sorrowful moods. The Ramayana is a complex epic with magnificent usage of literary symbols. Much remains to be explored. Reading Ramayana is a textual odyssey indeed!

BUDDHA

Chapter 7

A Layman's Guide to Buddha's Enlightenment

Born in the year 623 BC, Siddhartha Gautama, the Shakya Prince of Kapilvastu got disenchanted with the world of suffering and renounced the world at the age of 29. He left the city on a white horse, *Kanthaka* accompanied by the charioteer Channa. It was a night of the full Moon in the nakshatra of *Uttarasadha* (June-July). At this moment, Mara appeared and tempted him not to depart. The legends mention that Mara promised that on the seventh day from that moment, the jewel-wheel empire would appear and Gautama could rule over the four great islands and two hundred small islands. Siddhartha did not heed attention. Mara replied, "whenever you have a thought of lust, I shall know." Since then, Mara followed him, like a shadow.

When Siddhartha was to finally bid good bye to even his horse and the charioteer, a desire to have a look at the city arose in his mind. Pali legends mention that the great earth turned around so that Siddhartha did not have to look back. This site became the Kanthaka shrine. He crossed the river, gave all his ornaments to Channa and cut off his hair. Finally he parted to seek instructions from Sramana teachers to attain nirvana, cessation of all suffering.

Meeting Sramana Teacher Alara and Udaka

Siddhartha met the famous Sramana teacher Alara Kalama who lived in the city of Vesali (Vaishali) with three hundred disciples and is said to have attained seven states of *dhyana*. Alara welcomed Siddhartha and gave him practical ways to realize Truth. Alara did not cite any text as authority or that he has heard it from some other master. He told what he knew personally based on experiences. This convinced Siddhartha to follow the path. Soon, Siddhartha attained the highest state that Alara could teach. Alara honoured Siddhartha by asking him to stay at his centre and guide half of the disciples. Siddhartha was staying there but the spontaneous thought arose in his mind. This doctrine does not lead to Nirvana, the end of suffering.

Soon, he decided to leave the centre and went to meet Rama, another Shramana teacher. Legends mention that Rama had attained all eight stages of *Dhyana*. Rama was no longer alive. Siddhartha could meet Udaka Ramaputta, his son residing in Rajagriha. Upon hearing about the accomplishments of Rama, a thought arose in Siddhartha's mind, "It is not only Rama who had faith, industry, mindfulness, concentration and wisdom. I also have them." It is believed that Udaka set Siddhartha as his teacher. But Siddhartha realized that even this doctrine does not lead to cessation of suffering and he departed from Udaka's centre.

Arrival at Senanigama

Siddhartha began to wander in the Magadha in quest of the supreme path of Nirvana, the end of all suffering. Siddhartha arrived at Uruvela near Senanigrama. There was a delightful grove, a clear-flowing river, Neranjara and nearby village for seeking alms. He sat down there and firmed up his mind that this place was suitable for the striving. It was the moment when the famous three similes occurred to Siddhartha spontaneously.

The incident is reproduced below in Siddhartha's own words as preserved in Pali text, *Maha Saccaka Sutta* (Saccaka was a debater whom, on an earlier occasion, Buddha had defeated in a discussion).

Buddha addresses Aggivessana :

"Then these three similes—spontaneous, never before heard—appeared to me. Suppose there were a wet, sappy piece of timber lying in the water, and a man were to come along with an upper fire-stick, thinking, 'I'll light a fire. I'll produce heat.' Now what do you think? Would he be able to light a fire and produce heat by rubbing the upper fire-stick in the wet, sappy timber lying in the water?"

"No, Master Gotama. Why is that? Because the timber is wet and sappy. Besides, it is lying in the water. Eventually the man would reap only his share of weariness and disappointment."

"So it is with any priest or contemplative who does not live withdrawn from sensuality in body and mind, and whose desire, infatuation, urge, thirst, and fever for sensuality is not relinquished and stilled within him: Whether or not he feels painful, racking, piercing feelings due to his striving [for Awakening], he is incapable of knowledge, vision, and unexcelled self-awakening. This was the first simile—spontaneous, never before heard—that appeared to me.

"Then a second simile—spontaneous, never before heard—appeared to me. Suppose there were a wet, sappy piece of timber lying on land far from water, and a man were to come along with an upper fire-stick, thinking, 'I'll light a fire. I'll produce heat.' Now what do you think? Would he be able to light a fire and produce heat by rubbing the upper fire-stick in the wet, sappy timber lying on land far from water?"

"No, Master Gotama. Why is that? Because the timber is wet and sappy, even though it is lying on land far from water. Eventually the man would reap only his share of weariness and disappointment."

"So it is with any priest or contemplative who lives withdrawn from sensuality in body only, but whose desire, infatuation, urge, thirst, and fever for sensuality is not relinquished and stilled within him: Whether or not he feels painful, racking, piercing feelings due to his striving, he is incapable of knowledge, vision, and unexcelled self-awakening. This was the second simile—spontaneous, never before heard—that appeared to me.

"Then a third simile—spontaneous, never before heard—appeared to me. Suppose there were a dry, sapless piece of timber lying on land far from water, and a man were to come along with an upper fire-stick, thinking, 'I'll light a fire. I'll produce heat.' Now what do you think? Would he be able to light a fire and produce heat by rubbing the upper fire-stick in the dry, sapless timber lying on land?"

"Yes, Master Gotama. Why is that? Because the timber is dry and sapless. Besides it is lying on land far from water."

"So it is with any priest or contemplative who lives withdrawn from sensuality in body and mind, and whose desire, infatuation, urge, thirst, and fever for sensuality is relinquished and stilled within him: Whether or not he feels painful, racking, piercing feelings due to his striving, he is capable of knowledge, vision, and unexcelled self-awakening. This was the third simile—spontaneous, never before heard—that appeared to me." (Reproduced from Majjhima Nikaya MN 36, cited in *Bhikku Thannissaro,* 2008)

Once Siddhartha realized that the austerities are the sure way to attain the supreme state of cessation of suffering, he began to practice extreme methods to crush 'mind with the mind'. In the same text, it is referred in following ways in the words of Buddha:

"I thought: 'Suppose that I, clenching my teeth and pressing my tongue against the roof of my mouth, were to beat down, constrain, and crush my mind with my awareness.' So, clenching my teeth and pressing my tongue against the roof of my mouth, I beat down, constrained, and crushed my mind with my awareness. Just as a strong man, seizing a weaker man by the head or the throat or the shoulders, would beat him down, constrain, and crush him, in the same way I beat down, constrained, and crushed my mind with my awareness. As I did so, sweat poured from my armpits. And although tireless persistence was aroused in me, and unmuddled mindfulness established, my body was aroused and uncalm because of the painful exertion. But the painful feeling that arose in this way did not invade my mind or remain."

Siddhartha was well-versed in various breathing techniques as evident from his own outpourings. He is said to have described the effect of Yoga over body when he tried to control the breathing forcefully, in the *Maha Saccaka Sutta:*

> "I thought: 'Suppose I were to become absorbed in the trance of non-breathing.' So I stopped the in-breaths and out-breaths in my nose and mouth. As I did so, there was a loud roaring of winds coming out my ear holes, just like the loud roar of winds coming out of a smith's bellows... So I stopped the in-breaths and out-breaths in my nose and mouth and ears. **As I did so, extreme forces sliced through my head, just as if a strong man were slicing my head open with a sharp sword... Extreme pains arose in my head, just as if a strong man were tightening a turban made of tough leather straps around my head**... Extreme forces carved up my stomach cavity, just as if a butcher or his apprentice were to carve up the stomach cavity of an ox... There was an extreme burning in my body, just as if two strong men, grabbing a weaker man by the arms, were to roast and broil him over a pit of hot embers. And although tireless persistence was aroused in me, and unmuddled mindfulness established, my body was aroused and uncalm because of the painful exertion. But the painful feeling that arose in this way did not invade my mind or remain."

This narrative clearly points to an awakening of Kundalini, the base energy resting at the spine in Siddhartha's body. The description of burning in body, piercing of head, extreme pain in head are the symptoms of Kundalini awakening. Siddhartha had undergone extreme dhyana and breathing practices. The solitude and extreme vow to achieve the Highest Truth made the coiled energy to fully awaken in Siddhartha. This fact is further affirmed symbolically in the next narrative.

In spite of this strong piercing, Siddhartha realized that no wisdom arose neither the Nirvana could be attained. Siddhartha thought, "What if I strive still harder, entirely abstaining from food?" The *Maha-Saccakka Sutta* mentions following words of Buddha :

> "I thought: 'Suppose I were to take only a little food at a time, only a handful at a time of bean soup, lentil soup, vetch soup, or pea soup.' So I took only a little food at a time, only a handful at a time of bean soup, lentil soup, vetch soup, or pea soup. My body became extremely emaciated. Simply from my eating so little, my limbs became like the jointed segments of vine stems or bamboo stems... My backside became like a camel's hoof... My spine stood out like a string of beads... My ribs jutted out like the jutting rafters of an old, run-down barn... The gleam of my eyes appeared to be sunk deep in my eye sockets like the gleam of water deep in a well... My scalp shrivelled and withered like a green bitter gourd, shrivelled and withered in the heat and the wind... The skin of my belly became so stuck to my spine that when I thought of touching my belly, I grabbed hold of my spine as well; and when I thought of touching my spine, I grabbed hold of the skin of my belly as well... If I urinated or defecated, I fell over on my face right there... Simply from my eating so little, if I tried to ease my body by rubbing my limbs with my hands, the hair—rotted at its roots—fell from my body as I rubbed, simply from eating so little."

But, Siddhartha realized that in spite of the toughest hardships and the striving, he did not attain any noble vision. There was no end to quest for the Nirvana. Upon realizing the futility of austerities, he was struck with another roadmap. He remembered how as a child, when his father was working, and he was sitting in the cool shade of a rose-apple tree (jamrul) and he entered and remained in the first blissful contemplation, a rapturous joy born out of seclusion. Siddhartha realized that this might be the path to Nirvana. The child like approach, innocence, awareness and unprejudiced is the path to attain the realization.

Siddhartha felt that his persistent attempt to drive away pleasure was not the correct practice since the pleasure arising out of child-like innocence and skillful contemplation was something to be cultivated. He wanted to relish the same rapture, that moment of childhood illumination. But, he realized that such a weak body could not relish the rapturous joy. He decided to take solid food again. His five companions left him thinking that Siddhartha has lost the path.

The departure of five monks provided the right atmosphere of seclusion to Siddhartha. He could strive again with the new found method to achieve final liberation. He built up strength with proper nourishment and practiced the art of cultivating contemplative joy. He was able to achieve the one-pointed-ness of mind after enjoying the pure state of non-sensual joy.

Siddhartha's Last Meal

It was going to be the Full Moon of *Vaishakha*, the day of Enlightenment. Siddhartha had five dreams during the night before the Enlightenment, all pointing to the significance of his efforts next day. The Scriptures list the five dreams as follows:

(1) The world appeared as a great couch, and the Himalayas as the pillow. His left hand was plunged into the eastern ocean, his right in the western, and his feet in the southern. This means that he would attain supreme Enlightenment.

(2) A plant called tiriya (i.e. kusa grass) grew out from his navel, and rose and touched the sky. This means that he would discover the Noble Eightfold Path which he would proclaim to human as well as heavenly beings.

(3) White worms with black heads crept up as far as his knees and covered them. These were white robed lay followers who find lifelong refuge in the Buddha.

(4) Four birds of different colours came from the four quarters, and falling at his feet became entirely white. These are members of the four castes who, leaving the household life to join the Sangha, became the Buddha's disciples and realized the highest freedom.

(5) He was walking to and fro on a mountain of dung but was

> not smeared by it. This meant that he would receive the four basic requisites of a monk (food, robes, shelter, medicine) and enjoy them without being attached to them. (*Mahavastu* 2:136)

Sujata, a rich woman of Senanīgrama had prayer before a banyan tree asking the tree deity to give her a son as her firstborn. When she did get a son, she was elated and wanted to make an offering to Tree-God. This points to the prevalence of Yaksha worship during those times, since Yakshas were the local deities residing in trees and one often encounters the figure of Yaksha in hagiography of Buddhist saints. While Siddhartha was radiating with a charm and sitting under the tree, Sujata and her maid mistook him as the Tree-deity and offered kheer (milk-rice) in a golden bowl. Siddhartha made all the rice into 49 small balls and ate them without water.

This was his last meal before the Enlightenment and the only one for the next 49 days. This number 49 holds lot of significance in the later tantras.

After his meal, Siddhartha made an act of truth. He urged himself, "If I will today become a Buddha, let this bowl go upstream; if not, let it go downstream!" Then he put the golden bowl into the river Neranjara. It shot upstream into the middle of the river and then sank into a whirlpool. The legends mention that the bowl went into the region of Black Serpent, Kala Naag and after striking bowls of previous three Buddhas, made the sound of *'killi-killi'*. The mention of serpent king as predicting the rise of another Buddha same day has an esoteric significance since the serpent-like Kundalini energy is said to exist at the base of human beings and whose role is vital in spiritual illumination. It is interesting to observe that great Buddhist saints like Nagarjuna and Padmasambhava too have serpents in their hagiographies. The sound *'killi-killi'*— was later deployed in the Buddhist tantras to achieve siddhis of various kinds.

Siddhartha passed the day in a grove of sal trees. While he was going towards the Bodhi tree, he met a grass-cutter named Sotthiya (Skt Svastika), who offered him eight handfuls of kusa grass which

Siddhartha spread out under the Bodhi tree on the east side. He sat cross-legged in *Padmasana* and took a resolve not to leave the seat before attaining final salvation.

The epic struggle of Mara and Gautama is well known. The Buddha describes his experience of enlightenment in these words as preserved in the *Maha-Saccaka Sutta* (M 36):

When the concentrated mind was, thus, purified he directed it to knowledge of the recollection of past lives. Then arose the first true knowledge of the recollection of past lives. It was during the first watch of the night (6.00-10.00 PM).

In the middle watch (10.00 PM-2.00 AM), he developed the second true knowledge, that is, the knowledge of the arising and passing away of manifold of beings which enabled him to see the cycles of death and rebirth of other beings according to their karma.

In the third watch of the night (2.00-6.00 AM), he developed the third true knowledge, **the knowledge of the destruction of the mental cravings**. He understood the nature of things as they truly are. Siddhartha reflected in his mind what causes the approach of old age and death. He discovered the cycle *(chakra)*. Old age and death are produced only when there is birth just as headache is possible only when there is head. The birth itself is produced by karma and not from creator, nature or any self or without any cause. The existence originates due to grasping, the way one always adhere to certain rules, vows, rituals, passion, views of self and false views. The grasping is caused by the thirst *(trishna)*. The sensation causes thirst. It is the contact (touch)/*sparsha* which is the source of sensation. The cause of contact lies with the six sensory organs. The origin of sense organs lie in the name and form *(nama-rupa)*. The cause of name and form is the consciousness. Now, consciousness arises from name and form and the name and form depends upon the consciousness. Ashvaghosha has explained this with a beautiful simile in *Buddhacharita*. Just as a boat a man carries while the man propels the same boat, so name-and-form and consciousness are the causes of each other. It is a mutual causality.

Siddhartha understood how the world is produced by the causality. He realized the way to suppress the rebirths. When there is no consciousness, there will be no name and form and the causal chain of Existence. He realized that there is no-self anywhere and he became serene. **The end of craving was attained!**

At the moment of the fourth watch when the dawn came, Siddhartha reached the state of omniscience. He became enlightened. He sat and looked at the Morning Star, Venus. It was shining bright in the eastern sky. He realized that like the Morning Star, his own illumination was boundless. Many schools believe that Buddha smiled watching the Morning Star. But many other schools believe that Buddha could not have laughed when he realized that the world is tormented by suffering.

After the illumination, Buddha continued to meditate under the Bodhi tree for 49 days. He was protected from the weather by the Naga King *Muchalinda.* After inner dialogue, he decided to preach the dharma to his former five companions and set the Wheel of Dharma in motion.

Did Buddha Laugh?

While delving upon the life-history of Second Buddha, one often encounters number 64 pregnant with significance, while in the hagiography of Buddha, its number forty-nine. Sixty-four is derived from the multiplication of eight with eight while forty nine after the same operation of number seven. It is said that Mara followed Buddha for seven years, he promised Buddha the jewel-wheel empire in seven days at the time of renunciation, Buddha prepared 49 rice-balls as the last meal before enlightenment and meditated at seven points for seven days each under the Bodhi tree.

It is beyond doubt that at the time of Buddha, there was a flourishing urban civilization in the Gangetic plain. There were strong Shramana movement as a counter-tradition against the Vedic tradition. This would have been a fertile ground for literary encounters and the flourishing of the Sanskrit language which was the raft of the Vedic tradition. In Sanskrit language, there are 33 consonants that signify the manifest existence and 16 vowels the unmanifest root of Existence. We often find mention of 33 Heavens in Buddha's hagiography or even 33 teeth which Buddha is said to have possessed as the mark of a great man. This may be construed as corresponding to 33 consonants beginning from */ka/* to */ha/*. The total number of phoneme in Sanskrit language is 49 if we exclude the conjoint consonants. Thus, number 49 represents, in a way, the world of word, and the world of naam-rupa.

This brings us to the controversy of Buddha's laughter after Enlightenment. Laughter is always taken as a token of self-realization in the East. Even the Jatakas are full of funny, strange stories. The Zen school believes that Buddha indeed smiled and transmitted enlightenment through wordless smile by succession of 28 patriarchs before Bodhidharma from the Pallava Kingdom took it to China. The wordless smile burst into laughter upon transmission to Japan. Buddhism is not averse to laughter per se. In the legend of 84 mahasiddhas, one thing that is common is the rapture of laughter. Nagarjuna laughed, Virupa laughed. Nagarjuna laughs at Nagabodhi for growing a horn on his head by the power of meditation. By the early sixth century, we find that the laughter became part of even esoteric tantra. The Chakrasamvara tantra has laughter mantra,

"Ha ha he he ho ho hum hum
iti devimantrenapy ashtavidhau hasah!"

In later tantras, the scholars finally established correspondence of phonemes with human consciousness. 'Ha' became the visarga, the last consonant with which the manifest universe ends. This 'ha' is mere grosser form of the visarga vowel 'ah', which is often employed in the mantras. In laughter, this 'ha' and the 'aa' that expresses the primordial joy gets combined to create the sound of 'haha'. Buddha having realized the way to the cessation of rebirth reached the point of visarga. He experienced the emission from the cycle of existence and, thus, realized the extreme serenity. In such an extreme state of emission, the visarga 'ha' must have touched Buddha's consciousness. This laughter might be the wordless sita expressing the regenerative aspect of new Being. Therefore, the narrative of Buddha's laughter seems to be founded not merely on pure speculation.

Nirvana makes one spontaneous and cheerful, spreading the sweetness of wisdom and fragrance of presence. Buddha was not averse either to non-sensual pleasure or to raptures of joy. His enlightenment is the source of jöy for hundreds of generations.

Reference

1. Bhikku Bodhi (2005). *In the Buddha's Words: An Anthology of Discourses from the Pali Canon* (Teachings of the Buddha), July 2005.
2. Bhikku Thanissaro *(2008). Maha-Saccaka Sutta: The Longer Discourse to Saccaka, Majjhima Nikaya.* Available at www. accesstoinsight.org/tipitaka/mn/mn.036. than.html

Chapter 8

Buddha's Dharma Chakra Pravartana: Philosophy of Action

Two months after his Enlightenment, Gautama Buddha set the Wheel of Dharma in motion at *Rishipatan Mrigadaya* Park (Deer Park) in Varanasi. Again, it was a Full Moon day of the *Asadh* lunar month. Five erstwhile companions were sitting in front of Buddha. Pali sources mention that merely on hearing the First Discourse, Kondanna, one of the five monks, attained arhatship. The Four Noble Truth and the Eight Fold Path are well known. The kernel of the First Discourse that's 'Setting the Wheel of Dharma', based upon Pali sources particularly, *Samyutta Nikaya* (56.11) in *Dhammacakkapavattana Sutta*, is reproduced herein:

Dukkham ariyasaccham
(This is Noble Truth of Dukkha/suffering)
Dukkhasamudayam ariyasaccham
(This is Noble Truth of Dukkha's origin)
Dukkhanirodham ariyasaccham
(This is Noble Truth of quenching of Dukkha)
Dukkhanirodhagamini patipada ariyasaccham. Ariyo atthangiko maggo.
(This is Noble Truth of path for cessation of suffering. It is Noble

Eightfold path.)
Ime cattaro
(These constitute Four Truths)

With the propounding of the Four Noble Truth and the Eightfold Noble Path, Buddha set the Wheel of Dharma at the Rishipatana which Buddhists believe not to be stopped ever by Devas, Mar, Brahma, Brahman or loka. When the Wheel of Dharma had thus been set rolling by the Blessed One, Pali sources mention that the earth gods raised the cry: "At Benares, in the Deer Park at Risipatana, the matchless Wheel of Truth has been set rolling by the Blessed One, not to be stopped by monk or divine or god or death-angel or high divinity or anyone in the world." *(Etam bhagvata Baransiyam Isipatne Migadaye Anuttaram Dhammachakkam Pavttitam.)*

Chakra as Buddha's Index

Buddha is believed to be imbued with thirty two major signs of great man *(mahapurisa lakkhana)*. One of those signs was thousand-spoked wheel mark on soles which made Buddha's hands and feet extremely flexible. Buddha moved on wheels even without chariots. Before Buddha's statue began to be carved and sculpted from Kushana period onwards in later centuries, Buddha was represented as spoke-*Chakra* only. *Chakra* was the indexical signifier of Buddha. Verily, the Chakra was Buddha. It is one of such chakra carving which has been adapted as India's national emblem.

Chakra had 24 spokes denoting 12 months in *anuloma* (ascending order) and 12 in *pratiloma* (descending order), signifying the unstoppable movement throughout the year and throughout time. Ashoka, who emerged two centuries after Buddha's *mahaparinirvana*, installed pillars with *chakras* atop in all corners of his Empire in his zeal to propagate *Buddha dharma* after his conversion at Dhauli, Kalinga.

Interestingly, in every inscription, image of lion too was put atop the pillars. Though, Buddha set the *Dharmachakra* at Deer Park, the symbolism of lion along with chakra looks paradoxical. But if one deciphers the multiple way through which Indian culture has been chiselled, one can see the connection. Lion in Sanskrit is simha (सिंह) The anadrome is himsā (हिंसा). Himsā is violence, so simha represents non-violence (अहिंसा). Moreover, whenever there is a lion in a jungle, the order is established and there is universal peace. Thus, things which appear unconnected on surface sprout fresh meaning when one takes into account verbal permutation and combination in which Indians excelled more than people of any other culture.

Nirukta-Buddha's Guide to Unravelling Wisdom

Buddha is stated to be a keen observer and very methodical in his quest for Truth. Even his step wise step unravelling of suffering, its cause and its treatment is in the vein of medical diagnosis and treatment. It's not that Buddha was the first innovator of reasoning method. Nirukta was part of six *vedanga. Yaska's Nirukta* and *Nighantu* might have pre-existed Buddha, since Buddha often mentions about Brahmins well-versed in *Nirukta* approaching him for dialogue. *Nirukta* is the discipline of etymology. Vedic concepts were dissected and various permutations and combinations done with the root word to understand the significance of words. In recent decades, Martin Heidegger picked up the same approach with various terms in western philosophy and declared the 'end of metaphysics'. Later, his successors like Jacques Derrida picked up the thread and deconstructed the very idea of fullness of meaning and Truth. No doubt, there is voluminous literature proliferating now that tries to trace parallel between Nagarjuna and Derrida. Nagarjuna can be considered as the greatest commentator on Buddha's philosophy.

I am undertaking this task of tracing the etymological roots of Buddha's *Dharma Chakra Pravartana* at Sarnath.

Examining the Etymological Root of Dukha

In Pali literature, Buddha is often mentioned elaborating on the First Noble Truth of Dukkha in following words:

"This, bhikkhus, is the Noble Truth of Dukkha: Birth is dukkha, aging is dukkha, sickness is dukkha, death is dukkha. Presence of objects we loathed is dukkha; separation from what we love is dukkha; not getting what is wanted is dukkha. In short, the five clinging-aggregates are dukkha. (*Samyutta Nikaya*, 56.11)

Buddha thus arrived at the very root of dukkha—the five clinging aggregates. The aggregates/skandhas are physical form *[rupakhanda]*, feelings *[vedanakhanda]*, perception *[sanjnakhanda]*, mental formations *[sanskarkhanda]* and consciousness *[vijnanakhanda]*. The first aggregate is physical; next four are mind-based.

Buddha's novelty lies in inscribing the very basis of existence as *dukkha*. Buddha said in *Samyutta Nikaya*, "What ordinary folk call happiness, the enlightened ones call *dukkha*." Buddha discussed three kinds of dukkha:

(i) *Dukkha-dukkha* (pain of pain) —pain, illness, old age, death, bereavement.

(ii) *Viparinama-dukkha* (pain of alteration) —suffering caused by change.

(iii) *Sankhara dukkha* (pain of formation)—subtler form of suffering arising as a reaction to qualities of conditioned things, including the skandhas, the factors constituting the human mind.

Buddha discovered *Dukkha* in the very aspect of existence since it is subject to change. Impermanence constitutes ground for dukkha. Dukkha connotes the experience that all formations are impermanent. For, Buddha, dukkha was a ubiquitous category. But, he also taught that whatsoever arises must cease and there is a path for cessation of dukkha which he offered to his five disciples as Ashtanga Marga.

Dukha term is derived from the experience of chariot riding. Whenever one held a pleasant experience in riding chariot, the experience was termed *Sukha* and similarly the unpleasant experience was dubbed *Dukha* in Rigvedic hymns. Life itself was compared with the movement of chariot. Like chariot, life moves on. Like chariot, life carries our bodies. Life too has either of two experience—sukha or dukha. *Sukha* and *dukha* are derived from the root kha' (ख).

What is *'kha'?* (ख)

'Kha' is the void in the wheel. The concept of 'kha' has its roots in *Rig Veda* Sukta VIII.91.7 which mentions:

Khe rathasya khe anasah khe yugasya shatakrato!
apalamindra trishputvaykrinoh surya tvacham!

"In the axle hole of the chariot , in the axle hole of the cart, in the hole of the yoke, O Wise Indra, have purified Apala thrice and have given her a skin like the Sun."

Kha was the term for the hole in the axle upon which the proper motion of the cart depended. When ancient men discovered the wheel, it meant phenomenal change for mankind. But, the solid cart-wheel did not offer speed. It was the discovery of spoked-wheel used in the chariots *(rathas)* which gave mankind the speed to move that resulted into Empire formation. In the Vedic civilization, solid wheels had paved way for the spoked-wheel. Rim was known as pavi, spokes as ani, and the central hollow aperture as 'kha'. The ratha was pulled by horses and had wheels with *ara* (spokes) varying in number from 4, 6, 8 or 12.

The spoked wheel was lighter and technically superior, since the centre was void. Philosophers pondered how the void moves the wheel and the wheel moved the chariot, and on chariot, the great men and the kings, devas and the Brahma moved. Even the sages composed verses for the Sun moving on a chariot in the sky. The *Rig Veda* says, 'Ratha is Deva'(RV IX.111.3). The verses further mention that Devas move on chariot and the *asuras* (demons) stay at home. The chariot was the pinnacle of civilization.

After the discovery of the *ratha-chakra*, 'kha' spread everywhere. 'Kha' did not remain merely a central hole. It became emblematic of the unseen Force that drives the movement. It was considered to be within our human bodies, in the sky, in things. 'Kha' came to signify any hole, void or opening through which something may pass and by extension applies to fountain-head or canal or river-bed and later on the bodily apertures. Any sky or *antariksha*, the space that pervades between this-world and the other world (heaven), either internal or external was known as 'kha' in ancient Indian tradition. Even the cavity within heart is called 'kha'. This was later utilized in tantric scriptures, particularly Kashmir Shaivism. The vacant space inside which a meditator experienced is 'kha' (chidakash). Thus, Buddha deployed the imagery from the highest technology prevalent at that time to explain the principles of Existence. In similar vein, if Buddha would have treaded contemporary world, he would have appropriated concepts from the cutting-edge technology like artificial intelligence or nano-technology to illuminate his new philosophy.

Kha is also the *Majjhim pada*. It is open to speculation what Buddha intended by his concept *Majjhim pada*. Was it to be the Middle path between two extremes of *kamsukha llikanuyogo* (life of pleasure) and *attakilamathanuyogo* (life of abstinence) or he intended to communicate multiple meanings of the Middle way like the Middle Way of 'Kha'—the void, which Nagarjuna clarified centuries later in his masterly work, *Mulamadhyamakakarika*.

Moving the Circle

Similarly, the wheel of Dharma set into motion also deploys the allegory from the chariots. Vartana (वर्त्तन) is derived from the root, vritta (वृत), to turn. Circle is vritta (वृत). Vartana is the 'turning'. This was the term used in Rigveda for horse-training... ekavartana, tri-vartana, pancavartana, saptavartana, navavartana etc. Parivartana and pravartana are related. Pravartana is to set into motion. Vartan and chakra fused to signify the unstoppable ruler. Chakravartin was the great ruler whose empire could not be stopped. Buddha is declared as Chakravartin as his Dharma Chakra cannot be stopped by devas, Brahmins, loka or Mara.

Rigveda derived many of the concepts from the terminology of chariots. In the First Mandala, the verse mentions about wheel of time (*chakram ritasya*) with its twelve spokes turn round and round (*varvarti*) in sky and never ages (verse 164.11). So much so that ratha was said to be born of the Rita itself.(Ratha is ritaj, *Rigveda*, III.58.8)

India itself is known as *Āryāvarta* (आर्यावर्त), the land of the Aryas. But, the root 'ṛ' (ऋ) and the vṛt, both associated with movement also signify that the land of Bharat is the land of perennial movement, impermanence. It is only in *Āryāvarta* that the wheel of existence moves constantly bound by the law of karma and rebirth. Buddha used the allegory of spoked-wheel (*chakra*) to communicate his teaching of impermanence. Even the term '*vartana*' has been appropriated form horse-training. Imagery from chariots was consciously utilized to emphasize the fastest way to achieve the enlightenment since the chariots were the fastest and magical vehicle, during those times.

It is seen that Ariya is pre-fixed with all four Truth in Pali literature. Most of the interpretations put Ariya as 'noble' (arya). But, again something is amiss here. Ariya is not only Noble, but it also denotes various aspects derived from the root-'ṛ' (ऋ). Ariya is the movement, incessant striving as well as the Way of ancient Life. A scholar on Buddhism, has listed 100 different usage of term Ariya in Pali texts in his work.[1]

Arya is derived from root ऋ. Though, it is a vowel in Panini grammar, it became a sacred sound for ancient Indians. Rishis (ऋषि) composed ṛcha (ऋचा) compiled under the Rigveda (ऋगवेद). Ritu (ऋतु), Rina (ऋण), Riddhi (रिद्धी), Rishabha (bull) (ऋषभ) all have this vowel in their roots. And all these terms denote concept that signifies change. The root verb of 'r'. (ऋ) means to 'go', 'to move'. Since Vedic people were always on move before they came to India and started settling, they were known as Arya in the Vedas. But what made Buddha to term the truth, *'Chattari Ariyasacchani?'* Aryan as a suffix may be used either to emphasize the Noble way or the ancient Way or a Way on the Move itself. *Abhidhanappadipika,* a Pali lexicon explains Ariya to mean 'surpassing'*(adhigato)*. But, in Pali texts, the compound usage has varying meanings.

Buddha termed the path of *Nirvana* as *Ariyo atthangiko maggo* (Noble Eight Fold Path). The entire teachings are termed as *Ariyadhamma*. Buddha used the term in various discourses in the sense of virtue *(sila)*, penance *(tapas)*, wisdom *(prajna)*, freedom *(vimukti)*.

Buddha advised five disciples to avoid the two path of extremes and to follow the *Ariyapath*, the *Majjhim patipada* or the *Madhyama Marga*. The suffering is rooted in three roots—lobha, dosa, moha. To eradicate the three roots, one requires the *Aryan Ashtanga Marg*. Buddha discovered the principles of 'action', a path requiring right conduct, effort, thinking, concentration. Buddha wanted disciples to follow the principle of 'movement', a principle of 'nobi!ity'. His path was rightly designated as *Ariya* or *Arya*. He also wanted to convey that even the Truth he discovered was *ariya* that everyone has to discover his own Truth. It was not a mere coincidence that this *Ariya* path of action was propounded at Rishipatan (ऋषिपतन), both containing the root, 'ṛ' meaning 'to move'.

One can now analyze the root of *chakra* in the Dhamma chakka. *Chakka* is a Pali word for Sanskrit *Chakra*. The root of the word is *'Ka'* (क) or *'kra'* (क्र), meaning "to move." Cha (च) is repetition. *Chakka* is also used in *Chakkavala*, Buddhist world-system, said to be in continuous motion. Thus, the concept of Chakra itself contains the principle of movement and action' as propounded by Buddha.

One will be surprised to notice the imagery of movement in Buddha's Enlightenment. Go-tama became Tatha-gat at Bodh-ga-ya. He crosses over the river Ga-n-ga (गंगा) and shows the Mar-ga to the world. We see the imagery of movement in all such terms. Ga is gaman. Ga is gata, gati. Ga is used in the term gatagat (to and fro movement). It was such a highly valued concept that Nagarjuna had to undertake examination of the concept of *Gatagat* in his masterly work, *Mulamadhyamakakarika*. Buddha attained the *paragat* state and became *Tathagat*, beautifully captured in the *Prajnaparamita mantra* (Heart Sutra)

(गते गते पारगते बोधिस्वाहा:।)

Gone, gone, gone beyond, gone utterly beyond, Enlightenment hail!"

Buddha takes up the imagery of 'kha' to explain his philosophy. *Kha, gati, chakra*... all form a complex etymological matrix pointing to the ubiquity of movement. In particular *chakra*, the spoked wheel of chariot, which was the highest technology prevalent at that time, seems to have enamoured Buddha. Even *Dharmachakra* is depicted with eight spokes corresponding to Eight Noble Path. One can fathom the psychological undercurrents prevailing in Buddha's mind.

Buddha was a prince and he had been riding chariots. Even before leaving the family and kingdom in pursuit of enlightenment, he was accompanied by Channa, the famous charioteer and the horse, Kanthak. At the time of departure, there was a great turning of the earth, where Kanthak Shrine had been built. It's the '*vartana*' Buddha could communicate in the cognitive matrix that he possessed and enhanced. For him, chariot, charioteer, movement was part of everyday life. Buddha knew what difference speed of a chariot and that of solid cart wheel had; since he was a Prince. He wanted to convey that his *Dharmachakra* was the fastest vehicle to move beyond the cycle of existence. Secondly, Buddha also realized that his contemporaries were preaching a principle of *akriyavada* (inaction). He wanted to propound the philosophy of Action. The *chakra* symbolism aptly suited the situation.

Contemporaries of Buddha

Most of Buddha's contemporaries believed in *akriyavada* (non-action). It was not like Taoist wu-wei. It was pure philosophy of materialism, with no scope for ethics, morality and transcendental signifiers. The Samaññaphala Sutta in Digha Nikaya contains attitude and philosophy of Buddha's contemporary preachers.

Purana Kassappa was preaching Akriyavada based on Cārvāka's materialism. He held that neither good nor evil deeds have any effect on human life. He maintained that the soul was not affected by action/deeds either good or bad and stated that everything vanishes with death-body as well as soul. Makhali Ghosal propounded Niyativada. He was an ajivika ascetic. He viewed life as a ball of strings. Just as a ball cannot move beyond how much string it has, life comes to end after fixed rebirths. No one can do anything or undo anything. Ajit Kesakambal taught the philosophy of Ucchedavada. Even he belonged to the school of akriyavada. He taught philosophy of annihilation. For him, soul must undergo rebirth during eighty-four lakhs of cycles of Mahakalpas. No one can do anything to escape from this cycle.

Pakudha Kacchyana taught non-relatedness. He preached that there are seven elements which go to make up a being, "that do not alter, do not change, do not interfere with one another, are incapable of causing one another pleasure, pain, or both pleasure and pain. Which seven? The earth-substance, the liquid-substance, the fire-substance, the wind-substance, pleasure, pain, and the soul as the seventh *(Prathvi, Apa, Tej, Vayu, Sukha, Dukha* and the *Soul).*" Each is independent and does not affect the other. These substances are also unproductive, neither can be made nor caused to be made. Sanjaya Belaputta taught Vikshepavada. Even his school taught a kind of non-action and encouraged extreme scepticism towards transcendental things. His two disciples Sariputra and Mogallana became Buddha's chief disciples. Nigantha Nathaputta taught Chaturyamsamvarvad. He taught that the rebirth is due to bad karmas done in past lives. One must not do any bad karma in this life, thereby, one can eliminate the cause for next birth. To do so, he asked disciples to pursue a life of extreme austerity by observing *chaturyama dharma,*—(1) not to kill, (2) not to steal, (3) not to tell a lie and, (4) to avoid any mistake and hence, possibility of rebirth.[2]

Buddha believed in human propensity for incessant striving since the five aggregates itself are afflicted with *trishna* (desire). He realized that the world is impermanent and everything afflicted with momentariness since the movement is at the root of the Existence which causes suffering. To seek a path of non-action cannot help mankind as non-action is erroneous view. Buddha realized that it is only through action that the dukkha can be annihilated. The action should be right and the path, a noble one.

Chakra Magic Spreads!

Chakra symbolism caught the attention of Indian mind as this explains the cyclic phenomena of lunar months and seasons. Indian mind always believe in recursiveness. Chakra movement signifies in simplest possible way the universal phenomena of cyclicity as well as recursiveness. Buddha himself claims to be preceded by 24 buddhas (*Buddhavamsa* in Khuddaka Nikaya narrates the lives of 24 Buddhas) corresponding to 12 solar months in anuloma and then pratiloma sequence. Similarly, his elder Mahavira was believed to be the 24th Tirthankar. Buddha puts himself into the recursive cycle.

We also find how Buddha taught through recursive phrases. Most of the text and phrases get repeated and new thought is appended only at the end in each of Buddha's discourse .

Buddha while propounding his eightfold Noble Path, hit the jackpot of Universe's structure, which appears to be recursive at various layers. It's like concentric sheaths with similar properties appearing at different interval of space/time and other dimensions. The universe is like a nested recursive hierarchy. We survive in a solar system that consists of 8 planets. Atoms have propensity to acquire mere 8 electrons in valence shell that determine the chemical properties of elements. Diamond, the purest and hardest substance that has always been in the focus of the human quest, is an octahedron. The computer technology based on grouping of 8 bits (octet) have become successful in integrating machine and intelligence. It is oxygen with 8 electrons that has become the life-force for living as well as non-living things. We have music instinct based on octave scale. Drosophila (fruit fly) with 8 chromosome led to unravelling of genetic foundation of living beings. In recent years, the 8-coordinate Lie algebra has been developed by Garett Lisi which, the physicists claim, is better equipped to derive a 'Theory of Everything'.

Number 8 seems to repeat at various scale of physical as well as trans-physical universe. Is this iteration itself a by-product of fractality of universe? It was Anaxagoras, a contemporary of Buddha who proposed self-similarity proliferating at different scale. For him, matter is composed of infinite material particles and the parts contain the whole. In fact, cyclicity is nothing more than repetition of regularities.

Perhaps, the Eastern sages realized the power of repetition that induces kindling effect and new properties of mind. Mantras were created later on not as mere mumbo-jumbo but to harness these wonderful properties. Every indigenous society has a non-linear conception of time and their stories are repetition of patterns. Katha, myth, legends are epiphenomenal byproduct of mind's propensity to derive power from process of repetition. Buddha's preaching reflect this repetition. Thus, cyclicity and movement is ingrained in Buddha's philosophy. Chakra became the allegory for this conception of ancients.

One can also discover how Buddha was steeped deep into India's ancient knowledge tradition. He had explained his own Noble Path as the path treaded by ancients in later discourses. His thought had novelty but structurally resonated ancient thoughts. Indian thinking repeats the pattern of 'catuspada' (four-step), a triad of the immanent world and fourth as the transcending step. One can find the influences of this structure over origination of Gautama's Four Noble Truths.

Gautama became the Buddha, the Enlightened One, by realizing that there is suffering in the world, the root of suffering is desire, all suffering can be ended; and the way to end suffering is by practicing the Noble Eight-fold path. Now, the nature of this Enlightenment is encapsulated within a catuspada with analogous 3+1 structure, where the fourth is the Way. Similarly, I will reiterate what Buddha might have intended with his Triratna (Buddha, dharma, Sangha) that the triad is necessary , but the way is beyond the triad. Way is in transcending triad. Way is the perpetual movement .... an eternal gamana.

Khaga is the Way

On deliberations made herein, I would like to term the way which Buddha intended as, 'Khaga' (खग)—to do gamana within 'kha' or to move with a void at centre. When one removes the lobha, dosha, moha, one becomes void of trishna but this is not what he intended. With such state of vacuity at centre (Buddha did not believe in soul), the noble man must strive to realize and spread wisdom and compassion. For him, the centre of man itself is a void like the spoked wheel and the movement in the samsaric world of existence can take one to the state of Paragate. One must engage in active work with the void within to realize the state. Buddha wanted followers to become 'Khagvan'.

The Sun is also called khaga as it moves in space. Like the Sun which gives light to everyone without discriminating, Buddha wanted his followers to hanker after similar paragat state. Buddha was the annihilator of akriyavad. He is the eternal moving Sun. His teachings continue to shine along with the rays of the Sun. We should practice his teachings in the way he intended us to do. The Dharma Chakra Pravartan set up in motion by Buddha himself echoes his Philosophy of Action.

Notes

1. Gupta, K Manohar (2005). *The Aryan Path of the Buddha,* Delhi: Sandeep Prakashan.
2. Samannaphala Sutta: "The Fruits of the Contemplative Life"; available at http://www.accesstoinsight.org/tipitaka/dn/dn.02.0.than.html.

Chapter 9

Buddha Taught in Ardha-Magadhi!

There is a common belief that all Buddhist works are authentically recorded in Pali. But, Pali language originated quite later as the language of Theravada School. Sanskrit remained the initial linguistic vehicle wherein Buddhism travelled to Central Asia and China. Dharmaraksha translated the Lotus Sutra in Chinese, *Zhenf fahua jing*, in 286 AD based on a Sanskrit palm leaf manuscript. Satkari Mukherji, a leading Sanskrit scholar mentions that Sanskrit language had seven principal scripts namely Gupta Brahmi Scripts, Kharoshti, Later Gupta Brahmi, Siddhamatrika, Central Asian Brahmi with its several variations like recently discovered Tocharian, Newari and Old Bengali or Gaudi. Pali language had various scripts like Sinhalese, Burmese, Thai, Cambodian and Tuatham of Laos. Except Kharoshti which was found in north western India, all the scripts either of Sanskrit or Pali evolved out of Brahmi script. The earliest record of Brahmi script is found in the rock inscriptions of Ashoka. Most of the new studies agree in assigning the origin of these scripts to a later period, i.e. the early Mauryan era (late 4th—mid-3rd centuries BC). Lastly, it is perhaps helpful to recall that public writing started during Ashoka's reign and, therefore, neither inscriptions nor letters could have possibly been written earlier.

During Buddha's time; in all probability there was no writing system in India in which religious texts were recorded. Even in oral tradition, it is unlikely that Sanskrit and Pali were in vogue to transmit Buddha's teachings. Buddha discouraged use of Vedic Sanskrit in teaching. The Vinaya relates an incidence where two monks, Yamelu and Tekula proposed that the Buddha's teachings be transmitted in Vedic verse (*Chandaso aropetabbam*). Buddha refused and stated: "I allow you, bhikshus, to learn the Buddha word in your own dialect" *(anujanami bhikkhave sakaya niruttiyavacanain pariyapunitum).*[1] Buddha's statement on 'One's own language' has been a subject of debate among scholars. While many scholars took it to mean the 'language of Shakyamuni himself', others took it for that used by the monks in their daily lives. In the fifth century AD, Buddhaghosha, a prolific Buddhist scholar on Pali scripture promoted the view that Buddha meant 'his own language' and Pali was the language Buddha spoke. By establishing the antiquity of Pali, Buddhaghosha was able to establish the myth of transmission of authentic teachings of Buddha in Pali.

Buddha neither wrote scriptures nor books. All his teachings were given orally to his disciples. It is unlikely that any of his immediate disciples wrote any of the Buddha's direct teachings, since there is no evidence of any script predating Brahmi script found in the inscriptions of Ashoka's rock edicts for few centuries, the teachings were transmitted through reciters (bhanaka) who specialized in memorizing and reciting the long teachings. What language would have Buddha taught? Buddha conducted his major activities in the region of Kapilvastu, Sravasti, Kushinagar, Varanasi, Rajagir, Bodh Gaya and Nalanda. These were the prominent cities in Magadha and Kosala. Magadhi was the language of common usage. Ashokan inscriptions included elements of several different languages and linguists like Ji Xianglin have established that some characteristic have been taken from ancient Magadhi used in the area around the Ganges where Buddha was most active. The scholars argue that the language of Buddha was Magadhi or a language akin to it. He taught in Magadhi where speakers were Magadhi and in ardhamagadhi in other regions. Buddha and most of his disciples originated from eastern India. Ardhamagadhi was the most prominent dialect in eastern India. It has distinguishing characteristics different from Sanskrit which has been found in the Lotus Sutra texts in Kashgar manuscripts.

There was renaissance in Sanskrit under the Sarvastitvadins. Ashvaghosha further Sanskritized Buddhism. It was the Sanskrit texts which carried Buddhism to northern regions through the translation in Tocharians and other vernacular language like Gandhari. Pali texts moved southwards and were translated into various vernaculars like Thai, Khmer, Sinhalese and Burmese. Many new scripts were created to transmit Buddha's teachings in vernacular. During 7th century AD, Thumi Sambhota and his team came to Northern India from Tibet to develop their own scripts out of Brahmi script with the help of Kashmiri pundits. It is how Bhoti/Tibetan script originated that helped to preserve the authentic Sanskrit texts in which most of the compositions were being done after the emergence of monastic universities like Nalanda, Vikramshila and Pushpagiri during 4-13th century AD through rigorous translation.

The earliest Lotus Sutra found in the Central Asian manuscripts show that the earliest teachings were in Magadhi as the sentences ended in 'ani', unlike Sanskrit, where the sentence ends in 'ha'. Imagine what Buddha would have actually stated to his five disciples the Four Noble Truth in Magadhi form and pushing the Wheel of Dharma 2,600 years ago. The Four Noble Truth in English rendition is as follows:

1. Suffering does exist.
2. Suffering arises from attachment to desires.
3. Suffering ceases when attachment to desire ceases
4. Freedom from suffering is possible by practicing the eightfold path.

In Magadhi, the discourse would have been as follows:

Jana ha na:

1. *Saunjhe jaga mein dukhe bani*
2. *dukh ke karan dher iccha bate*

3. *dukh ke nivaran la rah hau*
4. *okra khatir jey rah apnaval ja sakela; okar athon hissa hum tohni ke batavat bani.*

While celebrating 2,600th anniversary of his first turning of wheel of dharma, speaking in Buddha's tongue may invite ridicule by the anglicized followers of Buddha.

Note

1. Tan, Piya, trns., (2004). *Vinayapitaka, Cullavagga*, Volume 5.

Chapter 10

Sugarcane and Buddhahood!

The Iksavaku dynasty is seen all across Indian history. There is clear reference to the Iksavaku family in the Vedas. Iksavaku was the grandson of Vivasvan and the son of Vaivasvata Manu. Lallanji Gopal, a historian on sugar-making technology from Allahabad University, has suggested that the Iksavakus got name in the Vedas from its ownership of sugarcane plantation.[1] Etymologically, Iksavaku is derived from 'Ikshu' which means sugarcane. In Ayurvedic pharmacopoeia, Ikshu finds a certain mention. Iksavakus were later known as the Solar dynasty in contrast with the series of royal lineages belonging to the Lunar dynasty. Thus, the king Rama of the Ramayana epic belongs to the Iksavaku clan while Krishna of the Mahabharata epic belongs to the lunar dynasty of Yadu clan. We find the reference of the Iksavaku clan in the emergence of non-Vedic religions also. Out of 24 tirthankars in the Jain history, 22 are believed to belong to Iksavaku clan. Rishabhdeva, the first tirthankar, himself belonged to this clan. Similarly, Gautam Buddha's Shakya lineage belonged to Iksavaku dynasty. The last reference of the Iksavaku Dynasty is found in the post-Satvahana period in Andhra when Iksavaku dynasty came to power in the Krishna river valley.

It was during this time that Nagarjuna spread Buddhism across the Indian peninsula. The great stupa at Nagarjunakonda is witness to the ascendance of Buddhism. The Andhra Iksavakus also built stupas at Jaggayyapeta, Amravati and Bhattiprolu.

How did the dynasty named after Iksavaku come to prominence in shaping Indian civilization? There are surviving myth in Southeast Asia that mankind originated from the sugarcane. This myth might have travelled during the Indianization movement. Iksavaku as the primordial lineage emerged due to the association of sugarcane with sweetness. In earlier times, the source of sweetness was honey, which was limited in supply. But, sugarcane juice made it possible for common people to relish the taste of sweetness. The clan which spread the cultivation of sugarcane gained respect. Therefore, every individual who made significant contribution to the society and brought happiness, in one way or the other, got associated with legendary Iksavaku Dynasty.

The sugarcane, Ikshu, caught attention of sharp minds. Sugarcane became a simile in spiritual discourses and diplomatic exchanges. The Greeks during Alexander's time described sugarcane as "reeds that make honey without the agency of bees". Megasthenes, the Greek ambassador to the court of Mauryas had mentioned about the sweet juice of sugarcane in detail. He believed that canes absorbed water from the soil and the strong sunshine cooked the plant as it grew producing sweet juice.[2]

Sugarcane plantations were in abundance in Magadha and this might be the reason that Buddha often employed sugarcane as trope in his utterances. John Kieschnick has compiled those sayings on sugarcane in his work, *The Impact of Buddhism on Chinese Material Culture.*[3] He cites a saying from *Abhiniskramansutra*, in which Buddha tells his cousin brother and personal attendant Ananda, "World is filled with arahats, in number as dense as stalks of sugarcane, bamboo, reeds, hemp or rice."[4]

In *Nirvana Sutra*, Kashyapa addresses Buddha in following words: "Buddha, like the juice of sugarcane which yields various flavours when boiled various times, I listen to the Buddha speak."[5]

Bodhisattva is often compared with sugarcane:

"The great Bodhisattva is like sugarcane or sesame which, when pressed with a device, gives forth juice or oil". [6]

A homologous scheme is devised to explain Bodhichitta. "There are three types of bodhichitta beings, Arahat, Pratyekbuddha and Buddha just as sugarcane yields three type of product, sugar, half-sugar and syrup". [7]

The Chinese have been the excellent translators and the oldest Buddhist texts survive in Chinese translations which have helped to reconstruct the events of past with precision. In one of the text, *Saddharmasmrtyupasthana Sutra* which was translated into Chinese in early 6th century AD, the practice of cultivation of Bodhichitta by monks have been compared with the refinement of sugar. At initial stage, it is separated from impurities and is like phanita. At second boiling, it becomes heavier and is like guda. When boiled third time, it becomes white like shimi (sarkara). [8]

Chinese monks learnt the technique of making white crystal sugar, *shimi,* but did not share with the emperors. The Tang emperors were so enamoured by the taste of sugar that two Technology Missions were sent to India during seventh century to learn how to make sugar. In the twenty-first year of the Zhenguan period (647), Li Yibiao, the Tang ambassador who led the second Chinese embassy to Kanauj in AD 643, finally managed to obtain an audience with the Emperor Taizong. Li Yibiao and his entourage, with the sugar-making technology they had acquired, returned to China in late 645 or early 646, when the emperor was still engaged in the military campaign against Koguryo. [9]

The Mission failed in initial attempt, and were arrested with dramatic and funnier turn of events when Wang Xuance and Jiang Shiren were attacked by the usurper of Harsha's throne in Kannauj. The Tang Emperor Taizong was ill and he was in search for some longevity drug from Buddha's land. In all likelihood, the crystal shaped sugar which is both white and like infinite Indra's net of glittering and reflecting pearl, fascinated the Chinese emperor as something associated with the Nirvana.

Apart from Buddhism, sugarcane juice finds an important place in Jaina ritual also. After attaining enlightenment Adinath Rishabhdeva took vow to live a simple ascetic life, not even to eat cooked meal. Since he was the first ascetic, people did not know what to offer him in alms. They offered ornaments and material things. But, Rishabhdeva needed only some food and water to feed himself and he continued practicing harsher austerities. But, since no one could understand his needs, and he being an enlightened Tirthankar could not demand food, he remained in fast for years. It was his grandson, Shreyansha Kumar, who understood the dietary need of Tirthankar. He offered Rishabhdeva sugarcane juice. Thus, Rishabhdeva ended his fast. This was the third day of lunar month of Vaishakh and now celebrated as Akshaya Trittiya to commemorate the event. One can gauge the esteem sugarcane was invested with during the early times more particularly in contemplative practices.

Sugarcane juice was used in the Vedanta literature as a trope. It is said that higher the state of samadhi, less sweeter it becomes just as sugarcane root is the sweetest and the sweetness declines towards the tender shoot. In Krishna bhakti, sugarcane was again employed to produce similar effect. Just as sugarcane juice has different states like molasses, sugar or sugar candy after being boiled; similarly a Bhakta/devotee tastes the Rasa in different states. Naam-japa, continuous chanting of divinity's name has been explained by juxtaposing linguistics and sugarcane juice by one of the foremost proponent of devotional path during 20th century, Naam Avatara Sri Sri Sitaramdas Omkarnath.

"Vaikhari is the state of sugar-cane juice. Madhyama is the state of molasses which also has some juice left. Pashyanti is like sugar and Para is candy. But in these states the Naam does not dry-up. The liquid state goes away and it becomes thick and solid. But the person who tastes it in any state feels the sweetness. One does not have to chew candy. It is enough to keep it on one's tongue. If necessary, one can grind it to a powder like sugar, or dissolve it in water to make a drink. But the substance is the same. As the Bhakta progresses, he tastes the different state of the Juiciest of All i.e. Naam."[10]

Thus, we find how sugarcane, Ikshu, became all pervasive to explain the state of realization. In the experiential aspect of religious history, Ikshu remain unparalleled as a trope. I am of the view that the concept of rasa in drama compiled by Bharat Muni during 4th century might have been inspired by the imagery of sugarcane juice in spiritual realization of happiness. Rasa is the juice. Sugarcane and sesame were used to explain how these produce juice or oil when pressed, by the early Buddhists. Since, sesame oil lost the race in taste of sweetness, sugarcane juice entered the vocabulary of poets, writers and thinkers. There has been a steady spread of the concept of rasa/ jouissance in Indian culture after the codification by Bharat Muni. By 8th century, rasa became the soul of poetry. Then, rasa permeated the world of linguistics in the hands of proponents of devotion/bhakti. Enchanting of name of the god produces sweet taste in consciousness. This gave rise to the kirtans or an ecstatic group singing. The idea of juice entered the competing sects like Nath, tantras, Sikhism, bhakti.

The sect of Srividya that soon engulfed Indian geo-culture area revolves around Mother Tripurasundari. She is shown as holding a bow made of sugarcane reed. The cult of Tara that took over from here depicts Tara as holding sugarcane bow and so does iconography of Kurukulla, the red form of Tara, now the supreme goddess in Mongolia. Sugarcane with its graded knots containing sweet juice, correlated with the aspects of Kundalini, the psycho-physical axial mundi of human body. Sugarcane became part of popular ritual. In north India, the devotees carry back, the sugarcane reed after burning the effigy of Ravana, the ten-headed demon, on the day of Vijayadashami (Dushehra), which to my mind appears to be symbolic of carrying sweet nectar of victory and immortality into own home.

Ikshu and Iksavaku are deeply connected with the unfolding, ceaseless history of India's pursuit of 'happiness as sweetness'. It is not a mere coincidence that contemporary India excels in preparation of sweets and on each happy occasion, may be sacred or profane, guests are greeted with a pack of sweet.

With the growing incidence of sugar disease in a Post-materialist society, sugarcane has lost the appeal as trope. Sugarcane cultivators in India are fighting to survive in contemporary India and so are Buddhists. Bodhimind and sugarcane grow in abundance when there is bright sunshine. But, when the nation is under the dark shadows, growth falters. We do not know what connected the spread of Buddha's sweet wisdom and sugarcane cultivations. But, the connection is sweet and one can relish the sweetness without cutting the sugarcane from its root.

Endnote and References

1. Gopal, Lallanji (1964). 'Sugar-Making in Ancient India', *Journal of the Economic and Social History of the Orient,* Vol VII, No 13, pp 55-72.
2. McCrindle, JW and Dr Schwanbeck (1877). *Ancient India as described by Megasthenes and Arrian*, OUP.
3. Kieschnick, John (2003). *The Impact of Buddhism on Chinese Material Culture,* Princeton University Press.
4. Ibid, p. 249.
5. Ibid, p. 251.
6. Ibid.
7. Ibid.
8. Ibid.
9. Sen, Tansen (2003). *Buddhism, diplomacy and Trade: The Realignment of Sino-Indian Relations,* 600-1400, Association of Asian Studies and University of Hawaii Press, p 45.
10. Sri Sri Thakur Sita Ram Das Omkarnath, *Naam Rasaanubhava* (Taste of Naam).

TANTRA

Chapter 11

What is Tantra? Tantra as Text, Text as Textile!

What is tantra (तंत्र)? Though Tantra has emerged as a separate discipline in academics as well as spiritual techne to overcome existential crisis, the word is sporadically used as a suffix in almost every branch of governance in India. India is a democracy (prajatantra). The head of the State in India is elected. India is a republic (ganatantra). In common parlance, India is also known as janatantra. India was a colony of the British empire till 14 August, 1947. India became independent (svatantra-स्वतंत्र) on 15th August,1947. The whole governance structure is known as shasan-tantra. There is police-tantra for law and order enforcement, nyayik-tantra to administer justice, prashashanik-tantra for general administration of populace. Tantra is, thus, a particular techne that has now encapsulated every realm of structuring the bio-political realm.

It is important to reflect over the etymology of the word, Tantra. Tantra is a Sanskrit word which means 'to weave'. Sanskrit roots of tantra is 'tan' (तं) and 'tra' (त्र). 'Tan' is 'to stretch' or 'to extend' and 'Tra' means 'to cross over'. Tantra will mean 'stretching to cross over'. Tra has a great significance in Indian civilization. Indian civilization is obsessed with the ideology of tran (त्राण/salvation), to cross over the cycle of existence governed by law of karma, rebirth and causality. Tra is the root of 'trayate', meaning to preserve. Tra is also at the root of tran. But, all these are derived from the root 'tri' (त्रि) that is three. Let us ponder over the origin of numbers in Vedic philosophy. Sutra 3.9 of the Nirukta by great Vedic etymologist, Yaska(4th century BC) mentions as follow:

"One is the number gone a little (to go). Two is the number running farther (dru—to run). Three is the number gone across farthest (tr—to cross)."[1]

Yaska states, *trayastirnatama samkhya* (there is three since it crosses over the first two numerals). Tri is the swiftest (verse 7.13, Nirukta).[2]

Tri as suffix is used in many words denoting the path to salvation, like Gayatri. Gayatri is derived from the root gai (to praise, to sing—gana). Gayatri is a three-verse praise, which is believed to be a syllabic path to salvation. Similarly, Gangotri, which is considered sacred spot where the river Ganges is believed to descend from the heavens consists of two roots—Ganga and tri. Here, tri is in the sense of crossing over. The river Ganges crossed over the Milky Way to descend down the earth so as to carry believers to cross over the worldly affairs, towards salvation. Similarly, suffix 'tri' in the word, 'Pavitra' (sacred) that consists of two roots—pavi (पवि) and tra (त्र). Pavi is the Vedic name for rim in the wheel. Just as the pavi brushes away the mud/earth, similarly, pavitra brushes away sin and makes one to cross over the worldly cycle. Similarly, tri as suffix in Putra has a powerful impact on Indian rituals. Putra consists of two roots—Pu and tra. Pu is to protect by offering. Tra is the crossing over, salvation. Putra is the son who helps in moksha through sacrificial offerings. It is why in Indian civilization, there is singular focus on having a son as an offspring.

Similarly, ratri (night) (रात्रि) is composed of two roots—ra+tri. Ra is 'to give' and tri denotes the crossing over. According to Yaska, Ratri exhilarates the nocturnal creatures and causes the others to cease work, and makes them strong.[3] Avatar (reincarnation) (अवतार) and avataran (descent from Heavens) (अवतरण) have 'tr' as their roots signifying the crossing over. Ava (अव) meaning to go, ava is the release. Avatar is one who descends to take people to cross over to the other side. Similarly, avataran describes the descent of a sacred being.

Tr root (त्र) is also used in the Vedic quotations concerning banks of the river. Tira (तीर) is the bank of the river. Tira signifies 'crossing over'. Similarly, Tira is the name for the arrow. The arrow crosses over to enemy's side. Tra has been suffixed with Su to create another vibrant aspect of Indian civilization, Sutra (सूत्र). Su stands for 'to press'. Su-tra is a compressed verse. It's like Japanese art of chijimi, to compress thoughts, feelings, history and technology. Sutra can be interpreted as the compressed verse that contains the art of crossing over.

Similarly, 'Tan' (तं) is to spread, stretch, extend or expand. This root also relates to the word 'tantu' (तंतु), which means 'thread', suta/dhaga. Just like thread can be woven into a fabric, 'tan' denotes the act of weaving in the word 'Tantra'. Tan signifies continuity. Tanta (तांता) is the queue, continuous movement. Tan signifying expansion is at the root of tamas. [4] (Verse 2.17, Nirukta). Tan is spreading as in the word, distributing (Vi-bhaj-anti).

By invoking various meanings, Tantra signifies different things in different contexts. But, simplest meaning of tantra will be 'tan trayate' (weaving for preservation). Tantra can also mean 'weaving liberation', 'spreading liberation'. Tan is also the human body. Tantra is to effect liberation through human body. Tan also signifies thread as in the word, tantu (stem) (तंतु). Tantra is the art of engaging with liberation through esoteric tantu, i.e. Kundalini. Tantra is invariably liked in intricate relationship with 'tri (त्रि), the number three as well as tr. (तर), crossing over or liberation. It is observed, therefore, that tantra does not exist in isolation, but is intertwined with two other aspects of spiritual technology- Mantra and Yantra. The triad Tantra-Mantra-Yantra (तंत्र-मंत्र-यंत्र) co-exists. Interestingly, all three has the root, tr (in both aspects, as a number as well as goal).

Figure 11.1

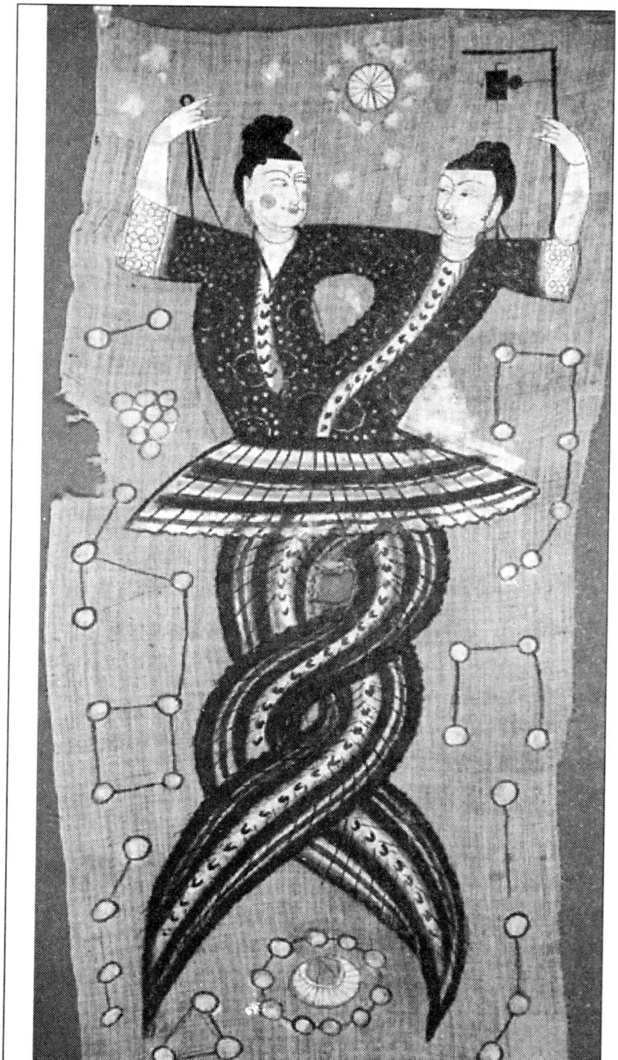

(Image of Nuwa and Fuxi—half-human, half-snake—mythological ancestors of Chinese people weaved on silk, also appear to represent Kundalini in Tantra.)

Fourfold Evolution of Indian Civilization

Tantra is used as double entendre. Tantra is 'to weave' a structure populated with humans, institutions, sound, phonemes, symbols, gestures. Tantra, in this sense, signifies perpetuity of a normative structure. Tantra in another sense stands for 'human propensity for liberation from samsaric realm'. Thus, Tantra simultaneously signifies the emergence of a structure and the way to destructuration of every possible structure. The semantics is a paradox. Tantra contains within its womb this paradox of manifestation and dissolution, srishti and pralaya. Tantra connects in a manifold universe in infinite ways. Tantra contains the full meaning of Nagarjuna's shunyavada premised on dependent origination of thing where everything in the Universe establishes interelationality with everything else. Thus, the Ganga in the sky (Milky Way galaxy is known as Akashganga) is connected with the terrestrial Ganga flowing from the Himalayas onto the subtle energy channel, Ida Nadi flanking Sushumna wherein resides Kundalini like a stem/thread (tantu) with knots at different layers of human existence. Tantra makes it possible to connect the nodes in a multi-layered, overlapping universe.

Tantra evokes the image of a string, sutra (Sanskrit). Both share common root, tr. Sutra, as discussed earlier, is also the compressed verse of wisdom. Sutra compresses wisdom. In earlier times, detailed commentary (bhashya) were written by great exponent of these sutras. One can take the case of one of the most important revelation in Kashmir Shaivism—Shiva Sutra. This was revealed to Vasugupta and his successors wrote extensive commentary on the sutras.

Indian civilization can be classified into four stages based upon the changing tradition of harnessing wisdom. The first phase was Sutra tradition as evident from the widespread use of this term as addendum in every branch of knowledge and ritual. This tradition can be traced from Buddha's time to Shankaracharya's time (Circa 500 BC—800 AD). Sutra is used in the sense of 'rules', though literally it is thread. Vedic tradition revolved around rituals. There were Shrauta Sutras concerning rituals. Sutra of Katyayani and

Baudhayana had major influences over ancient culture. Grihya Sutra concerning household ceremonies emerged later. There were some non-religious injunctions in sutra-style known as the Dharma Sūtras. The Dharma Sutras still has a major influence over contemporary Indian civilization as these determine the customs in everyday life.

There were six classes of the Vedic works—phonetics (shiksha), metre (chhanda), grammar (vyakaran), etymology (nirukta), religious practice (kalpa) and astronomy/astrology (jyotisha). In every Vedanga, major works were composed in sutra style. Panini is credited with Ashtadhyayi, a treatise on grammar in sutra style. Similarly, Yaska composed Nirukta in Sutra-style. All the kalpa-treatises that included Srauta and Grihya Sutras were in same style. The first Vedic mathematics was developed as Sulba Sutra to study architecture of sacrificial area. Similarly, in jyotisha, there are Parashar Sutra, Jaimini Sutra and Katyayini Sutra.

Even in post-Kushana period, one can see the proliferation of philosophical literature in Sutra style. Yoga Sutras, Samkhya Sutras, Nyaya Sutras,Vaishasika Sutra, Purva Mimamsa Sutras, Brahma Sutras of Badarayana upon which extensive commentary were written by great thinkers like Gaudapada and Shankaracharya. It is not only among the Vedic tradition that this style proliferated. One can see the same trend even among Buddhists and Jains. Panch Parmesthi Sutra or Panch Namaskar Sutra is recited in daily worship by Jains. Their holiest book, Tattvartha Sutra, is in sutra-tradition. The biography of Mahavir is contained in the Kalpa sutra. Similarly, early Buddhist literature is in sutras, which in Pali, was pronounced as Sutta. Tripitikas (Three Collections)—Dighanikaya Sutta, Majjhim Nikaya Sutta and Laghu Nikaya Sutta—are in Sutras. When Buddhism bifurcated into Hinayana and Mahayana sects, sutra tradition defined the course of spread of Mahayana. Hriday Sutra, Lotus Sutra Ugrapariprchha Sutra, Avataṃsaka Sutra, Triskandha Sūtra, Suvarṇaprabhāsa-Sūtra, Laṅkāvatāra Sūtra, Tathāgatagarbha Sūtra, Pratyutpanna-Sūtra, Samādhirāja-Sūtra, Śūraṅgama-Samādhi-Sūtra, Prajnaparamita Sutra spread Buddhism across Asia.

But Sutra tradition paved way for the Tantra tradition during

Pala period. It is like continuity of thread. Tantric literature flourished through Sutra-style. But, now Sutras were no more product of human imagination, The Sutras in the Tantric period were the revealed knowledge. The Tantras spread like tentacles across every belief-system. We observe, therefore, how Tantras emerged, collided, influenced and appropriated from each other among Buddhist, Shakta, Shaivite and Vaishnavites.

Tantras developed the new way of alliterative practice of mantras. Repetition of the mantras bestowed by Guru to disciples that appears as a continuous thread (again Tantra), also called lineage or kulas was believed to pave the path towards salvation. With the advent of Islamic rulers in Delhi (end of 12th century), Tantras paved way for the emergence of a Nama-tradition. Like a thread, the tendency to repeat mantras continued into new format. There was explosive creativity in composing in sahastranama (thousand names of gods/ goddess), like Lalitasahastranama, Vishnusahastranama. Mere repetition of the name of the god was sufficient to attain liberation. This became the foundation of emerging Bhakti movement as well as the new Sikh religion. Namjapa gained predominance over previous practiced Vedic ritual in later centuries and till now.

Present age has seen another compression. It is no longer necessary to even do repetition of nama or mantras (from Tantra tradition). The Vac has been expropriated from the everyday practice of dharma. It is the Pataka (Locket) Age. Liberation is in amulets, lockets, jantra. People believe in tying propitious threads around wrist, keeping pictures of god in purses, tattooing the image of god or some sacred word on surface of body. A Hindu wife wears mangalsutra in the form of an auspicious black thread or even a gold chain with black stones. Sisters tie rakhi around brother's wrist. Love has become a connection of raw thread between two hearts, not only metaphorically but even literally. Thread is omnipresent in our ritual.

The history of Indian civilization has finally arrived at the juncture which recuperates the initial conditions. Thread has remarried words in the new space-cyber universe and has become pure and unembellished with the power of the word in real social world.

From Textile to Text—Journey of Tantra

In ancient times when proper script did not emerge, memories transferred orally passed on from generation to generation like a continuous thread. Ethnographers are conclusive now that it is the intricate weaving pattern over the textile that is the repository of group's custom, tradition, legends and identities. Textile emerged much earlier than text and the weaving pattern can be decoded as cultural DNA to establish migration history among contiguous ethnic communities. Though, the earliest known woven fragments was excavated in Southern Turkey at Catal Huyuk and dated to over 9,000 years ago, the earliest known basket-weaving dates around 13,000 years ago. New York Times report that the oldest known twisted fibers, which could have been woven into basketry or textiles, were found in Israel and date to about 19,300 years ago. But paleo-anthropologists have to push back the date of weaving to 25,000 years ago after discovery of clay fragments embossed with textile pattern, discovered in 1995 in the Pavlov Hills in the south-eastern Czech Republic by a team led by Dr Olga Soffer of the University of Illinois and Dr James M Adovasio. A group of archaeologists have arrayed to establish the origin of textile technology before the Neolithic period (8000 B.C.) when human species learnt to domesticate plants and animals.[5]

There have been recent criticism against earlier generation archaeologists for over emphasizing stone tools and implements used by the male members in interpreting human history and ignoring technology of signification like textiles which are perpetual from very early times where women had dominance. They charge them with patriarchal gaze in telescoping present prejudices over recollection of past. It is being debated that textile predates text and there is a connection between textile (weaving) and text (language). Roland Barthes, the French philosopher whose work on the discipline of writing is immense, sums up the relationship beautifully that, 'etymologically the text is a cloth: textus, meaning woven".[6] Textile historian, Kathryn Sullivan Kruger goes one step further and claims that

"Because weaving constitutes one of the first signifying practices that recorded the world's ancient myths and symbols, I propose that reference made within a written text or to the weaving process recalls this history. Towards this view, the written text is a recent form of textile, ancillary to those primary texts 'told' or 'tooled' in cloth."[7]

Textiles emerged as important activity of primordial society as weaving was a laborious activity. The priests, village heads, tribal chiefs carried the authority signified through different drapings. In fact, different weaving pattern became hallmark of clan identity in egalitarian societies. Not only human bodies, but even deities and totems were decorated with various drapings. Weaving became an exercise in sacred ritual activity to propitiate. The textile and sacredness got so much intermingled from the earliest time that Buddhists all across Asia engaged in weaving Buddha robe as a path of liberation. Buddha image was weaved with precious silk. The evidences are still extant in the Dunhuang cave discoveries in China. Textile is offered as part of sacrificial act to deities among Hindus and Buddhists. The sacredness and textile became intermingled to such an extent that among Tibetan Buddhism followers, the High lamas offer kata (white scarf woven in silk) which is considered one of the 8 auspicious symbols. Among highland societies of Asia, traditional shawls carrying the thread of continuity of weaving pattern is offered as a mark of respect. Elizabeth Wayland Barber, an anthropologist mentions that, "Cloth, from our first direct evidence twenty thousand years ago, has been the handiest solution to conveying social messages visually, silently, continuously."[8]

This is so true for contemporary times also with different dress code for nurses, lawyers, military and police. The cloth as a text speaks about the identity bypassing the medium of spoken word. Kruger in her meticulously researched book establishes that the ancient production of text first occurred in the form of text. In fact, every culture, primordial or postmodern, records the symbols of its own heritage on the body of a textile.

Dr Angela Sheng, an art historian from McMaster University in Hamilton, Ontario, Canada has documented costumes from the

Miao, Yi, Dong, Tujia, Shui, Zhuang, Dai, Buyi, Yao, Wa, and Zang in South West China and explored variations in "myths of origin and heroic combats, communal memories, and wish fulfillment" among these communities. In the book, "*Writing with Thread: Traditional Textiles of Southwest Chinese Minorities*"[9] Angela Sheng, discusses in her essay, "Reading Costumes as 'Texts' and Decoding Ethnic Visual Culture of Southwest China", how to decode the myth and narratives of the community in the weaving patterns. I have tried to read the connection between various communities of Zomia through discovering commonalities in the weaving pattern over puanten, woman's lower garment.[10]

It is not surprising that first documented texts in India belonged to sutra tradition. Sutra is not only the compressed verse, but also the thread. Sutra is a formula, cultural code as well as material, tangible thread used in rituals. First evidence of written script in India dates back to Ashoka's time, (3rd century BC). Written texts emerged much later than massive production of texts transmitted orally in India either in Vedic or Buddhist or Jaina tradition. Weaving was the most sophisticated technology for ancient Indians and weaving became metaphor for Creation. Everything owes analogy to weaving. Possibly, weaving itself emerged as an imitation of the act of spider in weaving intricate web. Thus, primordial act of creation of Universe was imagined to be woven by Brahma. The whole terminology of weaving sneaked into the Vedic Sutras. Frits Staal has rightly observed that the terminology like grantha (knot), tantra (loom), nibandha (tying), prabandha (band) have their origin in textile technology.[11] All these terms spatter the Vedic as well as Tantric texts.

Spider Weaving and Prana as String in Vedic Texts

In the Mundaka and the Shvetashvatara Upanishad, the emergence of Universe has been explained using analogy from the spider web.

"From this Eternal Being, this world, this universe, has emanated. How does the world come from God? We have seen a spider spitting threads from its own body. From its saliva, as it were, threads come out, and it weaves a web around itself. Or we have seen trees spontaneously growing from under the earth, or we have seen hair growing on the head. In some such way is the manner of the creation of this world."

Mundaka Upanishad (1.1.7)

"May the non-dual Lord, who, by the power of His maya, covered Himself, like a spider, with threads drawn from primal matter, merge us in Brahman!"

Shvetashvatara Upanishad (VI.10)

It is interesting to note that even in mythology of most of the North American Plains, Indian tribes and many African tribes, spiders are considered as the Creator or a helpful creature. The Vedic seers viewed Brahma as the spider and the Universe as a textile with strings woven in the warp and woofs. There is an elaborate dialogue about the structure of existence between sage Yajnavalkya and other knowers of Brahman.

Sage Yajnavalkya is challenged by Gargi, daughter of sage Vachaknavi.The episode is described in the sixth Brahmana of the Brihadaranyaka Upanishad, and frequently mentioned to examine the contribution of women during Vedic times. Swami Krishnanada narrates the episode eloquently while giving a discourse on Brihadaranyaka Upanishad. Gargi asked the sage about the origin of different elements in the Universe and narrated to the sage that everything is capable of being designated as resolvable to water because the element of cohesion is necessary for the appearance of any physical object. What is behind this cohesive principle i.e. the water principle, she asked? The sage explained that it is the vayu, the air principle since it precedes the manifestation of the Water principle in the process of creation. Gargi asked "In what is Vayu (air) woven like warp and woof? What is its source?" This is the question. The sage replies—Antarikshalokesu (the atmospheric world). Here, we can observe how Vedic sages viewed the Universe as a woven fabric.

Gargi kept on asking about the underlying principles of antariksha loka, Gandharva loka, Aditya loka, Chandra loka, Nakshatra loka. The sage went on explaining in series the substratum of each substratum like sheath of onion peels. The sage explained that the Nakshatra loka, the physical universe is merely an external appearance of internal reality, Deva loka where gods live. Gargi raised the ultimate question:

Kasmin nu khalu deva-loka otas ca protas ceti

(Where is, again, the Deva-loka, or the world of the gods woven, like warp and woof?)

Sage replied, Indra loka. Indra is the King of gods. Indra loka itself is based on the substratum of Prajapati loka which is Virat (The Great Infinite) Himself. Beyond it is the world of Hiranyagarbha or Brahma loka. Brahma is the creator of the Universe and there cannot be anything beyond the Brahma loka. The sage explained how everything is strung in this Ultimate Being. Therefore, it is called *Sutra-Atman*. Sutra is a string. As beads are strung on a thread, so is everything that is created hanging or strung, on this thread of the Cosmos, or the *Sutra-Atman, Brahma* or *Hiranyagarbha*. Ultimate Reality is that in which everything is included in one form or the other. When Gargi further asked about the location of Brahma loka, the Sage warned that if she asked too much, her head would fall down and convinced her not to go beyond permissible limits of logical argument, because it is inadmissible to ask the cause of the Cause of everything. Gargi became silent.[12]

In Badarayana's *Brahmasutras* upon which Gaudapada and Shankara wrote brilliant commentaries, Prana is known as the Sutra-Atman. Sutra-Atman is also the Brahma. Thus, it is the same thread from the ultimate creator, Brahma to Atman in each Jiva. Each prana is connected to the Brahma through the vital life-principle, prana, which is the string. Tantras utilized the weaving metaphor more intimately and in a way tried to regain the space which women enjoyed in a pre-textual community (pre-Vedic community) with their dominance over textile technology. The textual tradition of the later Indic sects displaced women to the margin after appropriating the terms and techne which women utilized in creating material things to bind the community and propel the communitarian identity in perpetuity. Now, it was the world of men who "weaved thoughts to clothe the society with the fabric of belief."[13] Women being the master-craftsmen of human civilization with mere hand-technology of weaving, were reduced to spinsters. Slowly, when machines were deployed in textile industry, women lost the little autonomy they enjoyed during pre-Industrial days.

Tantra, Textiles and Women

Tantra itself means 'to weave.' Tantras re-established primacy of women as Shakti. Not only that, the tradition is supposed to be orally transmitted just like textile tradition during pre-textual times. In Kashmir Shaivism, it is mentioned in many sects that the authentic teachings can be transmitted only through Yoginimukha, a female tantric adept. One can also see in tantric literature mistrust towards written words or textual tradition. The secrecy of teachings is to be maintained. There is lot of abracadabra of language in tantric rituals which conforms to the latent tendencies against the language. Though, mantras do have structures and the whole emphasis is on understanding the structure so as to realize the unity of self with the cosmos. The whole concept of Kundalini in Tantra emanates from the craft of weaving. Chakras are like granthis (knots), and provide string that forms the warp and woof of our consciousness. These strings are the prana-shakti (life-principle) as Sutra-Brahman and in turn weave individual self to the Absolute, Brahma.

Tantra teaches us to understand the inter-relationality and the commonalities among us. Ultimately it is the same string which weaves our self and the other selves. There is no ground for hatred. Tantras espouse love as a medium to connect since love is as extra-lingual act, as is Tantra. Like a beautifully woven draper where patterns in multiple colours produce beauty, tantras teach us to co-exist in harmony. If the harmony gets disturbed, the string cannot weave. Finally, tantra teaches us that Truth is not to be read and studied. It is in the act of building connectivities and creating recurring structures during which one can get the glimpses of Truth.

This can be Srishti Krama. Some may experience truth by going in reverse mode by untying all knots. This is the Samhara Krama. Tantra is this paradoxical double entendre-the simultaneous act of creation and dissolution. Who else can signify the discipline than a woman who creates and nurtures new life in its womb and thence, cut the placental knot to release its creation to struggle against the vagaries of time in another sheath!

References

1. Sarup, Lakshman (1998). *The Nighantu and The Nirukta: The Oldest Indian Treatise on Etymology, Philology and Semantics,* Delhi: MLBD, p. 45.
2. Ibid, p. 119.
3. Ibid, p. 32.
4. Ibid, p. 41.
5. Fowler, Brenda (1995). Find suggests weaving Preceded settled Life, *New York Times*, May 9, 1995. Accessed on 3.8.2013 at http://www.nytimes.com/1995/05/09/science/find-suggests-weaving-preceded-settled-life.html?pagewanted=all&src=pm.
6. Barthes, Roland (1971). *From Work to Text,* reproduced in Josue V Harari, ed., (1979). *Textual Strategies : Perspectives in Poststructuralist Criticism,* Ithaca, NY : Cornell University Press, pp. 73-81.
7. Kruger, Kathryn Sullivan (2001). *Weaving the Word: The Metaphorics of Weaving and Female Textual Production, Susquehanna University Press,* p 33.
8. Barber, Elizabeth Wayland (1994). *Women's Work—First 20,000 Years: Women Cloth, Society in Earlier Times,* New York: WWNortan & Co.
9. Sheng, Angela, ed., (2009). *Writing with Thread: Traditional*

Textiles of Southwest Chinese Minorities, University of Hawaii Art Gallery.

10. Kumar, Niraj and CN Biak (2011). *Zomi, Zomia, Nomadia—Landscape, Handicraft and Statecraft*. Available at http://ariseasia.blogspot.com/2011/09/zomi-zomia-nomadia-landscape-handicraft.html. Aslo see Kumar, Niraj and CN Biak (2014). Textile, Text, Territariality-Weaving a Pan-Himalayan Identity, *Journal of Indian Research*, Vol. 2, No. 2, pp. 50-74.

11. Staala, Frits (2008). *Discovering the Vedas, Origins, Mantras, Rituals, Insights*, New Delhi : Penguin, p 262.

12. Krishnananda, Swami (1977). *Discourse on the Brihadaranyaka Upanishad*, 1st March 1977.

13. Kruger, n. 7, p 2.

Chapter 12

Chhinnamasta, Full Moon and Lunar Eclipse!

The Full Moon coincided with a total lunar eclipse in the year 2011. This was an opportune time to reflect over the narrative of the Goddess Chhinnamasta. She is a tantric deity worshipped by both Hindus as well as the Buddhists. While Hindus consider Chintapurni, near Kangra district in Himachal Pradesh as a major Shaktipitha as they believe the head (mastak) of Parvati, Shiva's consort fell there; Nyingma sect in Buddhism considers her as the severed-head form of Vajravarahi. The Full Moon under total lunar eclipse, represents principles behind propitiation of Chhinnamasta form of Shakti.

Chhinnamasta is one of the ten manifestations of Shakti (Das Mahavidya). Her iconography is frightening and awful for the common seeker. She is shown as a sixteen year old girl holding her own severed head in her left hand and accompanied by two attendants, Dakini and Varnini for Hindus; and Vajradak and Vajravarnini among the Buddhists. The triad of woman are depicted nude with dishevelled hair. Chhinnamasta wears garland of 51 skulls and carries a cobra around her neck. In all images, Chhinnamasta is depicted as drinking her own blood spewing from severed head. Now, here is the pictorial depiction of non-duality of Universe. Chhinnamasta herself is the sacrificer, sacrifice and partaker of sacrifice. There is no duality between receiver and giver of sacrifice. She devours herself to renew herself. This is the cosmic process of simultaneous creation and dissolution. Chhinnamasta signifies the process of creation, destruction and re-creation, the whole schemata of Existence. The full Moon with a total lunar eclipse can be viewed as severing of the fully blown head of the Shakti (Moon represents woman principle) and re-emergence of the Full Moon from the eclipse as the renewal of the Shakti. Therefore, it was a special celestial occasion to intune oneself with the cosmic principles encapsulated within a short span of time.

The work of Raoul Kopelman who led a team of researchers in the University of Michigan and discovered strong electric fields inside cells can be seen in the context of understanding the goddess Chhinnamasta in the modern idioms. Kopelman's colleague, Tyner's measurements revealed that cytosol—the jellylike material that makes up most of a cell's interior had as high as 15 million volts per meter electric field. This discovery was against traditional wisdom that there are zero electric field inside cell. The electric field strength of cytosol five times stronger than that present in the lightning bolt has been found![1]

This makes one dizzy and cause one to rethink about Chhinnamasta. Chhinnamasta is visualized as possessing the dazzling brilliance of a lightning bolt. She shines like lightning (vidyullekheva bhasvara). Her Buddhist name, Vajravairochaniya, is derived from this characteristic. She is the force (Vajra or thunderbolt) of Vairochana (luminous). Vairochana is the primordial light, Prakasha and Chhinnamasta is the source of its power.

In Saundarya Lahari, Shankaracharya mentions the lightning-like Kala as Sadakhya Kala (Verse 21) to denote the Primordial Shakti. This is the First Cause, and goddess of three aspects of existence, Nada, Bindu and Kala emerges. In creative aspect, the Shakti is Mahatripura and in destructive aspect, it is Mahakali. But, as we have seen Chhinnamasta represents all aspects simultaneously, creative, destructive and renewal. She shows the ability not only to sever her head but also to restore it. Thus, she is Mahatripura and Mahakali in unison. The visualization of Chhinnamasta as lightning is the dominant method in Tantras so much so that the lightning-Shakti is popularly identified with Chhinnamasta. There is an excellent work on the goddess' various aspects, *Chhinamasta: The Aweful Buddhist and Tantric Goddess* by Elisabeth Anne Benard (MLBD, 1994).[2]

With the recent discovery by the nano-technicians from Michigan, a whole new field to interpret the Chhinnamasta tradition gets wide open. If every cell within the body contains five times more powerful electric field strength than of the lightning bolt, can the tradition to visualize oneself as the Goddess to worship the Goddess induces certain activities in the electric fields within cell? Is there a linkage between Kundalini and the cellular electric field? Why awakening of Kundalini is often described as a lightning bolt from below? Does the neuro-chemical processes that accompany process of generation of lightning bolt within bodies lead to youthfulness, longevity and imagined immortality? Chhinnamasta is also the Goddess of immortality with her capacity to restore severed heads. But, is lightening like 'presence' within human body physically possible?

Coherence and Symmetry-Breaking

When the symmetry-breaking causes coherence, powerful new phenomena are created in the world. This is the case of super-conductivity and super-fluidity. Study of such coherence at atomic level is called Bose-Einstein condensate and it is a fast growing area of research. Laser and maser are industrially used phenomena of coherence which is produced by alignment of light waves in a single state and direction. Scientists have recently reported that even hadronic matter (proton) exhibit coherence properties. John Barrow and Joseph Silk in *The Left Hand Creation*,[3] has brilliantly demonstrated how the Universe is a manifestation of broken symmetries. The cooperative behaviour seen in the physical universe is an example of this kind of coherence. Another interesting observation is correlation of coherence and relative cooling. Water has rotational symmetry but in ice, it is lost and there is an orientation in space. With cooling of universe which is an on-going process due to dissipation of heat and ubiquity of thermodynamic laws, it is certain that more and more symmetries will be broken and cooperative behaviour of matter causing complex patterns would be manifest.

Symmetry-Breaking in Biological Evolution

If the symmetry-breaking explains the emergence of complexity and disappearance of opposite partners in the physical universe, the phenomenon is responsible for evolution of biological world. The chirality (mirror image) is a characteristic of biological world. The basic molecules of origin of life are glyceraldehyde. These molecules can exist in two forms: right-handed or left-handed, each a mirror image of the other. These are called enantiomers. Now, D-glyceraldehyde was favoured in biological evolution after the symmetry-breaking and this is the molecule that helped create life.

All amino acids are chirals. But, proteins are built up exclusively from L-amino acids. Similarly, RNA and DNA form only right handed helices. It is not that left-handed DNA helix cannot be formed, but these are rare. Snails have both l- and r-amino acids. Nature produces both kind of DNA but symmetry-breaking determines the difference in their distribution.

With DNA, there is a directionality caused by symmetry-breaking. DNA replicates only in one direction, 5'-3' pairs with 3'-5'. Biological systems have near identical cells and there are pattern formation on the surfaces of biological organisms. This cause symmetry-breaking and is a result of bifurcations in a dynamic system. It is suggested that even creation of new species is due to this process that favours one group and their dominance. This is known as sympatric speciation.

We know that every biological organism live for a certain period of time and then die. There is symmetry-breaking in biological process itself. All living beings tend to die but vice versa is not physically possible. Within organism, cells cooperate with a purpose to survive. This directionality entails yet to be ascertained break in symmetry. In higher animals and mammals, there is lateral symmetry but it is approximate and broken. Our right hand gloves will not fit in left hand even though we have similar halves. Mammalian brain was symmetric. But, in man, the symmetry has been broken. We have two hemispheres of brain with left hemisphere being the dominant part. Similarly, there is symmetry-breaking in our parity. Mirror image does not fit with the original. In human species, right-handed individuals are the dominant population even though left-handed individuals do exist. Even our thought process is dynamic and determined by bifurcations producing Duality. But, morality and ethics always emphasize to follow one set of pair and neglect the other. We want to be good, truthful, happy, peaceful, prosperous; not the opposite. Though, some also practise the other set as their philosophy of living.

Similarly, symmetry-breaking inside our bodies produce powerful phenomena. Visual cortex has symmetric network of neurons. But, neurons firing synchronously cause directionality. Networks of neurons oscillate and synchronize even when cells are not identical so that perfect symmetries are broken.

Cooperative Phenomena in Nature and Culture

In biological world, flocking of birds, swarm of locust, group of fish, herd of wild animal, wasps, ants, honey bee, migratory birds, flying cranes where coherent movement of a group of autonomous parts emerge from mutual cooperation is similar to the way symmetry-breaking produce directional and powerful phenomena in physical world like superconductivity. We know that in human history the revolution is the most powerful manifestation of human power which is nothing but synchronized action of random individuals. Facebook is such a phenomenon of synchronized oscillating interaction. Strong coherence and directionality always produce super-properties.

Signs of Enlightenment and Coherence

What insight do we gain from the phenomena discussed above

in quest of spiritual enlightenment for mankind? We know now the EEG patterns of long-time meditators. This is associated with 40 Hz synchronized gamma waves. When the full set of neurons in brain begin to fire synchronously breaking higher form of symmetry, that state produces the voidness in mind. What is kundalini awakening? Why is there horripilation, tingling and experience of crawling ants? Why is there epileptic-kind of seizure associated with kundalini awakening? The explanation lies in the synchronous neural firing of complete cerebro-spinal system that may entrain simultaneously even different sets of cells in bodies. We have seen how symmetry-breaking and directionality is associated with low temperature. Superconductivity and ferro-magnetism is possible only at low temperature. If those are heated, the directionality is lost and symmetry regained. Similarly, it is found that state of awakened kundalini is followed by experiences of cool breeze, cool drizzle, cool shower inside. Every mystical outpouring orbits around experience of coolness. When the stage of shithli-karan is achieved, the body sets in hypothermic condition. The coolness of body is one of the signs of an Enlightened personality. Sexuality entails increase in body temperature. But, low body temperature is not conducive to sexual excitements. Hence, the Enlightened beings have very poor appetite for sex. Similarly, there is no anger or similar heat-associated behaviour.

Synchronized firing of neural and other cells cause a self-sustaining magnetic field (moving electric currents in body due to directional firing producing magnetic field by induction as per Faraday law) which makes them so charming that this attracts feeble individuals (all of us have iron in our blood and magnetite present in region above nasal bone).

Now, it is increasingly becoming clear that induced coherence may cause symmetry-breaking and make cellular electric field to arrange in a direction causing lightning like experience, which further induces strong bio-chemical processes with an irreversible effect over consciousness. The alliteration prevalent in rituals may through certain quantum-mechanical phenomena induce this coherence.

This coherence can further cause quorum-sensing which partitioned tissues with specialized functions cannot do in isolation. The biologists have observed the phenomena at as low scale as bacteria. Bacterial cell start doing things as a colony that no bacteria has the energy to do on its own. It is how bacteria builds bio films inside our guts and on coral. The fossils of even bacterial colonies have been found in Australia (stromatolites) as the bacterial colonies managed to survive the process of weathering. We notice the phenomena in ant hills, bee hives, locust-swarms. It is this aspect of quorum sensing that now slime molds are used in artificial intelligence. Thus, once coherence induced within body makes cells to align their individual electric field in specific way, the body as a whole starts working as a unit, as an oscillator and the cells develop the extra-ordinary abilities which correspond to what biologists claim to be quorum-sensing. ESP and the extra-ordinary abilities of memorizing, stamina, blissfulness may suddenly dawn.

There is another interesting twist in this harvesting of electric potential within each of us. In a normal human body (75 kg), with metabolic efficiency of 31 per cent, calorie intake of 2,000 calories/ day translates into 620 calorie converted to ATP (Adenosine Tri-Phosphate coenzyme that is the 'molecular unit of currency' of intracellular energy transfer), motor behaviour and protein mass. Rest of the intake calorie is lost as heat or undigested matter. At this rate, biologists predict human longevity at 88 years. But, if the ATP and protein synthesis is increased through electro-chemical stimulation, effective calories from food may increase to 786 calorie. This puts the metabolic efficiency at 39 per cent and increase the longevity to over 200 years. The biologists though warns against capture of energy, using ATP synthesis from electro-chemical stimulation, as it is limited with same restrictions that govern exercise.

But, imagine a process by which a perennial source of electro-chemical stimulation is tapped through visualization; the protein and ATP synthesis increases and makes metabolism more efficient. The result will be massive slow down of ageing and increased longevity. The legends about siddhas like Nagarjuna living for few centuries no longer will appear superfluous.

To me, Chhinnamasta appears as the visual representation of the principles of achieving coherence within body and with the outer world and to harness the principles of life lying dormant within body to renew oneself and then beyond. She is the lightning Shakti that dazzles the sky and the inner eye. She is the Goddess of Kundalini. She is the emerging Full Moon from the total lunar eclipse carrying the *amritakalsh* that bestows immortality to seekers and peace to believers in the cosmic schemata of creation-dissolution-renewal.

References

1. Tyner, Katherine M, Raoul Kopelman, and Martin A Philbert (2007). "Nanosized Voltmeter" Enables Cellular-Wide Electric Field Mapping." *Biophysical Journal.* Volume 93, August 2007, 1163-1174. Available at http://www.dcsonntag.org/Electric-Cell-Papers.pdf.
2. Benard, Elisabeth Anne (1994). *Chhinnamasta: The Aweful Buddhist and Tantric Goddess,* Delhi: MLBD.
3. Barrow, John and Joseph Silk (1994). *The Left Hand Creation: The Origin and Evolution of the Expanding Universe,* OUP.

Chapter 13

Panchastavi and Abhinavagupta

Panchastavi is a collection of five devotional hymns. The first is the Laghustava which is the shortest one and contains 21 verses. Next are the Charchastava with 31 verses, Ghatastava with 24 verses, Ambastava with 32 verses and the last one Sakal-janani-stava as the longest comprising 38 verses. It is a prashashati poem (panegyric) to the Goddess Tripura Sundari. Panchastavi has been popular among Kashmiri Pandits . It is more than a thousand years old.

According to Janakinath Kaul Kamal, the earliest extant reference to verses of Panchastavi are found in the *Saraswatikanthabharana* of King Bhoja, who ruled from Ujjain, Malwa (1010 to 1060 AD). The probable date of the composition of Saraswatikanthabharan is between 1030-1040 AD. *Saraswatikanthabharana* is a work on Poetics in which King Bhoja compiled wide range of human experience and knowledge and discussed the poetics in details to lay down the rules of poetic composition to maximize the aesthetic delight. Many believe that Panchastavi must have been composed much earlier, for during those times it took years for ideas to travel and get popular to be noticed. Most pit its origin sometimes between the Sandarya Lahari, which was composed by Shankaracharya (788-820 AD) and the notice taken by Bhoja. Saundarya Lahari appears to be the inspiration for the devotional hymns in Panchastavi.

While great commentator on Tantra treatises, Lakshmidhara claims that Panchastavi was composed by Kalidasa, possibly noticing how the text finds earliest mention in the works of Bhoja, both belonging to Ujjain; some like Pandit Natharam Sastri pleads authorship for Abhinavagupta (950-1020 AD), a contemporary of King Bhoja. Some attribute its authorship to Adi Shankaracharya, while many to Dharmacharya from Kashmir. Janaki Nath Kaul Kamal and Laxman Joo Maharaj puts their weight behind Dharmacharya, since Laxmidhara who includes the Panchastavi text in his commentary upon Saundarya Lahari refers to the author as Dharmacharya. Nityananda, another commentator on Tantra mentions the name of Dharmacharya as the composer of Laghustava. Vidyaranya, mentions about Dharmacharya and Laghustava in his work, *Srividyamavatantra* (Chapter 31). Vidyaranya was the high priest of Harihar and Bukka Raya, who founded Vijayanagara empire and propagated the Srividya tradition. He wrote a treatise, *Sarva-darshana-sangraha* in which a chapter was devoted to Pratyabhijna thought from Kashmir. His engagement with thought-currents from Kashmir would have acquainted him with Abhinavagupta's work in greater measure.

Madhava Vidyaranya, who became the 12th Shankaracharya at Sringeri mentions about the encounter between Adi Shankaracharya and Abhinavagupta in Shankar-Digvijaya, which clearly is figment of his imagination since the two great Shaivite scholars were not contemporary and lived centuries apart. Local tradition of attributing origin of Panchastavi either to Shankaracharya or to Abhinavagupta appears from the story of this imaginary encounter.

Mammata, the great commentator on poetics profusely quotes the Panchastavi verses in his Kavya Prakasha (12th century) text. It is amply clear that thinkers on poetics like Bhoja and Mammata were quite conversant with the Panchastavi. This can be possible if we put up the authorship of Abhinavagupta to the Panchastavi. Abhinavagupta was a great synthesizer of tantras and aesthetic theories. His influence on subsequent generation of thinkers on poetics had been immense. Thus, even if the text might not have been popular with the people at large, this would have reached the hands of thinkers on poetics at the earliest. Secondly, local stories are not merely by-product of imagination. Exaggerations do creep up, but the cultural memories are grounded in some event of gigantic proportion. It appears that one of the Shankaracharya might have visited Kashmir during Abhinavagupta time. The author of Shankar-Digvijaya mixed the different stories of Shankaracharyas' travels into Kashmir.

Abhinavagupta wrote five hymns to Shiva towards the end of his life: The *Parmarthcharcha* viz. "Inquiry into Ultimate Reality"(There is a corresponding Charchastava (IInd stava) in Panchastavi), *Mahopadeshvimastika*, *Dehastha-devatachakra-strota* (Eulogy on the wheels of divinities existing in the bodies); *Bhairavastava* (Eulogy on the Absolute Reality) and *Anubhavanivedana* (The Offering of the Direct Experience of the reality). The last one is devoted to the bhairavi-mudra, the attitude of the mystic who has found his own self. This has resonance in the Panchastavi also.

Even in his lifetime, Abhinavagupta was eulogized by his disciples. Madhuraja, a yogi from south, wrote *Gurunatha-paramarsha* where Abhinavagupta is described as avatar of Shiva. Abhinavagupta's popularity crossed the Vindhyas during his own life-time and Ujjain being a creative culture centre would have noticed his great composition at the earliest. Bhoja rewarded a Pandit Purantaka, a worshipper in the temple of Mahakali for a poem *Shyamaldandaka*, a poem eulogizing Sarasvati, in 1001. (*Jane Gonda*, p. 259) Five decades is quite a long time for Abhinavagupta's short beautiful poetic composition to reach in the hands of a polyglot like Bhoja, who had fondness with the Shringar Rasa in literature.

Prof K.N. Dhar mentions that in various manuscripts in the Kashmir Government Research Library, the name of Acharya Prithvi

Dhar, a disciple of Shambhunath (Guru of Acharya Abhinavagupta) finds mention as the author. Many texts mention about Kalidasa. And most agree that it is one Dharmacharya. Dharmacharya, Prithvi Dhara and even Kalidasa are merely assumed name. The worshipper of Mahakali were also termed Kalidasa. Since the composer of Panchastavi eulogizes the Goddess in her red as well as dark complexion unlike Srividya texts from the South, it is assumed that the poet was Kali-worshipper. We already know that Tara worship was quite popular among both Buddhist and Hindus by the time Abhinavagupta came onto literary scene of India. In the very first canto, Laghustava, name Tara along with Jaya, Laxmi and Tripura has been mentioned (Laghustava:Verse 18). Verse 13 and 37 of the fifth canto, Sakal-janani-stava is dedicated to the dark coloured form of the Goddess. Thus, the appearance of the name of Kalidas in no way is contradictory to the Kashmiri belief about composition of Panchastavi by Abhinavagupta, since Abhinava was a great Kaula sadhak and wrote extensively on the rituals performed in the cremation ground. Kali is also the ishta-devi of Kashmiri tantriks. Dharmacharya itself is an honorific and a great mystic-thinker like Abhinavagupta would surely have held many other honorifics. Moreover, history records Abhinavagupta as the worthy disciple of Shambhunath. There is no confusion once Abhinavagupta is credited with the masterly work, since that also bridges the divide between popular perception and scholarly references.

Dr B.N. Pandit argues for the domicile of Dharmacharya in Kerala. He has different point of view that Panchastavi resembles Saundarya Lahari of Shankaracharya in technique and content, that it alludes to Sabri as the form of the Goddess. Sabri holds an important position in tantrik tradition of Kerala (Sabarimala is one of the most sacred sites in India), that the hymns does not mention about Trika or Kaula Yoga popular in Kashmir but alludes highest importance to Kundalini. Dr Pandit has missed the essential points. Tara is not worshipped in Kerala tradition or southern tradition. It is a north Indian deity that spread further northward across the Himalayas. Southern tradition worship Supreme Goddess in the form of fair complexion. Shaivism in south India is predominantly dualistic.

Panchastavi posits absolute non-duality and it is unlikely that it would have been composed in the south and gained popularity at Ujjain and Kashmir at the same time. There is also mention about Vatuk Bhairava (Charchastava: 29), who was popular deity in Kashmir and not Kerala.

The references made in the hymns about snow, pomegranate, blue lotus and herbs like trupsi and priyangu establishes further the Kashmiri origin of the composition. In the verse 14 of the last stava, the mention of Goddess form of Kundalini appearing dark as Priyangu is an important mark that indicates the proof.

प्रियङ्गुश्यामाङ्गीमिरूणतरवासः किसलयां
समुन्मीलन्मुक्ता फल बहुलने पथ्य कुसुमाम्।
स्तन द्वन्द्व स्फारस्तवकनमितां कल्पलतिकां
सकृद्ध्यायन्तस्त्वां दधति शिवचिन्ता मणि पदम्॥१४॥

(Those (devotees) who meditate constantly on Thee with Thy limbs dark-blue in colour, like the Priyunga creeper, dressed in red, resembling its (unopened) buds, and Thy form bent with (the weight of) Thy two voluminous breasts (bulging out), like massive bunches of its Pearl-like fruit, adorned with fully blossomed flowers, the bestower of all desires, like the wish-fulfilling creeper, they (those devotees, O Goddess) attain to the Chintamani state (all-desires-fulfilling gem) of Shiva Consciousness.)

(trans. by Gopi Krishna, 1975)

Priyangu (*Callicarpa macrophylla*) literally means that which is lovable or charming. It is one of the herbs mentioned in ancient scriptures of Ayurveda. Its synonyms are derived from the common etymological root, Priya, like phalapriya, priya, priyavalli. Other synonyms are streyasa, syaama, subhaga, nandini, mangalya. There is a belief that Priyangu puts forth blossom only when a woman touches it. This establishes a direct connection of the form of Shakti and the Priyangu. Its fruit are dark blue that represent infinite consciousness in experiential (anubhava) spirituality. The plant grows only in the South Himalayan belt from Kashmir to Bengal and Assam. Then, there is mention of another creeper trapushi (Laghuvastava, II). Janakinath Kamal mentions that trapusi is a kind of fern whose first sprout is tender and beautiful and resembles the rising Kundalini. In Kashmir, it is locally known as 'gyavthir'. Though, trapushi is also the Sanskrit name for cucumber. This makes it abundantly clear that it is unlikely that Panchastavi would have been composed in Kerala.

The most important hint Abhinavagupta, about being the composer of the Panchastavi is the use of tribija—aim, klim and sauh. We know how Abhinavagupta himself established bija 'Sauh' as the heart of Bhairava in *Para-Trisika-Vivarana (Verse 9-16).* Generally, the three bijas used in the Goddess worship are 'aim', klim, hrim, signifying the three aspects of goddess: jnana, kriya and iccha (wisdom, action and will). The three great goddess—Mahasaraswati, Mahalaxmi, Mahakali are the primary manifestation of the Para-shakti, Tripura. The Goddess is also known as Hrimkari (Laghustava:18). But, the substitution of the 'hrim' bija with the 'Sauh' bija could not have been done before Abhinavagupta. It is only Abhinavagupta who established 'sauh' as the amrit-bija, the seed of immortality. Abhinavagupta mentions that one who is not born of Yogini or united with Rudra cannot comprehend this supreme seed. This is the hridaya-bija of the Param-Shiva, and confers liberation. Thus, 'sauh' representing the Mahakali form of the Goddess Tripura substituting 'hrim' brings in valuable resolution between Monistic Shaivism and the Shaktism in Kashmir. This could have been done only by a person of stature like Abhinavagupta.

Importantly, Abhinavagupta wrote pentad for Shiva. He is the progenitor of the idea of bimba-pratibimba. The subtle to grosser manifestation operates like the mirror-image. In this theory, reflection is not identical, but one in which there is separate form, like triangle and inverted triangle, thereby having same structure in different form. It is the eternal recursion of the characteristics. The existence itself becomes a mosaic fractal. There is difference in sameness, and then recurrence of earlier forms. Thus, a pentad for Shiva ought to be followed by pentad of Shakti.

We also find extensive use of imagery of bimba-pratibimba in Panchastavi. Kundalini is described as the coiled tendril of the creeper plants. Kundalini is further described as the lightning creeper, the endless bifurcation in the lightning (tadi). It is this establishment of his own principle and attempt to resolve the divide that Panchastavi mentions about shata-chakra (6-chakras) and kundalini as piercing the shata-chakra by the grace of the Goddess. Shata-chakra brings coherence to the picture of bimba-pratibimba. The Shiva-triangle and its mirror image, an inverted shakti triangle interlocks to form a shata-chakra. It is to bring coherence in the whole system that 'sauh' became more apt as a bija than 'hrim', though hrim with curved 'ha' is used to represent coiled kundalini. The three bijas are the best way to offer salutation to the Tripura.

ऐंन्द्रस्येव शरासनस्यदधती मध्ये ललाटं प्रभां
शैक्लीं कान्तिमनुष्णगोरिव शिरस्यातन्वती सर्वतः ।
एषाऽसौ त्रिपुरा हृदि द्युतिरिवोष्णांशोः सदाहस्थिता
छिन्द्यान्नसहसा पदैस्त्रिभिरघं ज्योतिर्मयी वाङ्गमयी ॥१॥

(May the Goddess Tripura, who is of the nature of light and sound, shining in the forehead like the lustrous bow of Indra (ie the rainbow) in the crown of the head like the luminous white shine of the moon, and in the heart like the never-setting splendorous sun—may She, by means of the three mighty syllables 'Aim', 'Klim', and 'Sauh', speedily destroy all our impurities.)

(trans. by Gopi Krishna, 1975)

All three bijas themselves contain trines. Letter 'Ai' in the bijamantra, Aim, has triangular space. Letter 'Ka' in the bijamantra 'klim' written in old devanagari or Bengali shows a triangle in the left. The crooked portion on the right resembles like a goad which represent Kundalini. The empty space is the Yonimandala which is the seat of Tripurasundari. In the Sharda script, Ka is written in the same way. The third letter 'sauh' has the fourteenth vowel, 'au' which appears like trident. Thus, the three bija-mantras with which the pentad Panchastavi begins, itself represents picturesque view of the triadic nature of Existence. This might be seen as extension of chitrakavya for adulation to the divinity making it to be taken note of by Bhoja who formulated rules for chitrakavya.

The bimba-pratibimba aspect has appeared in various simile used by the composer. Kundalini resembles lightning and is also of the form of lightning. The most important aspect in the Panchastavi is the narration of effect of divine grace upon a bhakta. This could have been described so succinctly by Abhinavagupta only. Abhinavagupta describes in his magnum opus *Tantraloka* (Chapter V, 30-31) the seven blisses produced after penetration of cakras. In the stage of 'parananda' (supreme joy), the body is motionless, with eyes closed for breath having pierced the talu (palate) where it whirls continuously producing tears of love and yawning. *Tantraloka* describes ten successive states towards attaining Shivahood-trembling, revolving, whirling, flight, stability, light, bliss, vision, wonder and indescribable ecstasy of being settled in the Supreme self. In the fourth stava, Ambastava of the Panchastavi, the state of realization of divinity is described:

आविर्भवत्पुलक सन्ततिभिः शरीरै-
निष्यंदमानसलिलैर्नयनैश्च नित्यम्।
वाग्भिश्च गद्गदपदाभिरूपासते ये
पादौ तवाम्ब भुवनेषु त एव धन्याः ॥४॥

O Mother, with hairs on their bodies standing on end, with tears streaming down from their eyes and with their voices quivering with emotion, those (devotees) who ceaselessly worship Thy feet in their heart, they are, indeed, blessed.

आनन्दलक्षणमनाहतनाम्नि देशे
नादात्मना परिणतं तव रूपमीशे।
प्रत्यङ् मुखेन मनसा परिचीयमानं
शंसन्ति नेत्रसलिलैः पुलकैश्च धन्याः ॥१९॥

O Empress of the World: Those blessed ones who inwardly experience Thy blissful aspect at the place known as Anahata (heart chakra) in the form of Nada (Cosmic sound—the source of all speech) express the ecstasy of this encounter with their hair standing on end (through the intensity of emotion) and tears (of joy) pouring from their eyes.

(trans. by Gopi Krishna, 1975)

Thus, standing of hair on roots (pulakan) and tears of joy are the manifest expression of delight when the shakti touches the heart of the devotee. It is the 'touch' which mediates between the immanence and transcendence. Skin/Touch (tvak) is both a gem and sensory organ. Body is considered the island of nine gems. These are seven dhatus namely—rasa (chyle), mansa (flesh), rudhira (blood), shukra (semen), majja (bone marrow), asthi (bone), meda (fat), roma (hair) and tvak (skin/touch).

These are produced by body and grow on food. Touch appears to be unique because without it the sense organs cannot experience. Sparsha pervades all other sense. Hence, it is most primordial. The corresponding body organ for sparsha is skin and the same is called 'sparshana'.Thus, whenever the organ of touch skin bears some change, it is assumed that the body has been touched. If there is no external stimulus, the practitioners believed that they have been internally Touched, antahsparsha. It is the touch over the skin that causes hair to stand on roots. Sparsha is the paramount sense in the tantras.

Panchastavi's very second verse in Laghustava exhort this sense of touch:

या मात्रा त्रपुसीलतातनुलसत्तन्तूत्थिति स्पर्धिनी
वाग्बीजे प्रथमे स्थिता तव सदा तां मन्महे ते वयम्।
शक्तिः कुण्डलिनीति विश्वजनन व्यापार बद्धोद्यमा
ज्ञात्वेत्थं न पुनः स्पृशन्ति जननी गर्भेऽर्भकत्वं नराः ॥२॥

We, Thy devotees, always meditate upon the vowel in Thy first syllable (Aim) resembling the fine first shoot of maiden-hair (a kind of fern) just beginning to sprout which itself is of the shape of Kundalini always engaged in the work of creation (of the universe). Realizing Thee in this form, man does not touch the womb of a mother again (ie is not reborn in this world).

(trans. by Gopi Krishna, 1975)

The allegory of trapushi creeper itself reflects the bimba-pratibimba in operation. Trapushi creepers are covered in fine white hairs, appearing to be standing like pulkan. As stated earlier, the opening of the coiled tendril appears as unfolding of Kundalini. Similarly, we find mention of another plant, Priyangu. These bear dark blue seeds, but all over the petals and the stems, the white hairs appear as pulkan. There is belief that only when a woman touches the plant, it flowers. Thus, touch, standing hair, creeper, coiling everything that is associated with esoteric kundalini has allegoric presence in priyangu.

Panchastavi is compilation of hymns to Goddess, *Tripura Sundari*. The composer has described Tripura as the goddess who resides in three places in the very first verse. She is of the nature of light (jyotirmayi) and sound (vangamayi), who shines in the forehead (lalat) like the lustrous bow of Indra (the rainbow); in the crown of the head like the luminous white shine of the moon, and in the heart like the sun. As sound 'aim', it resides in the forehead, as 'klim' in the crown of the head and as 'sauh' in the heart.

ऐन्द्रस्येव शरासनस्यदधती मध्ये ललाटं प्रभां
शैक्लीं कान्तिमनुष्णगोरिव शिरस्यातन्वती सर्वतः।
एषाऽसौ त्रिपुरा हृदि द्युतिरिवोष्णांशोः सदाहस्थिता
छिन्द्यान्नसहसा पदैस्त्रिभिरघं ज्योतिर्मयी वाङ्गमयी ।।१।।

In the Verse 16 of the Laghustava, the composer explains the triple nature of the Existence in detail. There are three devas—Brahma, Vishnu and Shiva; three Vedas—Rik, Sam and Yajur; three fires—grihapatya (household), ahvaniya (sacrificial), dakshinagni (crematory); the three Shaktis-lccha (desire), jnana (Knowledge) and Kriya (action); three sounds—Uddat (tenor), anuddat (low) and svarita (medium); three worlds—bhu, bhuvah and svah; three-syllabled Gayatri—a, u and m; junction of three rivers—Ganga, Yamuna and Saraswati, three Brahmas—Om, Tat and Sat and three castes—Brahmin, Kshatriya and Vaishya. The poet declares that all these and others that are modelled in three ways (i.e. which are threefold in nature), truly follow in trika-principle that flows from the Goddess Tripura. Thus, the composer has sung in praise of the Kundalini having three coils (Sakaljnanistava: 29), and the three deep lines marking the body of the Goddess (Laghustava: 11). There are triple symbolism—Pujasamketa (secret of worship), Chakrasamketa (secret of chakra) and Mantrasamketa (secret of mantra) throughout the text. In the hymns, the Tripura Sundari is shown in three aspects—sthula (gross), sukshma (subtle) and para (transcendental). Thus, ritual is also of three kinds—kayika (body), vachika (speech), manasa (mind) or Bahayaga, Antaryaga and Bhavana. In the Laghustava, the mantra as the sound aspect and various dazzling objects as light aspect are described. This is the Bahayagya. In the second hymn, light as the inner contemplation aspect is provided. The third is the bhavana aspect—bhakti. In the Fourth canto, the experience and prayers to the Goddess in the form of kundalini has been described. In the fifth canto, there is the description of the Cosmic Mother, the shata-chakra and their identity/correlation.

देवानां त्रितयं, त्रयी हुतभुजां, शक्तित्रयं, त्रिस्वरा-
स्त्रैलोक्यं, त्रिपदी, त्रिपुष्करमथो, त्रिब्रह्म, वर्णास्त्रयः।
यत्किंचिजगति त्रिधा नियमितं वस्तु त्रिवर्गात्मकं
तत्सर्वं त्रिपुरेति नाम भगवत्यन्वेति ते ततत्वतः ॥१६॥

Even the seed mantra, 'aim klim sauh' has been chosen to complete the triple symbolism. One would have expected that once Shankaracharya's Saundarya Lahari was already extant which explored about the panchakshari and shodashskahsari seed mantra for seeking blessing of Tripurasundari, further treatises on Goddess Tripura would continue with the syllabic formula. Only an authority like Abhinavagupta would have substituted 'hrim' with para-bija of Trika Shaivism, 'sauh'. But, again this requires the genius and authority of an Abhinavagupta to bring in a trikakshari replacing extant verses, to bring in more coherence of Trika Shaivism and Tripura Shaktism.

One is tempted to ask why pentad? Why did the poet not compose a triadic hymn to bring more coherence? Again this has to do with the fusion of Trika Shaivism with Tripura Shaktism. There are five main powers of Param Shiva, viz. cit (consciousness), ananda (bliss), iccha (will), jnana (wisdom) and kriya (activity) as described in *Para-Trisika-Vivarana*. Similarly, there are five-fold acts—srishti (manifestation), sthiti (maintenance), samhara (absorption), vilaya (veiling) and anugraha (revelation). Composing a pentad for triadic Tripura brings the complete fusion of two paths.

Panchastavi, not only reveals the three-fold nature of the Universe and the three-letter seed mantra to seek divine grace, it is one of the sweetest and most beautiful compositions that establishes absolute non-duality. It is a text which can be grasped by common man and still has hidden secrets that can lead philosophers on a quest. Panchastavi is the living proof of the Indian propensity to settle conflicting paradigms under the banner of Advaita. In the 32nd verse of the last canto, even Buddha and Jina Mahavira, are described as the different names by which righteous persons call the Goddess Tripura.

विधुर्विष्णुर्ब्रह्मा प्रकृतिरपुरात्मा दिनकरः
स्वभावो जैनेंन्द्रः सुगतमुनिराकाशमनिलः ।
शिवः शक्तिश्चेति श्रुतिविषयतां तामुपगतां
विकल्पैरेभिस्त्वामऽभिदधति सन्तो भगवतीम् ॥३३॥

Thou art Brahma (the Creator), Vishnu (the Preserver) and Thou art matter, the embodied Soul, ego-consciousness, the Moon, the Sun, Nature (of things), the Lord of Jains (Mahavira), the illumined sage (Buddha), sky, air, also Shiva and Shakti. By these different names, O Goddess, Thou art heard of and called by the righteous.

(trans. by Gopi Krishna, 1975)

What an excellent thought that sprout from the land of Kashmir to propel the unity in plurality of Indian civilization!

References

1. Kamal, Janakinath Kaul (2001). *Pancastavi*: the pentad of hymns of Kundalini Yoga, Srinagar: Sri Ramakrishna Ashrama.
2. Krishna, Gopi (1975). *Panchastavi*: A Pentad of Devotional Hymns to Super-Energy, Central Institute of Kundalini Research.
3. Swami Laxman Joo Maharaj (1974). (trans. from Sanskrit to Hindi) "Sri Panchastav", Dharmacharya-krit, February 1974.

4. Krishna, Gopi (1995). *Ancient Secrets of Kundalini* (Hidden in Panchastavi).
5. Singh, Jaideva (1988). *Para-Trisika-Vivarana of Abhinvagupta*, New Delhi: MLBD.
6. Gonda, Jane (1977). *A History of Indian Literature: Epics and Sanskrit Religious Literature*, 1977.
7. Pandit, Dr BN, *Panchastavi in Kashmir*, downloaded from ikashmir.net/panchastavi/article2.html.
8. Dhar, KN, *Panchastavi—A Brief Study*, downloaded from ikashmir.net/panchastavi/article1.html
9. Awasthi, Shiva Shankar (1966). *Mantra aur Matrkaon ka Rahaasya*, Varanasi: Chowkhamba.

CAMATKARA

Chapter 14

Anandavardhana and His Theory of Poetic Suggestion

One of the most brilliant aesthetic thinkers of India, *Anandavardhana* has made an immensely significant contribution to the development of the Sanskrit literary theory. His famous treatise on poetic suggestion, *Dhvanyaloka,* is a seminal work in the field of poetics and is regarded almost as highly as Panini's *Ashtadhyayi* in the field of grammar. It is in fact a paradigm-changing work that revolutionized aesthetic thinking in India, its ideas providing parameters for appreciation of not only meaning in poetry but also beauty in other arts. If one can sum up in one sentence Anandavardhana's core concept of *dhvani* or poetic suggestion, one can say that what is explicit is mere expression of the implicit; what is seen is mere manifestation of the unseen; what is imminent is merely the unfolding of the transcendent; what is saguna has a nirguna aspect. It is, thus, a kind of encapsulation of the Indian way of thinking. There is always a non-empirical reality which cannot be grasped by ordinary sense. The extra-ordinary transcendental reality can be experienced in an intuitive flash by a few adept and so can poetic meaning. Moreover, the objective of comprehending the extraordinary implicit sense in poetry is *rasa* or savouring of aesthetic delight.

Anandavardhana was born in a Kashmiri Brahmin family. He was a courtier of King Avantivarman (855-883 AD) of Kashmir, as mentioned in Kalhana's *Rajatarangini*. Thus, his works can be attributed to the mid-ninth century. Besides being an aesthetician of high merit, he was also a poet with several poetic works to his credit. These include *Arjunacharita* and *Devishataka* in Sanskrit, and *Vishambanalila* in Prakrit. But, of these only the *Devishatak* is available now. Strangely though, it is not a good work of high poetic merit, but chitrakavya or pictorial poetry, a type that he himself described to be of a very inferior kind in *Dhvanyaloka*. *Vishambanalila* is an epic in Prakrit in which Kamadeva is shown frolicking with his friends. Anandavardhana was a philosopher and a scholar too. His philosophical works include *Tattvaloka* and his vritti on *Viniscayatika-dhararmottara*. But, it is *Dhvanyaloka*, his epoch-making work in poetics that won him fame. The treatise fame served as a lighthouse in the vast ocean of Sanskrit creativity. The *Dhvanyaloka* consists of two parts—the gnomic verses (karika) and the exposition (vritti). There has been a long controversy about the real author of the karika part. While many like Jacobi, SK De and PV Kane are of the opinion that the vritti and karikas have been written by two different authors, most scholars agree about single authorship of the two parts following Abhinavagupta's indication in the *Abhinavabharati* that both the karikas and the vritti are written by Anandavardhana himself.

Anandavardhana's Cultural Milieu

During the times of Anandavardhana's postulations, India was passing through a post-imperial phase when there was no single authority to keep it politically united. There were no unifying empires like the Kushana or Guptas but regional kingdoms of the Palas, Cholas, Pratihara, Rashtrakuta, Senas and, of course, the Utpalas in Kashmir. The collapse of the Gupta Empire led to the breakdown of a strong support system for the earlier sophisticated cultural enterprises. According to Edwin Gerow, Sanskrit drama lost its audience (never more than the society of sophisticates attracted to the imperial courts and cities) and its means of support (wealthy literati). Though, plays continued to be written, these were now rarely performed. (Gerow, 1977, p 251). Gerow continues, "On the side of strophic poetry, changes too were taking place, reflecting the new contexts in which poetry was used. We see growing devotionalism, and the employment of song, and also music, even marked shifts from Sanskrit to vernaculars." (Gerow, p 252)

It was the period when poetry was increasingly getting available to masses and hence, losing the sophistication. The rise of devotional sects created the need for expression. Poetry and devotional songs were undergoing fusion. In fact, ardhamagadhi dohas (couplets) used by the Jain monks during the 8th-9th century crept into Sanskrit. Gerow traces the genealogy of the first medieval poetry of Jayadeva, the *Gita Govinda* (12th century) to such borrowing from the non-Sanskrit popular sources. (Ibid)

The Bhakti movement emerged in the southern peninsula during the 6th and 7th centuries with most of the Bhakti saints belonging to the lower castes. The hymns and sermons were composed in vernacular Tamil language by the Nayannars (Shaivism) and the Alvars (Vaishnavism). It spread gradually to other parts of the country as a strong wave. Among the Shaiva saints, the foremost were Appar, Sambandar, Manikkawasagar, Cuntarar and Sundarar. The contemporary Vaishnava Alvar saints like Poykai, Putan, Peyar, Tirumankaiyalvar, Andal, Periyalvar, Kulacekarar, Tiruppanalvar, and Nammalvar were also great composers of devotional songs in vernacular languages. There was also the opening up of spiritual space for the woman saints. Andal preceded the later century women bhakti saints of medieval India. Bhakti movement was derived from the ideas in the Upanishads, and from the Buddhist idea of Bodhisattva beings. The mode of worship and the iconography was appropriated from the pre-Buddhist religion of yakshas and nagas. The religious hymns and music were sung during temple rituals. Dancing was also included, henceforth. From Pallava period onwards dancers were maintained by major temples. The medium of dancing in the ritual for theistic gods reiterate the connection with the yaksha-worship. The new devotionalism sought a more direct contact between man and God, a delightful love for the theistic deity, who bestows grace upon man. The popular need for a laukika deity in the time of fragmented polity to stem over the turbulence was catered by the devotional sects. Yakshas were the laukika deities believed to be in direct contact with man. The devotional movement, thus, merely imitated the pre-existing mode of worship in new avatar with new gods, new hymns, new tales and new Puranas.

It was the time of emergence of the cult of eighty four Siddhas among Buddhists in the eastern part of India with the centre at Nalanda. The Siddha tradition emerged in the South (Tamil Siddhas) as well as North (Nath siddhas). The Siddhas like the bhakti saints mostly belonged to lower castes and composed their poems in vernacular languages. The charyapada verses composed by them are regarded as the earliest composition in the emerging vernacular languages like Assamese, Bengali and Oriya.

In the post-Gupta, pre-Islamic period, the religious landscape was undergoing massive transformation. As a result of millenarianism, the concept of avatara held sway across the religious spectrum. The Puranas were being composed by the revivalist Hindu sects and Buddhism was undergoing a major schism. In *Dhvanyaloka*, Anandavardhana alludes to the three-fold division of kathas, the narrative of the new gods referred to in Haribhadra's (730-780 AD) '*Samaratcchakaha*'—divya, manusa and divya-manusha.

The fragmentation in the polity had its *dhvani* (resonance) in the religious realm. It is the time when one finds a major shift from ancient order to new order. The iconographies of yakshas were being appropriated to develop images of new gods. Various statues of alaukik (extra-ordinary) gods were being built on the foundation of statues of yakshas and yakshi (laukika demi-gods). The nomenclature of 'Bhagavat' was used for yakshas and only later on borrowed by emergent theistic Hinduism to signify gods. Scholars have traced the cult of Tara and Hariti among Buddhists and the cult of Balaram and Kartikeya or even Ganesha to pre-existing yaksha tradition.

Yakshas continued to straddle in imagination, but they were reduced into the demi-gods guarding the temple complex, caves, stupas of the major gods and as carrier of water. Theistic Hinduism as well as idol worship among the Buddhists was taking proper shape. There were endless multiplications of divine images and for each deity or the Bodhisattva, certain purana, or devotional shatakam, were composed separately. Since performance of drama was becoming difficult in the meltdown of support structures, the vernacular poetry and songs were emerging as the best form of expression for propitiating new gods.

In Anandavardhana's Kashmir, a wide range of Tantric cults, both Hindu and Buddhist, which had started emerging from the 5th century itself, enjoyed a wide popularity and impacted every aspect of social and religious life. Of particular importance was the upsurge of the non-dualist Shaivism, derived from Shaivagamic traditions which it shared with the dualist Siddhanta Shaivism.

Thus, the time of Anandavardhana was a period of flux in which the monopolizing tendencies were withering away. There was creative plurality with Sanskrit itself beginning to face the challenge of vernacular languages which were soon to become the preferred medium of creative expression. Anandavardhana himself was a participant in this flux. He was a great connoisseur of Prakrit poetry and wrote a narrative poem in the language, the *Vishamabanalila*.

It was in this situation of flux and intellectual ferment that great debates on *rasa* or aesthetic emotion were taking place among poetic theorists and scholars, each interpreting Bharata's famous *rasa* sutra or definitive aphorism about what constitutes the aesthetic experience according to his own philosophical standpoint. While agreeing generally that the ultimate objective of kavya was the evocation of *rasa* or aesthetic delight, they differed widely about the nature, location of the *rasa* experience. By the time Anandavardhana expounded his revolutionary *dhvani* theory, Sanskrit poetics had developed along two distinct traditions of poetic appreciation and evaluation—*rasa* and alamkara. There was also the Riti school with gunas or stylistic qualities as its basic parameter. Both Alamkara and Riti schools were more concerned with structural or stylistic aspects than evocation of feeling which forms the core of the *rasa* theory. A universally accepted literary theory had still not come into existence and it was here that Anandavardhana was to play a very significant role.

Meanwhile, the need for an overarching theory of unity at the intellectual level was strongly felt. If unity was not possible in the political or religious sphere, could it be posited in the realm of literature? Mimamsa and Vedanta philosophers both vied with each other for postulating such an over-arching concept of unity. Shankaracharya, only few decades before Anandavardhana, had propounded the philosophy of Advaita Vedanta. The Vedantists drew inspiration and ideas from the great linguistic philosopher, Bhartrihari (450-510 AD), who founded the shabdadvaita (word monism or linguistic monism) school of thought. Looking at the problem from the linguistic angle, Bhartrihari tried to explain pluaralities of the phenomenal world in terms of the unity generated by shabdatattva or the word-principle in his famous treatise, the *Vakyapadiya*. If the Word is the Brahman and if the Universe is the manifestation of the Brahman, the Word identified with Brahman or Reality is the subtler ground for all-pervading unity. The meaning of the pada (sentence), the speech-unit, is indivisible (*akhanda*). Meaning cannot be reduced to its parts. Individual words are distinguished only for the purposes of convention or expression. This whole-meaning (*sphota*) is intuited in a moment of instantaneous flash (*pratibha*).

Anandavardhana had to grapple with the new situation and he had a path burst forth before him. Concept of *Sphota* could provide him with the desired tool to postulate a unity. Anandavardhana must have faced multiplicity of issues before he decided to systematize the science of poetics in *Dhvanyaloka*. Some of which can be framed as follows:

Could laukika plurality be understood as manifestation of alaukika unity? Could devotion and cognition be fused? Could there be a science of poetics that could explain the popularity of new poetries which lacked the classical ornaments of poetries? Could the popularity of new poetries like caryapada with emphasis on obliqueness be traced in the sense of aesthetic delight? Was *rasa* limited only to Sanskrit drama and not to new vernacular poetries? Why do resonances (*dhvani*) of bells, mridanga, musical instruments produce delight, even though these are mere sounds without phonetic shabda? If shabda is the carrier of delight, how do gestures in dances, mudras in rituals produce delight? Can there be a way to fuse logo-centric thinking and gestural thinking? Does repetition of mantras produce a *dhvani*-effect (resonance) which might lead to the state of liberation, Moksha and production of the associated *rasa*, santa *rasa*? Does repetition of name of the new divinities create similar experiences? Could *dhvani* (resonance) hold the key to moksha? Could there be a new path of salvation, *rasa-dhvani*, resonating Buddha's path to Nirvana? Anandavardhana had a tough task to accomplish. How did he accomplish the path?

Alamkara Shastra and *Dhvani*

As said earlier, there were two major theories in vogue in Sanskrit poetics, as B.K. Matilal has pointed out. One was centred on alamkara or embellishment of word and meaning by means of figure of speech, and the other on *rasa* or evocation of aesthetic emotion. There were also theories pertaining to guna or poetic qualities and riti or diction, but the science of Sanskrit poetics was broadly designated as alamkara shastra. Bhamaha was the founder of this rhetorical school with Udbhatta, Dandin, Vamana, Rudrabhatta etc. contributing significantly to it, all being predecessors of Anandavardhana. This school believed in the poetry alamkara or ornamentation as the dominating feature. Describing poetry as "well matched form and content", Bhamah was of the view that vakrokti, deviation from the ordinary mode of expression, is the best alamkara for it. For Vamana, the founder of the Riti school, alamkara meant beauty itself and not just ornamentation. 'Saundaryam Alamkarah' (alamkara means beauty), he states in his *Kavyalamkarasutravritti* (KASV). Dandin on the other hand says in his *Kavyadarsha*, "Kavya shobhakaran dharman alamkaran prachakshate" or "characteristics that makes poetry beautiful are called alamkara."

Alamkaras or figures of speech, it may be pointed out, are two types—shabdaalamkara or figures of speech and arthaalamkara or figures of sense. The number of alamkaras was, however, by no means fixed and went on multiplying. Where as Vamana describes only two shabdaalamkaras and regards all arthaalamkaras as aspects of upma or the simile, Mammata defines 61 arthaalamkaras and 6 shabdaalamkaras in his *Kavyaprakasha*. Rajasekhara in his work *Alankara Makarandah* (the nectar of alamkar) discusses 63 alamkaras. Chandraloka extends its scope to 100 arthalamkaras.

Whatever the case be, there are three major kinds of shabdaalamkara or the figures of speech: anup*rasa* (alliteration), yamaka (pun) and shlesha (paronomasia, double entendre). Some frequently used arthalamkaras or the figures of sense are upma (simile) and rupaka.

However, the art of poetry did not remain confined to listing of alamkaras or structural elements alone but was also subjected to a deeper inquiry about what constituted its essence. The metaphor about the body made more beautiful by ornaments was extended. If the poetry is externally a body, it was argued, and alamkaras are the ornaments that enhances its beauty, what constitutes its soul became a major issue that was confronted by rhetoricians like Vamana. Anandavardhana, while not dispensing with the use of figures altogether, thought it more important to draw attention to the significance of the emotive import of poetry. Making what proved to be the most significant development in the whole discourse, he came up with his seminal concept of *dhvani* or poetic suggestion, through which he felt the emotive power of poetry could be best brought out. It was *dhvani*, he declared in the very first verse of the Dhvanyaloka that was the soul of the poetry—"*kavyastatma dhvaniriti*". (DL, I.1)

Language being the medium of literary expression, earlier critics had emphasized the essential unity of shabda and artha or word and meaning. In poetic context or in ordinary discourse , they had pointed out, meaning of word operates through two or rather three semantic powers. The first of these is abhidha or denotation that gives the literal or lexical meaning. In certain instances where the denotative power does not give the appropriate meaning in the context, the second power called lakshana or indication comes into play which modifies denotation to provide the metaphorical sense of a word. There is a third one also known as the tatparya or purport through which the integral meaning of a linguistic statement emerges from the context. Anandavardhana's theory of *dhvani* or resonance, however, made a major departure by positing a special power of words—vyanjana or suggestion. It is the suggested sense, he declared, that operates in poetry at a deeper level than either denotation or the literal sense, or indication or the metaphorical sense, and unravels poetic beauty. Abhinavagupta, who wrote a brilliant commentary 'Lochana' on the *Dhvanyaloka* says that *dhvani* or suggested meaning is the fourth power of the word—"*Chaturthyam tu kakshayam dhvanana-vyapara*". (Dhvanyalokalochana, I.4)

Anandavardhana's theory was severely criticized and opposed by some scholars of grammar and logic, who vehemently argued against the necessity of positing vyanjana as a linguistic power for communication of meaning in poetry. Abhidha or denotation was sufficient to lead it through the process of anumana (inference) or tatparya (purport), they said. The *Dhvani* theorists fought back with equal vehemence to establish that the suggested meaning in a poetic construction did not come within the ambit of any of these linguistic powers but beyond them. They likened it to ripples of resonance produced when a metal is struck or to an echo subtly produced by a voice.

Many are of the view that the roots of Anandavardhana's concept of *dhvani* can be traced to Vamana's conception of vakrokti or obliquity of poetic expression (on which Kuntaka later based an entire theory). Anandavardhana, however, went beyond the semantic meaning and sought to unravel deeper mysteries of poetic beauty by linking the suggestive mode to *rasa* or aesthetic delight and thus combined the two into a 'unified theory of aesthetic response'. Later, Abhinavagupta established the pre-eminence of the *rasa-dhvani* theory on a firm footing in the '*Locana*'.

To explain his concept of *dhvani* or the suggested sense,

Anandavardhana used the analogy of lavanya or charm in ladies. He wrote: "But the suggested aspect is quite different from this. In the words of the first-rate poets it shines supreme and towers above the beauty of the striking external conditions even as charm in ladies. (DL, I.4)

The lavanya of a lady, he said, is always more than the beauty of her different limbs or her physical appearance, more than the beauty of ornaments and the dress. It is intrinsic and beyond expression. Similarly, *dhvani* in a poetic composition is the charm of the poetry. It is beyond every explicit sense. It is suggested and cannot be reduced to mundane meaning, either ordinary or embellished. It delights the reader just as a lady's charm delights the admirer. Anandavardhana uses various illustrations from Prakrit as well as Sanskrit literature to describe the nature of *dhvani* which is implicit in a poetic composition. Anandavardhana refers to the suggested sense as the soul of poetry and says:

"That alone is the soul of poetry; and so it was that, of yore, the sorrow of the First Poet (Valmiki) at the separation of the krauncha couple took the form of a shloka."(DL, I.5)

Sometimes the suggested meaning, i.e. *dhvani* may be of the nature of prohibition while the explicit meaning is of the nature of positive approval. Anandavardhana explains the karika with an example:

"Ramble freely, pious man! That dog today is killed; By the fierce lion that dwells." (DL, I-4, p 9)

Here the idea suggested is in the sense of prohibition, but the explicit meaning is the idea of moving freely.

A Primer to Dhvanyaloka

Dhvanyaloka consists of the verse as well as commentary portions. It is divided into four udyotas or flashes (chapters) containing therein 19, 33, 47 and 17 verses, respectively. In the first udyota, various views criticizing the concept of *dhvani* have been discussed. The nature of *dhvani* as suggestion has been explained and it has been sought to establish that *dhvani* is the soul of poetry. In the second udyota, different types of *dhvani* have been discussed in terms of the role of the suggested meaning (vyangyartha). The importance of *rasa* and various associated metaphors are also described and discussed. Arguments of the opposing schools of rhetoricians have been refuted and demolished. The third udyota is the longest. Here *dhvani* have been discussed from the point of view of the suggested word (vyanjaka). The fourth udyota describes the wider scope of the applicability of the concept of *dhvani*. Here Anandavardhana establishes that like the principle of unity of action in drama, unity of *rasa* is necessary in a poetic composition. A poet ought to strive for evocation of a single *rasa* in his work. And if another *rasa* is necessary, it should be treated as mere auxiliary to the main suggested *rasa*.

The concept of *Dhvani* had its root in the *sphotavada* of Bhartrihari. In the *sphotavada*, the pada or words are not taken separately by splitting a vakya or sentence. *Sphota* is manifest from the last sound together with the impressions produced by preceding sound. *Sphota* is thus, equivalent to the power of visarga, where there is emergence of manifest universe only at the end of the vowel-series. Similarly, *dhvani* is a suggested meaning that echoes and carry within itself the impressions produced by all other forms of meanings—lakshana, abhidha or tatparya. It is like the intuitive flash of *sphota* that *dhvani* is comprehended in a poetic utterance. *Dhvani* incorporates within it the abhidha and lakshana aspects. One can arrive at the suggested meaning (*dhvani*) either through abhidha (literal meaning) or lakshana (metaphoric or indicative meaning). Abhidha and lakshana are the ways and the vyanjana (suggested meaning) the end. *Dhvani* is so termed because it reverberates. *Dhvani* is the implicit meaning and more than either the literal meaning or the indicative meaning. Just like there is krama (sequence) by which a word gathers meaning, similarly there is a krama by which the *dhvani* is revealed. The sequence in grammar is from sound to word, from word to *sphota* and from *sphota* to meaning. Similarly, in poetic creation, the krama is from abhidha to lakshana and then to vyanjana/*dhvani*. Anandavardhana mentions in the karika given below:

"Just as the purport of a sentence is grasped through the meaning of individual words, the knowledge of that sense is got at only through the medium of the explicit sense". (DL, I.10)

The suggested meaning manifests suddenly to the intelligent minds when they turn away from the literal meaning. Anandavardhana describes, vyangyakavya as the poetic compositions where the ordinary literal or conventional meaning becomes secondary and the secondary meaning in turn suggests the implicit meaning. (DL, I.11). In the commentary, Anandavardhana sums up the position in detail:

Where the suggested meaning is not important and mere ancillary to the expressed meaning, these are mere instances of vachya-alankar (metaphor);

When the suggested meaning merely follows (anugami) the vachyartha (literal meaning), there is no *dhvani* poetry;

When both the shabda (word) and artha (meaning) are solely directed towards the suggested sense, only then does *dhvani* emerge. There should not be any confusion on this account.

Dhvani and Sphota

In *Dhvanyaloka*, Anandavardhana himself admits that the very term, '*dhvani*' has been borrowed from the grammarians who maintain that sound in its eternal form of *sphota* is identical with the Brahman i.e. Ultimate Reality. *Sphota* is a genus of which *dhvani* is like species. *Sphota* is the permanent element in the sound whereas *dhvani* refers to transitory elements of speech manifest in temporal universe. *Dhvani* articulates *sphota*. When a sound is produced by contact (sparsha), it is called *sphota*. And from the mother sound wave, succeeding sound waves are produced. These succeeding sound waves are *dhvani* which is audible when it comes, giving it a kind of ripple effect. These successive sound waves are *dhvani* which is audible when it comes in contact with auditory organs. Since audible sounds are produced from initial *sphota*, *dhvani* is said to be suggested by *sphota*. Thus *dhvani* becomes the suggested and *sphota* as the suggester. Anandavardhana took up the idea of *dhvani* as suggested (vyangya) from this discussion of *sphota* and *dhvani* in Bhartrihari's work, the *Vakyapadiya*. Whereas in the *sphota* theory, *dhvani* is the vyanjaka of the *sphota*, i.e. initial sound; in the *Dhvanyaloka*, Anandavardhana used the concept of *dhvani* as suggested by both shabda and artha (word and meaning). It is on this basis of *dhvani* as vyangya-artha that Anandavardhana classified *dhvanikavya* into three major types—vastu *dhvani* where it is the object that is suggested, alamkar *dhvani* where the figure is suggested and *rasa dhvani* where rasa forms the suggested sense.

The *sphota* doctrine emphasizes the ultimate unity of word and meaning. Pashyanti vak represents the stage of ultimate unity. The differentiation of word and meaning takes place at the stage of madhyama vak, but here the word and the meaning are not manifest externally. Vak as consciousness is a temporal unity. It is akrama, beyond temporal sequentiality. But, its third stage, vaikhari is the audible external sound that functions in time hence governed by krama, temporal sequentiality. *Vaikhari* reveals the madhyama. Here the audible phoneme is the vyanjaka and the internal *sphota* is the vyangya or the suggested. Varna or the audible letter as *dhvani* reveals *sphota*. *Dhvani* also has the quality of resonance. Thus, the two-sided function of *dhvani* as having the power of revelation and process of resonance made it an apt concept to be adopted by Anandavardhana. Just like the echo in the audible sound, there is echo of various levels of meaning. Just as sound-waves reach our ears in temporal sequence like waves, similarly the meaning is revealed in sequences.

There is homologisation and correspondences between stages of shabda in *sphotavada* and stages of artha in *dhvanivada*. In both, pratibha (intuitive flash) is the guiding instinct. There are three stages of shabda—pashyanti, madhyama and vaikhari. Similarly, there are three stages of meaning in the *dhvanivada*, abhidha, lakshana and vyangya. Abhidha (literal meaning) corresponds to audible sound in the form of varna (vaikhari), lakshana (indicative meaning) corresponds to the madhyama stage of shabda where meaning and shabda even though are separated, but it is not manifest. The vyangya or the suggested meaning corresponds to the highest stage of pashyanti where meaning and words are undifferentiated. It is a non-duality of linguistic universe. The vyangya suggests the non-duality of semantic universe. Finally, the vyangya merges into pashyanti. Here the *sphota*, *rasa*, Brahma, shabda merges into a monistic universe. This is the non-dual Absolute. The criss-crossing discourses on nature of reality in Indian tradition if read together, reveals the tendency towards the absolute unity of every climax—visarga, *sphota*, *dhvani*, *rasa*, moksha, Brahman. Indian thinking is inherently non-dualistic.

There is another interesting relationship between *sphota* and *dhvani* doctrine. It is in inverse order of functionality. It is like anuloma-pratiloma sequence which is found in abundance in Indian culture. Just like krama and vipareeta krama is often juxtaposed together to generate a cycle and embellishes poetic compositions, *sphota-dhvani* are in similar relationship. In the philosophy of the grammarians, *sphota* in succession reaches the stage of *dhvani* which is the audible and manifest aspect. *Sphota* is permanent, but in *dhvani*-school, the lakshana (literal meaning of words) is permanent and the suggested meaning i.e. *dhvani* as the manifold manifests on the other end of the meaning-spectrum. In *Dhvanyaloka*, the manifest subsumes in succession under the *dhvani*, which is implicit. It is like anadrome sequence of manifestation. Whereas *sphota* is a unity, *dhvani* assumes innumerability and multiplicity. *Sphota* is permanent, *dhvani* is playful. In *sphota*, there is no delight in realizing unity, but in *dhvani* there is delight. *Sphota* is Brahman, *dhvani* is playful Lalita. *Sphota* is Vedantic in nature, *dhvani* is agamic/tantrik in nature. In *sphota*, there is silence and stillness. In *dhvani*, there is synthesia and creative play. *Sphota* is Shiva, *dhvani* is its Shakti. Thus it is not an inconsistency to claim that *dhvani-sphota* are in a relationship like anadromes (not in literal sense, but in functional sense).

Conception of *Dhvani* as a *Dhvani*

The concept of *dhvani* itself has multiple suggestive meanings. *Sphota* is called *dhvani*. When a drum is beaten with the stick and the stick is separated while beating, sound is produced nearest the drum. This sound is not heard. What is heard is the succession of waves which strike the ear. This last sound that strikes the ear is called *dhvani. Sphota* is manifested by the contact of the last of the sound of the word together with the unified impressions of all other previous sounds. Such sounds that manifest *sphota* are called *dhvani.* When the first sound (*prakrit dhvani*) is heard, the subsequent sounds (*vaikrit dhvani*) generate in them impressions through changes in speaker's voice or peculiar manner of expression like fast, slow, high or low tone. This makes the manifestation of *sphota* much clearer. This additional activity of the speaker is also called *dhvani.* Then, vyangyartha or the suggested sense which is the essence of poetry is also called *dhvani.* Those words (*vyanjak shabda*) and senses (*vyanjak artha*) which are capable of manifesting the suggested meaning are called *dhvani.* It is not the literal (abhidha) or the indicative (lakshana) sense, but the third activity inherent in word, and different than the previous two which is known as *dhvani.* The poetic composition where suggestive words and suggestive sense are primary is also called *dhvani.* Thus, *dhvani* is used in these five senses even though the nomenclature is borrowed from the *sphota*-grammarians where it is used in limited context.

Types of Dhvani in Poetic Composition

Having established vyanjana or suggestion as a distinct linguistic power, Anandavardhana classifies different categories of poetic creation in terms of the predominance of the suggested sense. The highest and the best kind of poetry is that in which the suggested sense has dominance over the expressed sense. This is called *dhvani* kavya in which beauty lies in the resonance (*dhvani*) of the suggested sense and not the expressed. There can be poetry in which suggestion may be present but the suggested sense may not dominate the expressed sense. This kind of poetry is called *gunibhuta-vyangya-kavya* or poetry of subordinated suggestion. This kind of poetry has been given the name of chitrakavya or pictorial poetry and is regarded as the most inferior kind. After according *dhvani* the most predominant place in poetry, Anandavardhana categorizes it into three types according to the nature of what is suggested-vastu *dhvani*, alankara *dhvani* and *rasa dhvani.*

If what is suggested is some idea or material fact then it is a case of vastu *dhvani*. If the suggested sense is some poetic figure, then it will be alamkara *dhvani*. If what is suggested constitutes *rasa* or aesthetic delight, it is called *rasa-dhvani*. There are two more main varieties of *dhvani* described in *Dhvanyaloka*, the *avivakshita-vakya* and *vivakshitaya-paravakya*, from the point of view of the suggestive element. In the former, the explicit sense is avivakshita i.e. inconsistent and in the latter it is consistent. In both the varieties of *dhvani*, all five aspects of *dhvani* are expressed. These five aspects in the former case are as follows:

1. *Vyanjaka*: Those suggestive words whose primary sense is useless,
2. *Vyangyartha*: the suggestive sense, which makes primary meaning redundant,
3. *Vyanjana*: The suggested meaning for whose sake the explicit meaning is rendered useless,
4. *Vyanjanavyapara*: The suggestive function through which the primary sense is discarded,
5. *Vyangyakavya*: A poetic composition where the primary sense is discarded,

This can be explained by examining the famous lines from Shakespeare's Julius Caesar, "Brutus is an honourable man". Mark Antony in his funeral speech for Julius Caesar says,

"The noble Brutus".
"Brutus is an honourable man."

It was because of Brutus that Caesar was killed. Here the address, 'honourable' is a vyanjaka word signifying 'respect'. But, the vyangyartha is the crooked act of Brutus. The vyanjana i.e. suggested meaning which Shakespeare intends to convey is that despite praise of Brutus, it is he who was responsible for Caesar's killing. The word functions to suggest the speaker's intention to publicly ridicule Brutus as a crooked man. This is vyanjanavyapara. The speech has predominance of suggestiveness and hence it is a vyangyakavya, (Bhavana Bhalla, 2008).

Like the types of *dhvani* classified according to the suggested sense, there is a large number of varieties and sub-varieties of *dhvani* based on the relationship between the suggester and suggested, vyanjaka and vyangya, mentioned in the *Dhvanyaloka*. The two main varieties of *dhvani* according to this system of categorization are the avivakshita-vachya *dhvani* and the vivakshitaya-paravachya *dhvani*. The avivakekshitavachya *dhvani*, which means unintended denotation, is lakshana or indication-based. Here the literal meaning is discarded. The vivakshitanya-paravachya *dhvani*, means suggestion of extended denotation. In this type, based on the denotation mode, the literal meaning is not discarded but is used to express the suggested sense. This type of *dhvani* operates in all five aspects viz. suggestive words, suggestive ideas, suggestion and the composition where these are predominant.

These two varieties of *dhvani* are further subdivided into two sub-varieties each in the *Dhvanyaloka*. The avivakshitavachya *dhvani* comprises of atyanta tiraskrita vachya *dhvani* and artha-antar-samkramrit-vachya *dhvani*. The vivakshitaya-paravachya is divided into samlakshya-krama vyangya *dhvani* and asamlakshya- krama-vyangya *dhvani*.

The atyanta-tiraskrita-vachya encompasses all cases where some fact or idea is suggested by completely discarding the primary sense due to utter incompatibility. Anandvardhana discussed this type by examining a verse given below in translation:

"The moon whose lustre has passed over to the sun and whose orbit is covered with the mist does not shine forth just as a mirror that is rendered blind by long heaving."

The context is the appearance of the Moon in the early morning in the winter. It is like a mirror that is covered with cloudy warm vapours that comes out while heaving in the winter. But, the Moon is not a person with eyes which can be blinded. The mirror does not have eyes and it cannot be described as being blind. There is incongruence. But, if one looks for the suggested meaning, the picture becomes clearer. The mirror covered with the vapour is like a blind person which cannot see the external object. The mirror has lost its power to reflect and rendered useless. The Moon is in similar predicament after having lost its lustre in a misty morning. Thus, the primary sense being incompatible has been discarded in this case and then by resorting to the secondary sense arises the suggested meaning.

The artha-antara-samkramita vachya-*dhvani* presents a case of progressive denotation. Here the primary sense is not incompatible. The literal meaning of the sentence on consideration of the text is given up in favour of the suggested sense. This has been explained by examining a verse by Anandavardhana:

"Good qualities become really so only when they are appreciated by cultured minds; indeed lotuses become lotuses only when they are favoured by the rays of the sun."

The primary sense is that excellence should be recognized by cultured people. The suggestion comes from the second 'lotus' in the expression 'lotuses become lotuses'. This suggests that when the ray of the sun falls properly, the lotuses bloom and become the seat of Lakshmi. Here, the primary sense is not completely discarded but, it does lead to suggestion of other idea. The artha-antara-*sankramitadhvani* is the category where the primary sense slowly fades away and the suggested idea appears.

Let us now turn to the samlakshya-krama-vyangya-*dhvani* sub-variety. Here we have suggestion of a perceptible process of transition from the expressed sense, vachyartha to the suggested meaning, vyangyartha, in a distinguishable sequence. In asamlakshya-krama-*dhvani* or suggestion of imperceptible process, Bharat Muni's *rasa*-theory and the *dhvani* concept get fused together. Here the primary meaning (vachyartha) generally constitutes a configuration of vibhava, anubhava and vyabhicharibhava and *rasa* or aesthetic delight is realized not by any words denoting it, but is suggested in the form of the vyangyartha. But *rasa* cannot be evoked by simply naming it. For instance if one hears the word 'karuna', it does not evoke the feeling of pathos in his mind. But, when one listens to the first verse of that Adikavi Valmiki uttered about the pain of the separation of the pair of krauncha birds, when one of them is killed by the hunter, the feeling of pathos is at once aroused. Anandavardhana rightly observes that while suggestion of *rasa* is the ultimate end of poetry, idea and figure, vastu and alamkara, can also be suggested like *rasa*. Establishing the pre-eminence of *rasa*, which according to him is the soul of suggestion, he asks poets to employ alamkaras only with the aim of evoking *rasa-dhvani* and not disregarding *rasa*. He considers *rasa-dhvani* as the ultimate goal of poetic creation.

Suggestive Elements

In *Dhvanyaloka*, Anandavardhana points out that while the primary meaning is based upon shabda or words only, suggestiveness is related not only to words but also to the sense. Though suggestiveness is not unrelated to verbal functions like abhidha or lakshana, it transcends them. Thus, while the first two are expressed by direct meanings and are laukika *dhvani*, *rasa-dhvani*, which is the highest form of *dhvani*, is inexpressible and can be only experienced. This experience is alaukika and not just an ordinary, everyday experience. Linking suggestiveness and feeling, Anandavardhana's doctrine goes beyond verbal construction and can be applied to other areas of art experiences, like music and dance, as well.

Suggestiveness in a poetic construction is not exclusive to words alone. The word, the letters, the sentence or even the whole composition all can possess suggestive power in a poetic context and help in producing aesthetic relish. Words are composed of letters which though by themselves do not convey sense, can however act in various arrangements as suggesters for expressing meaning and nourishing *rasa*. For instance, combinations of soft and pleasant sounding letters are helpful in suggesting shringara or the erotic *rasa*. Similarly, combination and conjunction of harsh and high sounding letters are of help in vira *rasa* or the heroic sentiment. But if harsh consonants like palatal or cerebral 'sha' are used in conjunction with 'dha' and 'ra', they become a hindrance in the evocation of the shringara *rasa*. He also says that even letters can be suggestive. However, when these same letters are employed to describe the feeling of disgust, these will intensify it. Thus, even letters suggest sentiments, *rasa*, as do words, sentences and other elements of a poetic construction.

For Anandavardhana, there cannot be a poetry without *dhvani*. *Dhvani* is the soul of poetry and the *rasa* is the soul of *dhvani*. In fact, Anandavardhana turned his own life into a poetry. He wrote in Sanskrit and Prakrit. He took up diverse themes like playfulness of Kamadeva on one hand and hymns to Goddess, *Devishatakam* on the other. He wrote prose and poetry. Though, he espoused for *dhvani* kavya, he was not critical of alamkara kavya. It's a paradox that he composed *Devishatakam* in chitrakavya which is a very inferior kind of poetry even though he advised the poets to make *dhvani* as the soul of the poetry. He borrowed ideas from his predecessors Bhamaha, Bharat, Bhartrihari, names appearing as an anuprasa alamkar. He took up the idea of *dhvani* as audible sound and transformed it into non-expressible, non-communicable vyanjaka. He centered his analysis on the nature of language and propounded the trans-linguistic unity.

Poetic Genius

In the very beginning in *Dhvanyaloka*, Anandavardhana speaks in glowing terms about poetic genius. The creative genius of great poets, he says, is extraordinary and their speech is suffused with sweet and suggested meanings. Anandavardhana puts only two to three—at the most five or six—in the category of great poets that include Kalidasa. The verse is as follow:

> "The speech of the first-rate poets streaming forth that sweet content reveals clearly their extraordinary genius which is as unearthly as it is ever bright". (DL I. 6)

Anandavardhana uses terms like 'swadu', 'aloksamanya', 'sphurantam' and 'pratibha' to describe the compositions of great poets. From the selection of such vocabulary, it is clear that he considers a great poet to be extraordinarily talented and his creation having the qualities of sweetness as well as brightness. The word 'sphurantam' denotes a flash of lightening, a sudden awakening. This quality, he explains, cannot be acquired by having more knowledge of grammar or looking into the lexicon. The basic requisite for a mahakavi is creative imagination, the skill to use words which are rich in suggested meaning. In this context, Anandavardhana refers to the concept of mahakavi. In this verse, Anandavardhana has referred to the concept of pratyabhijnana , showing an attempt to incorporate concepts of Kashmir's local philosophical tradition and the aesthetic discourse.

Anandavardhana cautions that if a word is used erroneously either because of the lack of poet's education or genius, it should not be regarded as *dhvani* even if the secondary meaning is generated. In this manner, Anandavardhana makes it clear that *dhvani* poetry cannot be composed by all and sundry. It requires either a poetic genius or the constant training of mind and sensibility to compose poetry.

In the fourth udyot, most verses are devoted to describe the characteristics of good poet and the way to maximize the delight in poetic composition. Some of the relevant verses in this context are reproduced below:

> "By a mere touch of even a single variety of suggestion (among the many that have been enumerated), the poet's expression will acquire novelty though it might perhaps embody only a trite idea." (DL IV.2)
>
> "Even trite subjects in poetry will put on a new freshness if they get into touch with sentiment just as the same trees appear quite new with the advent of spring." (DL IV.4)
>
> "Though several varieties of the suggested-suggester relationship are possible, the poet should be most intent upon one of them in particular, viz., that relating to the delineation of sentiments etc." (DL IV.5)
>
> "So long as these varieties of principal and subordinate suggestion are utilized in a work and so long as the poet has the gift of creative imagination (in so utilizing them), there can be no dearth of poetic themes."(DL IV.6)

"Infinitude is achieved by the expressed content also even when it remains in its pure and natural state by reason of the considerations of circumstance, place, time, etc." (DL IV.7)

"Like the resources of primordial Nature herself, the infinite possibilities of poetic themes can never be drained off even by a million Brhaspatis composing with all their might simultaneously."(DL IV.10)

"There are bound to be plenty of coincidences amongst great minds." (DL IV.11ab)

"But all of them should not be regarded by the wise as being identical." (DL IV.11cd)

"Even when the already existing elements of poetic themes such as arrangements of letters etc are utilized, it will certainly not smack of a flaw so long as the poetic theme as a whole is shining with novelty." (DL IV.15)

"Though it might smack of earlier usages, a theme can very well be utilized by a good poet. He will never become an object of censure by so doing." (DL IV.16cd)

"The Goddess of Speech, Sarasvati, herself will provide the desired ideas of a good poet whose mind is averse to borrowing the belongings of another." (DL IV.17cd)

Tumultuous Impact of Concept of *Dhvani*

Anandavardhana is the hinge between two different orders in India's cultural and religious history. He formulated the doctrine of suggestion at a time when the theistic Hinduism was taking shape. The cult of yakshas was finally bidding adieu. The new form of religions borrowed most of the ideas for performances, rituals as well as iconography from the yaksha-worship. From hymns, incense burning, music to idol worship, the stamp of this lost tradition is clearly visible. But, it was the time when there was emergence of the monistic ideas in philosophy. Advaita Vedanta was the high mark and so was the proliferation of the concept of shunyata among Buddhist schools.

The paradox between popularity of idol-worship and the ascendance of monistic ideas was resolved by the *dhvanivada*. The Idol of the deity is the exoteric appearance corresponding to varna and the abhidha. The ritual decoration of deity corresponds to the alamkaras and the lakshana. But, the vyanjana is implicit. The Absolute God is implicit in the idol worship and this can be merely realized through *dhvani*. If *dhvani* was declared as the soul of the poetry, monism became the soul of the theistic Hinduism. This allowed mutual co-existence as well as growth of paradoxical ideas. The orthodoxy and orthopraxy developed independently, former among the masses and the latter among the literati classes.

Anandavardhana also established shringara *rasa* as the primary *rasa*. He discussed the need to cultivate santa *rasa* as the ultimate *rasa*. These formulations were deployed during the medieval devotional movements. The laity was encouraged to engage in ritual for decorating the deities. Evoking santa *rasa* became akin to suffusing one's soul with the nectar of salvation. Another synthesis occurred subsequently under the hands of the singers and poets. The sweet shringara *rasa* ultimately leads to the santa *rasa*. The suggestive meaning that emerged was that even by the 'seva-bhakti' (service of the deity), one can attain moksha. The old hierarchical categorization of moksha as the ultimate pursuit through the sannyasa ashram was thus, stultified. Moksha was attainable even by the house-holders. And to attain liberation, what was necessary was not the penances but even sincere devotion through adoring and decorating the idols of the beloved gods was enough. This was a severe blow to the survival of Buddhist religion. Buddhism offered salvation through the Middle path. Buddhism spread as it was simpler in operation than the older Brahmanism. Moreover, Buddhism had incorporated the earlier belief in the yaksha worship from the time of Buddha making it palatable to the masses. The Veda and Upanishad-based belief system with complicated fire-ritual to transact with the plethora of gods had lost the ground. But, Anandavardhana affected a paradigmatic shift. Now onwards, the path of emancipation was simplified and it also incorporated the major characteristics of popular yaksha-belief and practices. Buddhism didnot appeal to masses, more particularly after the rise of complex esoteric sects. On the other hand, theistic Hindu sects were making everything exoteric for mass consumption.

There is direct transmission of ideas from Anandavardhana to various bhakti saints through Abhinavagupta. Jnaneshwar developed the concept of *amritanubhava* (nectar of experience) and incorporated many of the ideas of Kashmir Shaivism like *shivashakti samaveshan*. Bhakti movement which was already the dominant trend in southern India now took the north with storms. Jnaneshwar composed the philosophy in poetic language unlike the earlier trend of writing sutras. He inspired poet-mystics like Namdev, Janabai, Eknath, Tukaram. Most of these compositions were done in the vernacular languages. The hierarchy between vernacular and Sanskrit was effaced by Anandavardhana by positing the ultimate meaning, the suggested *rasa* as an experience of emotion and not any communicable, verbal object. Most of the bhakti saints sang and composed hymns in vernaculars thereby deepening the textual tradition.

Anandavardhana de-Sanskritized the poetics, Even the meaning was de-verbalized and it began to encompass the realm of experience, and *rasa* theory gained prominence. The highest suggested meaning ought to evoke *rasa*.

Anandavardhana and Poetics in Contemporary Asia

One finds many affinities between Anandavardhana's theory of *rasa-dhvani* and aesthetic thinking in neighbouring Asian countries, particularly China and Japan. About the same time when Anandavardhana was engaged in bringing about a paradigmatic shift in the thinking about poetry, music and other forms of aesthetic delight that heralded new revolution in the sonic and non-sonic communications; the Chinese poet-critic Ssu-k'ung T'u (837-908 AD) and others were engaged with redefining aesthetic experience of poetry. Ssu-k'ung remarked that the aesthetic experience of poetry comes from what he called 'flavour beyond flavour' and 'image beyond image.' (Frijda and Sundararajan, 2007). How close is this to the doctrine of 'suggestiveness' propounded by Anandavardhana which says that in poetry where suggested meaning gains primacy and *rasa* is evoked. The Chinese critics developed and refined the theory of savoring (*pin-wei*) which incorporated various kinds of emotional experiences that are different from the ordinary, everyday emotional response to things. Chinese poets of the time believed in preserving the principles of harmony in their works. It is on grasping what constitutes harmony in a poetic composition that a poet engages himself in the act of searching for harmony. This act is what they called savouring. In this act of savouring, there is self-reflexive awareness in which the object of emotion is the experience rather than the experienced object. The adept in savouring primarily relishes the delightful taste and not the tasty food, delightful smell and not the smelling flower; delight produced by music and not the delightful music. It is a second-order comprehension and experiencing of aesthetic rapture. One finds echoes (*dhvani*) of a similar idea in the *rasa-dhvani* concept of Anandavardhana, where intuition of the higher order comes into play and one experiences the *rasa* generated by the suggestiveness in poetry, music or even other non-auditory forms of expression like gestures, paintings, smell etc. The process of savouring is a self-initiated act and it does not require any mediation or effort. It is direct. The Chinese explained it with an analogy that the devil can be made to taste his own medicine, but not to savour it unless he is himself inclined to. Thus, savouring cannot be achieved without the intention and it requires the art of *zhi* (making distinction) for its function. This sounds similar to Anandavardhana's view that only sahridaya and people of refined sensibility can relish *rasa-dhvani* and his exhortation to poets to write *dhvani*-poetry.

In the concept of savouring, the contemporary Chinese scholars formulated various stages and classified the process systemically. *P'in-wei* is the distinction of flavour, *zhi-wei* is the cognition of flavour and *hui wei* is the memory of flavour. Then, there is *yi-wei*, or flavour corresponding to *rasa-dhvani* in entirety. Su-kung T'u is said to have savoured 24 poetic moods. The act of savouring involves lingering over sensory and non-sensory impressions. It is like the echo of the *dhvani*-theory. One casts a glance, turns away and casts a new glance again. This produces delight. One finds same example put forth to argue about suggestiveness in poetic composition by Anandavardhana in *Dhvanyaloka*. When savouring is done of meaning of events or any object, insights is produced which is different than what the perceived object signified. This insight is inexpressible, non-communicable just as *rasa-dhvani*. Ssu-k'ung T'u wrote:

> "An image beyond the image, a scene beyond the scene-can these be easily verbalized?"

This is again very close to the concept of suggestiveness. Savouring produces pleasure and the feeling of harmony between things which enters one's consciousness. This resonance (*dhvani*) of the idea can be found in a beautiful verse of Ssu-K'ung T'u:

> "As if just about to echo;
> Those who recognize already understand;
> But seek it and it will move further away."

In Japan, there was a tradition of miraculous poetry, *kotodama* (magic spirit or power of special word). A contemporary of Anandavardhana, the Japanese court poet Kino Tsurayuki (905 AD) compiled an anthology of poems—*Kokin Wakashu* (Collection of Japanese Poems: Past and Present) and stated in the introduction that the poetry has the power to "move heaven and earth, stir feeling in unseen demons and gods, soften relations between men and women, and soothe the hearts of fierce warriors". This is like the resonance of *rasa-dhvani*, the extraordinary effect that suggestiveness can induce in poetry by evoking an emotive response transcending ordinary experience. The Japanese tradition abounds in the stories of the poets who used poetry to heal people, inspired love, end droughts, exorcise demons and bring back dead into life. Such tales are called *kakotu setsuwa*. It is this early tradition which later became a force with the advent of waka poetries. Waka is a five- line verse of 31 syllables and is believed to possess miraculous powers. But, waka from which other variants like haikus emerged has its roots in the works of Kukai Kobo Daishi (774–835). Kobo Daishi had a lasting influence on the development of subsequent Japanese poetry and poetics. For him, writing was a sacred technology necessary for creating and maintaining the cosmic order. All literature expresses the universe of the Buddha. It is like the shabda-Brahma in Bhartrihari's *sphotavada* doctrine of grammarian philosophy. Kobo fused poetry and mantra and made poetry a means of achieving enlightenment.

Kobo introduced the idea of combining the exoteric and the esoteric in poetry, propounding that a poem has a subtle and deeper meaning below the surface meaning. The reader has to go beyond the surface meaning and delve deeper to arrive at the real meaning. This bears a similarity to Anandavardhana's idea of *dhvani* or the suggested meaning transcending the literal or figurative meaning.

Kukai propounded a general theory of language based on his analysis of exoteric and esoteric aspects of the Word. Just like the contemporary conditions in India, Japan was witnessing flourishing of various Buddhist, Taoist and local sects. Kobo employed two Buddhist ritual languages, dharani and mantra, both having words that short-circuit meaning in ordinary sense, to explain the dichotomic nature of the Word. Mantra is restricted to esoteric practice whereas dharani is found in both esoteric and exoteric ritual. Dharanis are the summary verse that operates as mnemonic tool which encapsulates the meaning of a section or chapter of a sutra or even the complete text. Dharanis are believed to possess miraculous powers like kotodama poetries. Both, mantra and dharanis are devoid of meaning. But, Kukai viewed mantra as a special class of dharani and postulated that every syllable of a dharani was a manifestation of the true nature of reality, that all sound is a manifestation of shunyata or emptiness of self-nature. Thus, though on surface the dharanis and mantras appear meaningless, there is implicit meaning in those and only true adept can grasp the intelligible cloaked beneath unintelligible. According to Kobo, Tathagata knows the true meaning of dharanis while lay persons straddling the samsara know only the outer characteristics of the word and not the inner meaning.

Dharanis are the words of Tathagata himself. His exoteric sermons were lengthy meant for those with exoteric merit. But, for those with esoteric merit, Tathagata preached dharanis, where each word embraces manifold meaning. Thus, dharanis even though are merely summary of the verses, suggest something else. There is a hierarchical dichotomy. Dharani itself is now exoteric whereas mantras are esoteric. Thus, Kukai set everything into two dimensional realities, one explicit and another implicit. One which is manifest, the other merely known through suggestion.

Like Anandavardhana, Kukai found the power of non-verbal communications. He stated that it is only in intonation that the meaning is grasped. This is true of the intonation of Chinese words. Kukai explored this aspect in his *Thesis on the Mysterious District of the Mirror of Writing*. His emphasis on sound was one of the reasons for introduction of phonetic writing system, the *kana*, in Japan. With the propagation of the new phonetic system, the possibility of synthesis of indigenous Shintoism and Buddhism, increased manifold. Buddhism became indigenized in Japan. It was the impact of Kukai Kobo Daishi that Japanese culture with emphasis on discovering meaning in seemingly meaningless everyday acts emerged. The hakka poetries or the Zen tradition had roots in this uprooting of meaning from the words and harvesting Truth lying hidden in the esoteric aspect of everything.

There seems to be a resonance, *dhvani* across Asian history. One is amazed at the similarity between the ideas about poetry and poetic creativity of these three contemporary geniuses-Anandavardhana, Kukai Kobo Daishi and Ssu-k'ung T'u. Their poetic theories appeared at similar times in different corners of Asia and the Asian literary scene did not remain same after that. In fact, the radical revaluation of poetic language across Asia had its roots in the new doctrines that burst forth during the ninth century with implications for cultural and intellectual enterprises later in time. Asia did not remain same before and after this paradigmatic revolution. Perhaps this is why the Ulatbansi verses of Kabir and the poetry of Japanese Zen poets bear such a striking resemblance. Was this an epistemological resonance which echoed in Asian thinking related to different areas of logo-centric as well as non-logo-centric creativity?

Why did this Asian poetic thinking, this simultaneous creative urge to link aesthetic delight, language, gesture, silence, non-verbal sounds, meaning, intuition, ultimate reality, remain esoteric to generation of Asians? Why did it succumb to western calculative, utilitarian thinking within a few centuries after poetries acquired the miraculous power to transform the visible as well as the invisible Universe?

One of the towering western philosopher Martin Heidegger, encountered Indian thought and proclaimed the need for a planetary thinking based upon 'poetic dwelling'! Heidegger was aghast with the march of western calculative thinking and the associated technicity that has uprooted man from the earth. He stated that the only possibility to save ourselves is by thinking and poetizing. Pointing to the nature of new poetic thinking, Heidegger characterized it as that which strives to ponder over the un-thought. The essence of poetry is to 'point to something' 'we cannot see', he said. And perhaps, this 'pointing to something' is what Anandavardhana termed *dhvani*.

Asian thinking and, in particular, Indian thinking is inherently poetic and roots man into this world by rooting him/her in own tradition, and pointing to the omnipresence of an esoteric reality. To save the planet is to save ourselves. The path is within our grasp. The tradition of poetic thinking to which Anandavardhana contributed so richly has to be revived. The tradition must find own dwelling to help stem the tide of planetary upheaval. The exiled bards must get back to their old homes before the buds of poetic compositions begin to bloom in the barren field of technicity. The thinkers must think the unthinkable before the questions are reduced into digital binaries! An epistemic rupture is the need of time. Does Anandavardhana's cognitive rapture (*rasa-dhvani*) hold the key?

(All translated verses of *Dhvanyaloka* are reproduced from the translation work of K. Krishnamoorthy.)

References

1. Krishnamoorthy, *K. (1974) Anandavardhana's Dhvanyaloka—Critical Edition with Introduction,* English Translation and Notes, Dharwar: Karnatka University.

2. Tripathi, Dr Ramsagar (1979). *Anandavardhanavirachit Dhvanyaloka,* New Delhi: Motilal Banarasidass.

3. Chari, VK (1993). *Sanskrit Criticism,* New Delhi: Motilal Banarasidass.

4. Kunjunni Raja, K. (1969). *Indian Theories of Meaning,* Adyar Lib. Series, Vol. 91, pp. 276-315.

5. Sankaran, A (1929). *Some Aspects of Literary Criticism in Sanskrit or the Theories of Rasa and Dhvani,* University of Madras.

6. Hota, Ajodhya Nath (2006). *Sphota, Paratibha and Dhvani,* Delhi: Eastern Book Linkers.

7. Gerow, Edwin (1977). *Indian Poetics in a History of Indian Literature,* Vol. V, Otto Harrassowitz, Wiesbaden, pp. 218-288.

8. Gnoli, Raniero (1956). *The Aesthetic Experience According to Abhinavagupta,* Series Orientale Roma, XI, Rome.

9. Sharma, Mukund Madhava (1968). *The Dhvani Theory in Sanskrit Poetics,* Delhi: Chowkhamba.

10. Bhalla, Bhavana (2008). *Dhvani and Rasa: Their Interrelation and Role in the Process of Poetic Creation,* LiCus4, pp.15-24.

11. Matilal, BK (1988). "*Vakrokti and Dhvani: Controversies about Theory of Poetry in Indian Tradition,*" Paper presented at World Sanskrit Conference, Leiden.

12. Hogan, Patrick C (1996). "Towards a Cognitive Science of Poetics: Anandavardhana, Abhinavagupta, and the Theory of Literature," *College Literature,* Vol. 23.

13. Toshkhani, S.S. (2003). "Kashmir's Contribution to Indian Aesthetics," *Kashmir Herald,* Vol.3 (3).

14. McCrea, Lawrence J (2008). *The Teleology of Poetics in Medieval Kashmir,* Harvard University Press.

15. Kimbrough, Keller R (2005). Reading the Miraculous Power

of Japanese Poetry, *Japanese Journal of Religious Studies, 32 (1)*: 1-33.

16. Eco, Umberto (2005). *Rasa and Taste: A Difficult Synonymy*, Lecture given in Pondicherry, October, 2005.

17. Frijda, Nico H and Sundararajan, L, "Emotion Refinement: A Theory Inspired by Chinese Poetics," *Perspectives on Psychological Science*," Vol. 2 (3), pp. 227, 241.

18. Sundararajan, L (2010). Two Factors of Aesthetic Tasting: Rasa and Savouring- A Cross-cultural Study with Implications for Psychology of Emotion, *Review of General Psychology*, Vol. 14(1), pp. 22-30.

19. Heidegger, Martin (1966). "*Only a God can Save Us*," Der Spiegel's Interview, published on May 31, 1976, five days after death.

20. Visuvalingam, Sunthar (2002). "Towards an Integral Appreciation of Abhinava's Aesthetics of Rasa" *Indic Colloquium*, July, 2002.

21. Avasthi, Shiv Shankar (1990). *Vakyapadiya*, Varanasi: Chaukhambha.

Chapter 15

Camatkara and Abhinavagupta's Aesthetics

Abhinavagupta (10-11th century AD) was the true genius and polymath who synthesized various strands of Indian thinking. He was a great yogi, philosopher and master of poetics. Abhinavagupta inherited multiple traditions of knowledge through a large number of gurus mentioned in his magnum opus, *Tantraloka* and altered those fundamentally. In this Chapter, his work on poetics will be discussed and his ideas on aesthetic experience vis-à-vis spiritual experiences will be situated.

Abhinavagupta's major works on Sanskrit poetics are the *Locana*, a commentary on Anandavardhana's *Dhvanyaloka* and the *Abhinavabharati*, a commentary on Bharata Muni's *Natyashastra*. The *Locana* was written before *Abhinavabharati* as there are references about the latter in the former. Abhinavagupta mentions Utpala as his Paramguru in poetics. He also quotes his teachers Bhatta Induraja in both *Locana* and *Abhinavabharati* and Bhatta Tauta. Bhatta Tauta is credited with the work, *Kavya Kautuka* on which Abhinavagupta wrote a commentary. But, Abhinavagupta seems to be much influenced by the triple formulations of Bhatta Nayak in *Hridayadarpana*, which appears to have touched deeply his own penchant for trika philosophy.

Before Anandhavardana, there were three schools in the field of criticism. Alamkara and Riti school in the poetics and the Rasa school of Bharat in dramaturgy. Bhamaha's Kavyalamakara is considered the first work of Alamkara school. For Bhamaha, '*shabdarthau sahitau kavyam*' or the words and their meaning, properly matched is the poetry. Bhamaha considered *vakratva* (deviation from ordinary mode of expression) as the best ornament of poetry. The alamkara school was further developed by the works of Dandin. The Riti school was developed by Vamana. Bharat Muni is credited with systemizing the Rasa school in the magnum opus, the *Natyashastra* (4-5th century AD). The theory of Rasa was discussed systemically by Bhatta Lollata, Sankuka and Bhatta Nayaka.

According to the Indian literary tradition, there are different layers of meanings in any literary work. These are, literal (shabdartha), indicative (lakshana/metaphoric), and the purportive (tatparya). But, the *dhvani* theorists emphasized there was an implicit meaning (vyangyartha) in every work of literature and art.

Abhinavagupta inherited Anandavardhana's theory of *dhvani alongwith* its criticism by Bhatta Nayaka who emphasized more on the evocation of rasa.

Abhinavagupta accepted Anandavardhana's categorization of *dhvani* and added certain categories himself. He reinterpreted the theory by referring to the fundamental question—What is *dhvani*?' '*Dhvanat iti dhvani*', that which sounds or resonates or implies is *dhvani*. '*Dhvanyate iti dhvani*' or *dhvani* is what is sounded or reverberated or implied. Abhinavagupta accepts the three-fold classification of *dhvani*. But, he brings in his own criteria for the same—*laukika* and *alaukika*. *Laukika* is that which one encounters in everyday life; the other is '*kaavya vyaapaara gocara*' and *alaukika*. It is to be found only in poetry. Abhinavagupta like his predecessor Anandavardhana holds that *rasa-dhvani* alone constitutes the soul of poetry.

The Rasa theory

The term *rasa* originally meant the essence, juice, sap of plant.

The term was known during Vedic times. In Indian culinary art, the separation of oil and the rasa of the preparation is the sign of generation of taste in food. Suddenly, the colour of the whole changes and the taste that emerges is quite different from that of its constituents. Similarly, chewing betel leaf has been a part of Indian culture since ancient days. The chewing (carvana) of the betel leaf along with lime, catechu, and areca nut produces rasa, something quite different in colour or taste than any of the constituents. But, the concept of rasa gradually became subtler. In Buddhism, the imagery of juice of sugarcane was often deployed to describe the state of Bodhisattva. Bodhisattva is often compared with Sugarcane: "The great Bodhisattva is like sugarcane or sesame which, when pressed with a device, gives, forth juice or oil." (Kieschnick, p. 251)

By the 4th-5th century, alchemy developed as a full-fledged science. The whole discourse of alchemy revolved around the rasa. It was also known as the Rasayan ... path of Rasa. But, in contrast to the juicy nature of rasa, the alchemists termed the ashes of different metals and gems as rasa. Mercury ash was termed as the rasadhiraj. Rasa was supposed to rejuvenate the heart, mind and body of the consumer. Can rasa subtler than even ash, rejuvenate the soul? This was the occasion when Bharata Muni extended the term to drama and developed a full-fledged theory of Rasa.

Bharata Muni says that which can be relished—like the taste of food—is rasa—*Rasyate anena iti rasaha* (asvadayatva). Any art -performative like dance or drama or literature like poetry or katha, is not complete without rasa. Rasa is the thing that mediates between the artists and the spectator.

Bharat formulated the Rasa theory in the Natyashatra (5th century) under the famous Sutra *vibhavanubhavavyabhicharisamyogad rasanispattih* meaning thereby that the birth of rasa takes place when the *vibhava, anubhava* and Vyabhichari or the transitory mental states unite. *Rasa* is said to arise when the *sthayibhava* in the individual is awakened by his perception of the *vibhavas, anubhavas, vyabhicharibhava* and *sattvic bhavas*. What are these different components that evokes Rasa as whole? *Vibhavas* have been termed as the determiner by R Gnoli.

Gnoli explains the process how *vibhavas* as external stimuli like the story, stage and the actor, awakens our latent sentiment. *Anubhavas* are the consequents-deliberate manifestations of feelings on part of the actor in accordance with the mood. *Vyabhichari* bhavas are the transient moods that arise along with the basic permanent mood. For e.g. if the basic mood is love (rati), joy in union will be the accompanying emotion.

The *Natyashastra* classifies eight sthayi Bhavas and corresponding Rasa:

Bhava	***Rasa***
Rati (Love)	*Sringara Rasa*
Hasya (Mirth)	*Hasya Rasa*
Shoka (Sorrow)	*Karuna Rasa*
Krodha (Anger)	*Raudra Rasa*
Utsaha (Energy)	*Veera Rasa*
Bhaya (Fear)	*Bhayanak Rasa*
Jugupsa (Disgust)	*Vibhatsa Rasa*
Vismaya (Wonder)	*Adbhut Rasa*

Rasa and *bhava* can be considered as Siamese twins: one without the other would not have a sensitive life. *Rasa* cannot be generated without *bhava* and vice-versa .

Following Bharat, the theory of *Rasa* was further expanded by Bhatta Lollata (9th century). Lollata examined it only in the context of performing arts like drama. According to him, "*Rasa* is a *sthayibhava* intensified by a poetic description or the histrionics of the actors through vibhavas, anubhavas etc." (Sankaran, p. 98) For Lollata, "*Rasa* primarily resides in the character and also in the actors on account of their imagining themselves for the moment to be those very same characters."(Sankaran, pp. 98-99). For Lollata, it is the actor that exhibit the *rasa* and so it is they who realize it. There is no consideration for either the poet or the audience. But how does the audience realize the *Rasa*?

Sri Sankuka criticized Lollata for equating *rasa* with *Sthayibhava*. Sankuka argued that when a spectator witness a perfect imitation/reproduction of the characters and their experiences, the spectator forgets momentarily the difference between actor and the character and inferentially experiences the emotion of the character. This experience of aesthetic emotion by spectator is a reflex of real emotional moods, sthayibhava of the characters. Inferential experience is the realization of *Rasa*. Sankuka brings in spectator in the realization of *Rasa*. But, how can it be said that either actor without knowing the original, imitate or the spectator without knowing the original, infer the imitation? (Sankaran, p. 99)

Then comes Bhatta Nayak. He says *Rasa* is neither known through the means of knowledge, nor produced nor manifested. If it be a known thing, then in *karuna*, one must experience pain and not pleasure. If it is known through shabda, there cannot be any sense of joy. Witnessing actual love-making of two lovers on stage may cause aversion in elderly spectators. Bhatta Nayak explores "that really constitutes realization of *Rasa*." (Sankaran, p 103)

Sankaran states that for Bhatta Nayak, the poetic language has three aspects:

1. *Abhidh*a or denotative
2. *Bhavana* or unificatory
3. *Bhojakatva* or Bhoga or enjoyment

All linguistic expressions have *abhidha*. Only poetry has bhavana. The gunas and alankaras generate bhavana in ordinary poetry. "Difficulty in realization of *Rasa* is the individualistic element of the spectator of Sahridayas on one side and actors and characters on the other." (Sankaran, p.103). Bhatta Nayak assumed the "unification of the character, sahridaya and the actor." There is complete unification of the three elements and this is called *Sadharanikarana*, a process which Abhinavagupta later made thorough use of in his own theory. When there is a powerful representation, individual loses the individuality and aided by imaginative sympathy undergoes sadharanikaran. When this emotion is universalized, the third aspect, viz. Bhojakatva operates. Bhatta Nayak says that Bhoga arises only through predominance of sattva guna over the other two gunas and, hence, is always pleasant. This resolves the problem as to how the karuna *rasa* is also pleasant.

Abhinavagupta follows Bhatta Nayak but only differs in the terminology. For Abhinava, it is the *dhvani* or the suggestion which is the essence of the poetry. Abhinavagupta brings *sadharanikarana* or *Bhavakatva* of Bhatta Nayak under concept of *vyanjana* and bhoga under *rasapratiti.*

Abhinavagupta now synthesized two different models- Anandavardhana's theory of *Dhvani* fully developed in the four udyots (flash) of the *Dhvanyaloka* and Bhatta Nayak's ideas on conception of aesthetic experience enunciated in the *Hridayadarpana.*

In Abhinavabharati, Abhinavagupta elaborated on the theory of *Rasa* in the sixth chapter. The points he discusses are: "Whose *rasa* is it that we are realizing? Is it that of the poet or of the great characters or that of the actors or only of our own? Moreover, what are the different emotions that produce *rasa*? Most problematic for Abhinava was to explain how the painful emotions appeal to us? Though, we cry on tragic scenes and also shed tear, why do we feel inspired to return to read or watch same tragic scene once again and like to shed tears? Man wants to relish the pleasure but why is it that painful emotions expressed in literature charm us?" (Sankaran, p. 97)

Abhinavagupta's Aesthetics

Abhinavagupta's exposition of *dhvani* and *rasa* in his two works, *Locana* and the *Abhinavabharati,* is remarkable feat of synthesizing the different theories prevalent in poetics and dramaturgy. Abhinavagupta formulated the solution to the problems that Bhatta Nayak had to face by reposing his belief in immortal soul. All souls have in them implanted certain *vasanas* (instincts) which was known as the Sthayibhavas, more particularly in Sahridaya (responsive critics or emotional community). "When there is vivid representation of the *vibhavas* (determinants), *anubhavas* (consequents) and *vyabhicharibhavas* (transitory mental states), this instinct is called forth and developed to that climax when it is realized by us, accompanied by thrill or joy." (Sankaran, p. 104) This is the realization of *Rasa*. *Rasa* is the emotional mood revealed in blissful knowledge, free from barriers that hinders its realization.

R Gnoli discusses seven barriers in the realization of *rasa* and Abhinavagupta's prescriptions to overcome those. Sahridaya through "imaginative sympathy identifies himself with the situation, and he realizes his own emotion that has been stirred and developed to a climax, free from all limitations and accompanied by thrill." (Sankaran, p.109) This realization is in the nature of pure joy and *alaukik*, transcendental. It lasts only during the time of realization and never beyond it and is different from the *sthayibhava* as it is not permanent state. This is the *rasa*.

Abhinavagupta distinguishes between the world of drama/ representation and the real life. In art, one moves from the gross to more subtle forms of expressions and experiences. There is a propensity to realize unity amidst multiplicity or what some Buddhist masters speculated, "to see a world in a grain of sand." Abhinavagupta also grappled with the old problem as to how the feeling that might cause pain in real life is capable of providing pleasure in an art form. Here, he again borrowed Bhatta Nayak's idea that *rasa* is *sattvic* and hence always pleasant.

Abhinavagupta now had to synthesize ideas from the Samkhya philosophy to explain the dichotomy of enjoyable pathos. The emotional mood pertaining to karuna is *Soka* or grief. During realization of *Karuna*, mind gets so much absorbed in the representation (*tanmayata*) that it achieves a certain equipoise (*sama*). When the mind attains balance, free from any disturbance, delight is produced that is what Samkhya thinkers had propounded. This explains how tragic scenes are pleasurable, though human nature abhors the experience of pain. This also put a question mark on Buddhist worldview that there is *dukha* in the world. A connoisseur can generate bliss in this very life if he becomes a spectator of cosmic drama and evokes the Karuna *rasa* by transcending his limitations and individuality.

Abhinavagupta deals with each *rasa* corresponding with eight Sthayibhavas in his sixth chapter of *Abhinavabharati*. All these are related to three ends of life in Purushartha system—*Dharma*, *artha* and *kama*. This was another stupendous feat of creative fusion. Abhinavagupta now wanted to fit in the highest purushartha, *moksha*, under his aesthetic gaze. This he achieved by pitting for another *Rasa*, shanta *rasa* whose emotional mood is *Sama* (quietude), related to the *moksha*. Sama became sthayibhava for the shanta *rasa*.

The greatest achievement of Abhinavagupta in the field of aesthetic philosophy is his incorporation of shanta *rasa* in the theory of *Rasa*. Udbhata and Anandavardhana both had accepted shanta as the ninth *rasa*. But, it was Abhinavagupta who incorporated this *rasa* in the emerging paradigm. He perceived shanta as the ultimate in the process of *rasa*-realisation.

Abhinavagupta also described how shanta *rasa* underlies all the other eight *rasas*. Shanta rasa pervades all rasas like the sixteenth digit of immortality of the moon. The shanta rasa is the ultimate rasa. All the other rasas emanate from the shanta rasa and resolve again into it. Bharat Muni says,

> "All emotions, when their respective conditions or excitants obtain, proceed from Shanta; and when the conditions are withdrawn they again merge or repose in shanta." (Sankaran, p. 116)

Since all rasa when realised are alaukika and free from sensual enjoyment, they are necessarily of the nature of shanta rasa.

Abhinavagupta's novelty can be summarized in these words: Rasa-dhvani form the soul of poetry. In Bhatta Nayak's classifications of realization of rasa in place of Bhavakatva, suggestion or Vyanjana (dhvani) should be substituted. Even painful emotions are pleasant and the shanta rasa is the predominant rasa among all the Rasas.

Abhinavagupta paved the literary path to moksha. Great literary works suffused with elements of rasadhvani finally lead to the experience of shanta rasa. This had tremendous impact over India's literary tradition. The bhakti movement emerged that thrived with the wonderful poetic compositions and mustic-saints harnessed the aesthetic delight for mystical ecstasy. Post-Abhinavagupta, tremendous outpouring of poetic literature in the form of chalisa, manas, doha, chaupai, namvalli, sahastranam emerged across length and breadth of India. Kavya or poetry became an alternative path to moksha.

Camatkara—an Alaukika Experience

The realization of rasa is alaukika or trans-mundane experience. It is different from ordinary experience which is produced by vibhava, anubhava and vyabhicharibhavas. In ordinary experience, even after the cause is destroyed, the effect continues to exist, just like the chak (potter-wheel) which produces a pot, even if destroyed, the pot continues to exist. But, in case of Rasa, realization ends when the vibhavas etc. are withdrawn. There are other ordinary experience in which causes reveal things that already exist. For instance, a lamp is the vibhava for revealing a pot that is kept in a dark room. But, in case of rasa, it is not correct to assume that rasa pre-exists the Vibhavas. Thus, rasa is not an ordinary experience. *Rasapratiti* is alaukika. Rasa is neither *gyanpak* nor *karak*, it is *carvanopayogi*. It can be realized and savoured only (Locana I. 18). Rasa is something which is produced *sui generis* like the experience of rumination (*carvana*).

Rasa is evoked when the senses are fully absorbed in something (tanmaya)to the exclusion of everything else. The objects which arouse this state may be food or drink, a song or dance. Aesthetic and mystical state of consciousness have particular kind of bliss. It is Purnananda or the Supreme bliss. These are accompanied by sense of *wonder*, camatkara. Camatkara is more than amazement. It emerges like lightening flash and fills one with thrill. It is also *apurva* and *alaukik*. Abhinavagupta deploys the terminology for the first time in the verse I.12 of the Locana where he discusses that *vismaya* is not *camatkara*. Vismaya is wonder. Sometimes alaukik words and their meanings generate curiosity (*kautuhala*) in us but these are not so intense as to immerse us in Rasa. Abhinavagupta takes up the example of chitrakavya. The structure, words and the meaning in chitrakar may cause curiosity and wonder in us, but it is not the principal Kavya. True poetry has such a powerful flow that sahridaya get immersed in rasa and loses his individuality. Such is the camatkar Rasa. V Raghvan mentions that the word "camatkara was originally onomatopoeic word referring to the clicking sound we make with our tongue when we taste something snappy, and in the course of its semantic enlargement, camatkara came to mean a sudden fillip relating to any feeling of a pleasurable type." (Raghvan, p. 269). But, the term 'camatkara' shares etymological affinity with 'chamak' (brightness). Camatkara involves act of sudden brightening, like the lightening flash, palpitating with enormous deindividuated joy. Camatkar is of the nature of Adi Shiva who has two aspects—Prakash (illumination) and vimarsha (also known as Anadashakti, the mother of bliss). The highest spiritual realization mentioned by Shankaracharya in Saundarya Lahari is that of Shakti in lightning-like Kala as Sadakhya kala (joyous lightening flash) (Saundarya Lahiri, Verse 21). Similarly, the Kundalini Shakti is described as resting in the ground within the body that rises like lightening and showers the aspirant with inexpressible, alaukika bliss. Camatkara as a concept is a paradigmatic invention to describe the ultimate experiential encounter of an individual.

Utpaldeva, guru of Abhinavagupta was the first to use the term in a technical sense. Bhatta Nayak also used it in his *Hridayadarpana*. Camatkara is synonymous with the Buddhist *Samvega* and *Vismaya* of the Spanda school. Here, the term is used in the sense that the ordinary laukika world is suddenly replaced by a novelty, an 'apurva' incidence. Abhinavagupta states that camatkara is present in every form of life. It is this that distinguishes conscious beings from inanimate matter. Aesthetic sensibility is nothing but capacity to wonder, more condensed than ordinary wonder. (Probably, this is the challenge for scientists working with machine consciousness. What after robots pass Turing Test? Can machine consciousness experience camatkara?)

For Abhinavagupta, camatkara provided a convenient solution for the unpleasurable rasa problem, since the spectator was now expected to feel a detached cognitive delight, regardless of the emotional value of the text. Rasa for Abhinavagupta involved a deindividuated affective state (sadharanibhava) occurring in the spectator's mind and extracted from a remembered personal experience of emotion. The immersion in delight (bhogavesha) is camatkara. It is a state of rasavesha—rush of rasa. The rasa gushes forth and pours into the being just as spark catches fire in dry wood. Even if a play is based upon the bibhatsa or karuna rasas, the resulting feeling in the reader or spectator is camatkara, which fills the individual with delight. This is the reason why the TV serials depicting fear as the predominant theme like *Fear Files*, continue to enthral the spectators and attract the viewer to repeatedly watch the ever new episodes. In real life, no one wishes to encounter such situation, but as spectator they derive the maximum joy out of the same situation.

The aesthetic experience is a direct experience, *sui generis*, free of every vibhava or anubhava, determinant and consequents. This form of consciousness without obstacles has been termed as camatkara. Abhinavagupta has discussed the physical effect of camatkara like trembling, horripilation, ullasana-joyful motion of limbs. Moreover, the aesthetic experience of camatkara appears each time the poetic expressions that aroused it, are evoked. Camatkara is svatantra (free) from the impediments. It is an absolutely independent state of joy. In *Tantraloka*, Abhinavagupta always invokes the imagery of camatkara to describe the esoteric energy lying dormant within our body. The divine resides within the human body (Deva-sadan-deha) and the lowest chakra, muladhar is soaked with camatkrit rasa that emanates the nectar of joy (*Tantraloka*: Chapter 29.176; Chapter 26.63). Rasa is the essence of cognitive chewing-carvana. It is immediate and not something that pre-exists before the cognition. Rasa is different from natural eight permanent mental states (sthayibhava). Rasa is alaukik. Rasa leads to experience of the camatkara.

Brahmanubhuti vs. Rasanubhuti

Realization of Rasa and the realization of supreme Brahman is said to be a similar experience. But, certain differences do exist. The brahmanubhuti is Oneness with the Absolute and without differentiation. The cognition of rasa is a delight evoked through different elements like determinant and consequents. While aesthetic delight is temporary and as soon as the things causing it are removed the same disappears, the brahmanubhuti is permanent. In rasanubhuti, there is lack of knowledge of the Absolute and the normal everyday life returns after the experience is over. Abhinava mentions that the two experiences are family-resemblances. Gnoli sums up Abhinavagupta's view, "the aesthetical and mystical bliss is nothing but a state of independence, of liberty from any extraneous solicitation and hence of rest 'lysis', tasting, gestation and bliss are strictly connected." (R. Gnoli, p. XLI)

While yogi achieves brahmananda through a tough life of renunciation, the sahridaya achieves the same level of ecstatic pleasure through the enjoyment of creative work of art.

Abhinavagupta further describes "rasa to be a clarification of a spectator's own latent emotional propensities, resulting in a momentary manifestation of an inner brahmasvada—the tasting of ultimate bliss" (Gerow, pp. 267-68). He further suggests that "the enjoyment of rasa was a semblance of only a particle of that bliss." (tadanandaviprunmatravabhaso hi rasasvadah) (Locana, Udyot 3.43).

There are two types of yogic realization. Yunjana is one who practices various yogic methods to attain brahmasiddhi like hathayoga. But, rasa experience is pleasant unlike yunjana's experiences. Similarly, Yukta is a saint that has attained unity with the Absolute. Yukta realizes Absolute which is neither compatible with life or death. On the other hand, Rasa is lively.

In *Locana*, Abhinavagupta likens rasa to milk that secretes forth from the Poet, as the 'Vac' from a Dhenu cow to satiate the desire of the sahridaya-calves. It is quite different from the yogis. There is no rasavesha in a yogi. The yogi has to make an effort to milk this realization of Rasa. Abhinavagupta borrows the metaphor from the *Kumarsambhava* of Kalidasa describing the Himalayas. In the text, the Earth is compared with a cow and it has been described how from the earth-cow, gems and medicines were milked by the Sumeru and at that moment, all mountains pushed the Himalayas as the favourite calf. Kalidasa was suggesting how the Himalayas is the source of best gems and medicines. Abhinavagupta takes the same description to compare the realization of Rasa by a sahridaya kavya-rasika and the yogi. The Kavya-rasika is the Himalayas and the Yogi is like another mountain (Locana 1.6).

Like his predecessor Bhatta Nayak, Abhinavagupta gives to the poet a status higher than that of the Yogi.

Critic = Poet / Reader = Writer

In S/Z (1970), Roland Barthes, leading figure of French post-structuralist movement, raised the issue of the 'writerly' (scriptable) text in which the reader involves equally as a kind of 'writer' to produce meaning and convert text into polysemic object. The 'text' in western literature was treated as passive for the reader with mere authority of the author (readerly text). Barthes writes, "the goal of literary work (of literature as work) [which] is to make the reader no longer a consumer, but a producer of the text. Our literature is characterized by the pitiless divorce which the literary institution maintains between the producer of the text and its user, between its owner and its consumer, between its author and its reader. This reader is thereby plunged into a kind of idleness—he is intransitive; he is, in short, serious: instead of functioning himself, instead of gaining access to the magic of the signifier, to the pleasure of writing, he is left with no more than the poor freedom either to accept or reject the text: reading is nothing more than a referendum. Opposite the writerly text, then, is its counter value, its negative, reactive value: what can be read, but not written: the readerly. We call any readerly text a classic text." (Barthes: 1974, p. 4).

The deconstructionists and post-structural theorists deployed writerly text as the means to transform literature into an emancipatory agenda.

> "We know that to restore to writing its future, we must reverse its myth: the birth of the reader must be ransomed by the death of the Author." (Barthes, 1966)

Barthes further sought to take literature beyond meaning, a non-semantic appreciation of literature. He stated:

> "Thus literature (it would be better, henceforth, to say writing), by refusing to assign to the text (and to the world as text) a 'secret': that is, an ultimate meaning, liberates an activity which we might call counter-theological, properly revolutionary, for to refuse to arrest meaning is finally to refuse God and his hypostases, reason, science, the law." (Ibid).

But, Indian genius developed the theory of the writerly text whereby the reader gains equal prominence as the composer and the reader is no longer lost in the endless chain of evaporating meaning or any ultimate meaning, but realizes the delight of reading and listening centred within himself. The author was long decentred in the Rasa-Dhvani School and the spectator/reader gained the centrality in realization of aesthetic experience, but the author was never non-existent. Indian masters believed in life-affirming predicament and the harmonious existence of different elements. The author and the critic, the performer and the spectator became co-partners as sahridaya. The text is to be savoured only by the person with a heart. The reading/ watching was no longer a dull passive exercise. It became a journey to realize the goals of the purushartha and ultimately the freedom from the ordinary, mundane existence.

The very first verse of the Locana pits for the parity of the poet and the critic. Abhinavagupta says:

> May the element of the Saraswati/Vāk which, without any cause, creates *apurva* (never known before) subjects and expands the composition, which infuse rasa into the inanimate stones and vivifies the whole universe, which with the power of prajna (intuition) and upakhya (expression) turns the world into a delightful place, and which gushes forth in the hearts of the poets and the sahridaya-critics, be ever Victorious!

Abhinavagupta claims that same element is present in both the poet as well as the critic. Abhinavagupta refers to Bhatta Taut, his preceptor and describes how spectator, poet and actor realize the same Rasa. (Locana 1.6)

Anandavardhana's *Dhvanyaloka* and Abhinavagupta's commentary on it affirmed the 'writerly' nature of rasa a millennium before the French post-structuralists forayed into the world of experiential literature. While, for Lollaṭa (early ninth century), this aesthetic flavour (rasa) was an augmented or enhanced stable emotion (sthayibhava) of a character and shared by the actor playing the part; for Shankuka (late ninth century), rasa is located in the character, but only imitated by the actor. But for *dhvani* theorists like Anadavardhana and Abhinavagupta, rasa resides in the sahridaya, the critics or the sharing affective community. This was liberative moment for savouring of aesthetic experience.

Abhinavagupta further describes rasa to be a catharsis of the spectator's own latent emotional propensities, resulting in a momentary manifestation of an inner brahmasvada—the tasting of ultimate bliss (Edwin Gerow: 267–68).

French post-structuralists sought writerly text in which bliss (*jouissance*) is produced and which transcends the pleasure of text (*plaisir*) produced merely by the verbal signification. Barthes writes in his essay, *The Death of the Author*, "We know that a text does not consist of a line of words, releasing a single "theological" meaning (the 'message' of the Author-God), but is a space of many dimensions, in which are wedded and contested various kinds of writing, no one of which is original: the text is a tissue of citations, resulting from the thousand sources of culture." (Barthes, 1966)

There is no originality that pours forth from the author out of pathos or similar impersonalized delight. Barthes further adds, "The writer can only imitate a gesture forever anterior, never original; his only power is to combine the different kinds of writing, to oppose some by others, so as never to sustain himself by just one of them; if he wants to express himself, at least he should know that the internal 'thing' he claims to 'translate' is itself only a readymade dictionary whose words can be explained (defined) only by other words, and so on *ad infinitum*."(Ibid)

Barthes was hankering after the writing that gush forth in rasavesh, that pours from the Being immersed in emotion (nivesha).

He was not apurva in his quest, since Indian theorists of poetics had long moved beyond the idea of pleasure of text to the ultimate experience of camatkara in literature. Abhinavagupta's concept of *pratibha* (intuition born from inspiration) as the motivating force of creativity and the resonance in the heart of sahridaya, where rasa burst forth through sparsha (touch) of hearts has given prominence to direct experience. Abhinavagupta says that great writings spill forth the soul struck by camatkara and no amount of mere weaving of text can produce true literature. Barthes was merely echoing (*dhvani*) Abhinavagupta's formulations.

The Sahridaya

Abhinavagupta seems to be deeply influenced by Bhatta Nayak's *Sahridayadarpana.* Bhatta Nayak had criticized Anandhvardana's concept of *dhvani* and developed a paradigm for the savouring of Rasa by an 'emotional community." He discusses in detail Bhatta Nayak's work, *Hridayadarpana* in his commentary of *Dhvanyaloka*, Locana. In fact, the two concepts that are central to Abhinavagupta's philosophy and aesthetics can be traced to the title of Bhatta Nayak's work. According to Abhinavagupta, hridaya is the predominant organ of experience. Rasa experienced by hridaya is higher and alaukika than cognition of knowledge. Similarly, his whole philosophy of pratyabhijnana is based upon the mirror analogy. It is the *abhasavada* based on bimba-pratibimba model. What we perceive is the reflection of our consciousness. The entire world is of the nature of reflection in mirror of cosmic consciousness, Prakasha which is svatantra (free). But, is pratibimba possible in the absence of real thing? Abhinavagupta says that existence of bimba is not necessary for pratibimba. In dream experiences, one perceives objects reflected in mind without real object outside. By analogy, Abhinavagupta argues that the world is reflected in consciousness without there being a real world outside. The world is the reflection of the Absolute consciousness, Shiva-consciousness. Nature of existence is light or prakasha. This is identified with *samvit. Samvit* is that which enlightens the object (artha prakasha rupa). It is itself light. It is *svatantra*, not limited by space or time. The samvit has anandashakti. Anandashakti has triple aspects—icchashakti, jnanashakti and kriyashakti. Samvit is the ultimate reality. In its absolute independent state of joy, it is ananda as desire called camatkara. Thus, aesthetic experience leads one to the experience of the Absolute momentarily, since camatkar is the nature of the Samvit. Everything is a reflection of the Absolute Shiva and hence, also has the nature of Shiva. When individual human soul recognizes itself (pratyabhijna) as Shiva, the soul reaches the ultimate goal.

We have seen how in *Locana*, Abhinavagupta observes that not everyone has the intrinsic capacity to taste a poem. It is only the sahridaya who has this aesthetic capability. An opaque heart does not wonder. Again the mirror analogy explains the whole mechanism. Just like a mirror reflects better when cleansed, analogously the reflection in consciousness as mirror gets progressively purified of memory and other vasanas until it perfectly reflects the Shiva-consciousness, which alone is the essential nature and perfect knowledge. The mirror of the heart of a rasika can be cleansed only by regular immersion (nimmajana) in aesthetic delight.

The sahridaya has a clear mirror of mind by means of repeated acquaintances with and practice of poetry. In *Abhinavabharati*, Abhinavagupta states that the mind and heart must be mirror-like, ready to receive all the images reflected in them (Gnoli, fn. p. XLIV).He further states that poetic sensibility of a sahridaya is the faculty of absorbing/ immersing (tadatmya) with the heart of the poet (kavihridaya-tadatmya-pattiyogyata).

Abhinavagupta observes that the pleasure of watching a spectacle increases when there are a large number of spectators. A spectacle seen by many people together at the same time generates a greater pleasure than those which are if it is seen by a single individual. It is considered that, when a group of people gather together in order to experience art or to perform spiritual practices, if they are all open, they are linked by a greater enjoyment and bliss than that of each individual when alone. Abhinavagupta explains this again using the analogy of mirror. In individual bodies, consciousness enters into contraction. But, in public celebrations, it returns to expansion since all components are reflected in each other. The joy of one's own consciousness is reflected in the consciousness of all the bystanders, as if in so many mirrors, and, inflamed by these, it abandons without its effort its state of individual contraction. For this very reason, in meeting of many people, fullness of joy occurs when every bystander, not only one of them, is identified with the spectacle. In virtue of the absence of any cause of contraction, the consciousness finds itself in a state of expansion, free of obstacles (vighnas), and pervaded by beatitude. But, when even one bystander does not concentrate on the spectacle he is looking at, and does not share, therefore, the form of consciousness in which the other spectators are immersed, this consciousness is disturbed, as at the touch of an uneven surface (Gnoli, pp XXXVIII- XXXIX).

Abhinavagupta extends the concept of the spectacle to the esoteric practices of spiritual realization. If a coherent spiritual community is created, it can accelerate the spiritual evolution of its members compared with individual practice through this mirroring of consciousness. The spectacle-techne pervaded his kula-yaga. Group practices involving music, dance, meditation and rituals, including tantric sexual rites all combined to create a spectacle, *melak* of the kula. The ultimate purpose of the group practices is the expansion of consciousness. And during the chakra ritual, no individual must be allowed to enter who does not identify himself with the ceremonies and thus does not share the state of consciousness of the celebrant; this would cause , a contraction of the consciousness (Tantraloka, Chapter 28: 373-378).

Universal Samvit which contracts due to differences of bodies, when unites in chakra (melak) ritual through mutual samghatta (friction) and reflection of each other in same act, achieves fullness after the doubt and shyness are removed. Moreover, in a chakra yaga, the individual consciousness gets reflected in the *samvit* like multiple images (pratibimba) and attains universality without effort.

Abhinavagupta elaborates the point in the context of public

performances like dance, music and drama. When everyone gets absorbed (*tanmayi*), the delight produced is not of an individual, but of the totality, the *samvit*. (Tantraloka, 28.375) The spectator who is sarvatanmayibhava (completely absorbed) and ahladit (filled with joy) is not of an individual, he experiences universal joy of samvit, the Purnananda.

In public performances like dance, the ever delightful samvit attains unity and realizes the Purnananda, total delight. When there is absence of the factors of contraction like envy, hate, jealousy etc. the doubtless samvit (viksvar) delights in its blissful aspect. Therefore, those who cannot attain the stage of complete absorption (tadatmya), may cause hindrance in full realization of samvit, just as a rough surface cannot properly touch the adjoining objects. The Tantraloka advises that admitting such persons would cause contraction of samvit in the chakra yaga.

Similarly, rasa-dhvani of poetry can be savoured by only sahridaya. If one is not sensitively equipped and is not fully absorbed in the poetry, one cannot realize the rasa-dhvani. The sahridaya cannot be general people. Abhinavagupta refers to the connoisseur of music and mentions how those who are not conversant with the knowledge of music cannot differentiate the sur and tala of the music. Similarly, the rasa-dhvani can be realized only by the experts in poetics. The rasa-dhvani is not verbal and those who spend the time merely to know about shabda and meaning, can never decipher the suggestion, the *vyangyarth* (Locana I.7).

The 'heart' (hridaya) is an important symbol for Abhinavagupta. His tantra treatises refer to the seat of knowledge in the Yoginihridaya (heart of Yogini). We also find how hridaya (heart) again holds the most important position in *Para-Trisika-Vivarana*. Abhinavagupta terms 'sauh' (सौः) as the hridayabija and sums up the trika philosophy in this hridayabija.

The conception of sahridaya arises out of this quandary. Only sahridaya can be fully absorbed in relishing the poetry (tanmaya) and lose their individuality and let the samvit expand in delight to experience camatkar rasa, through multiple reflection in the Samvit as the universal mirror.

Thus, Abhinavagupta has utilized the two categories used by Bhatta Nayak in Hridayadarpana to generate the aesthetic as well as philosophical ideas.

Primacy of Aesthetics over Mystic Experience

Edwin Gerow raises a pertinent question. Gerow writes, "We may better appreciate Abhinava's problem by asking how a sovereign aesthetics might help a Shaiva mystic develop a philosophically accountable notion of the Lord, who is, after all, at play." (Edwin Gerow, 1994, p 186) I would like to expand the question. How does one make aesthetic delight permanent like the spiritual experience? And, how does one make, mystic experience effortless? Can spiritual delight be generalized like aesthetic delight? How does one make spiritual realization in this very body as temple (deva-sadan-deha) without abdicating worldly life? Spiritual realization should not be beyond life and death, but life-affirming.

The Kula tradition, or at least Abhinava's rendering of that tradition, is expounded in *Tantraloka* Chapter 29. He prescribes the use of three makars only to express practitioner's inner bliss and to break down the wall between inner and outer bliss. By authentic initiation and above all by the grace of Shiva (*Shambhopaya*), one can attain the Bhairavic attitude, where the outer and the inner are the same. Such an adept does not oppose the external world vis-a-vis the internal world, subject and object, self and the other. Everything is equally the expression of the Shakti, the supreme word, *Paravac*. Abhinavagupta breaks down every wall between sacred and the profane, ritual and ordinary life, so that the Kula practitioner gets liberated while alive. Everything reflects everything else. The wall analogy is replaced by reflecting, shining mirror analogy in his aesthetics as well as philosophy. The adept attains the bhirava-mudra and his each act becomes a worship to the Param Shiva.

Abhinavagupta deploys the aesthetic categories to generate

Purna-ananda of spiritual realization to all the participant effortlessly like in aesthetic realization of Rasa by the sahridayas. He always emphasizes about *tanmayata* (complete absorption) and *tadatmya* (resonance) for the participant of the chakrachar and compares the same with drama in 28th chapter of the Tantraloka (Tantraloka: 28.18-20). Abhinavagupta prescribes non-entry for those who cannot immerse fully in the spiritual communion (Tantraloka: 28.375-377). For him, Kula is nothing but the Parmananda (Tantraloka: 29.4). Abhinavagupta elaborated homologous method of aesthetic delight to realize the Bhairava-mudra of spiritual bliss when camatkara pervades the inner as well as outward life, ordinarily in everyday life.

Kaula's basic method is the experience of the freedom of consciousness in the heart—in the first phase, the limitation of consciousness is removed and it enters nirvikalpa, then in the second phase consciousness manifests as a free force, entering the senses, and producing extroverted samadhi, and in the final phase, the body is divinized and immortalized—the effortless method—[S'] ambhavopaya—direct and immediate entry in nirvikalpa (Muller-Ortega, p 63).

Mark Dyczkowski sums up how Tantric experience itself may be identified with the aesthetic experience of the individual actor in cosmic drama, "the Self ... is an actor because it assumes every state of being. Inebriated with the juice of supreme bliss, the self sports in the world of daily life like an actor." (Dyczkowski, p. 113)

In this paradigmatic shift, one can trace the foundation of bhakti movement. The spiritual communion can be attained by all-householders and the sages alike. The nature of realization is bliss and the public ceremonies aid in the realization of the camatkara. Rasa is realized by way of sahridayas losing their individual selves through sadharanikaran and partaking in the expansion of blissful samvit. Abhinavagupta mentioned bhakti as an important component of the shanta rasa. He struggled hard against demolishing bhakti as a lakshana of *Dhvani* in the *Locana*, so as to establish the primacy of *rasa-dhvani*. Many contemporary thinkers had identified *dhvani* with bhakti. They deliberated that just as horseness separates horse from other genus, bhakti is the lakshana of dhvani. Abhinavagupta wanted to clear the mist engulfing the *bhakti-dhvani* semblance, but the concept of bhakti seeped into Indian consciousness from the literary genre. Bhakti became a catechism for the transformative movement in Indian society with rasa as its carrier.

The bhakti movement borrowed Abhinavagupta's mirror paradigm. The idols (pratima derived from pratibimba) were seen as pratibimba reflecting the Absolute Divine. The *sahridaya* sanghas proliferated. The aesthetic delight which was savoured by a select community of literary expert expanded through sadharanikaran. The sahridaya communes became vyapta and vyakta. The poetic traditions under the renewing Hinduism counted Bhakti (devotion) itself as being among the navarasa.

The poets and the spiritual luminaries, from beginning of the 11th century, provided a tremendous impetus to the Bhakti movement. Soon after Abhinavagupta's legendary disappearance, there appeared Ramanuja followed by Sant Jnaneshwar, Namdeva, Tukaram, Tulsidas, Surdas, Shankardeva, Chaitanya, Kabir, Mirabai, Vallabhacharya, Rupa Goswami, Purandar Das, Eknath and Ravidas.

The Kula rituals meant as the way to effortlessly realize the camatkrit rasa for a small group of the practitioner disappeared from Indian soil. And it was like a camatkara that the bhakti movement pervaded each and every nook of the continent and continue to expand by fusing the spectacular power of music, bhajan, kirtan in public sphere and the growing firm faith in the divinity revealing to a bhakta much easily than to a yogi or to a tantrik.

Primacy of Poetry

Why is it that most religious texts are written in verse? Why is it that Adikavi Valmiki when struck by shoka after witnessing the Krauncha bird bereaved from its mate caused by the killing of the mate during intimate union, let his Rasa of karuna (pathos) flow into the first verse of the Ramayana? Why did siddhas compose the caryas? Most religious experiences get communicated through poetic mode. Is poetry higher than religion? Can Higher Truth be known only through rasa-dhvani?

I have argued how the joy of spectacle makes the spectator to desire to participate in the deindividuated moment (sadharanikaran) again and again? The collective joy strikes as a camatkar to the participant. One can reflect over the intensity of delight when military marches in unison or when people gather in protest movement . The sahridayas reflect each other and touch with same intensity. This is what is known as resonance in the physical sciences. In the Sphota theory of Bhartrihari, *dhvani* is the term for such resonance of the speech sound. Though, the aestheticians used the term *Dhvani* in altogether different sense of suggestion, the rasa which is savoured through cognition of such suggestion expands when the individual is in communion with sahridaya. Sahridayas resonate at same frequency as they are completely absorbed (tanmaya and tadatmaya). But, the paradox arises again. If greater delight is experienced in the state of deindividuation, in the collective participation of aesthetic pleasure, why do we long for the freedom (svatantrata)? How does one reconcile the delight of svatantrata and intensification of Rasa in collectivity?

Herein comes the Poetry as the site of resolution of conflicting desire of svatantrata and the collective deindividuation! The Poetry gives the complete freedom to create and generate novelty. Anandavardhana compares the Poet with the Prajapati, the creator—Brahma. Everything is transformed in the way the poet envisions. Therefore, the very first verse of *Locana* mentions how even the stones become infused with the rasa in poetic creation. The Poet has this power to create apurva things (never heard of). The poetry is the manifestation of this everlasting power to create. Poetry is also something that can be relished by the sahridayas. The most spectacular delight is the camatkara free from any impediment, a *sui generis* delight, which is also the nature of the Universal consciousness viz. samvit. Poetry indeed is a camatkara that combines desire and joy, svatantrata and ananda.

Every religious text has these two paramount goals—to offer

a way of salvation from the bondage in form of Nirvana, moksha, end of time etc. as well as eternal deindividuated transcendental (alaukik) joy. Naturally, the poetic language is the only apt vehicle to communicate the message to the followers of religious faith. Poetry does not need religion to renew itself. Poetry is free from the impediments of discriminatory barriers. Poetry transcends walls. Poetry operates through mirror, religion survives through erecting wall.

Poetry is the vaccine against Walmart-culture. The consumerism and the mall-culture thrives over human propensity to enjoy novelty and collective deindividuation. The death of poetry preceded the birth of mall-culture. Only the renewal of the primacy of Poetry can rescue mankind from the narcissistic path of self-destruction and lead us to revaluate the authentic touch of poetry. Will that not be a camatkara? Poetry touches our heart. Our hearts have lost the touch of poetry.

References

1. Sankaran, A. (1929). *Some Aspects of Literary Criticism in Sanskrit or the Theories of Rasa and Dhvani,* University of Madras.
2. Raghvan, V. (1942). *Some Concepts of the Alankara Sastra,* Adyar.
3. Gnoli, Raniero (1968). *The Aesthetic Experience According to Abhinavagupta, Varanasi:* Chowkhambha.
4. Gerow, Edwin (1977). *A History of Indian literature, Vol. V: Indian Poetics,* Otto Harrassowitz, Wiesbaden.
5. Gerow, Edwin (1994). "Abhinavagupta's Aesthetics as a Speculative Paradigm." *Journal of American Oriental Society,* Vol 114:2.
6. Barthes, Roland (1974). *S/Z: An Essay,* trans. by Richard Miller, New York: Hill and Wang.
7. Barthes, Roland (1966). "The Death of the Author," trans by Richard Howard.

8. Barthes, Roland (1975). *The Pleasure of the Text,* trans by Richard Miller, New York: Hill and Wang.

9. Muller-Ortega, Paul Eduardo. (1986). *The Triadic Heart of Siva: Kaula Tantricism of Abhinavagupta in the Non-Dual Shaivism of Kashmir,* Albany: SUNY.

10. Dyczkowski, Mark. (1992). *Aphorisms of Shiva,* Albany: SUNY.

11. Urban, High B (1997). "Disinterested Judgement and Its Social Interests in Kant and Abhinavagupta: A New Approach" *Comparative Aesthetics,* Number 35, Winter.

12. Mukherjee, Ramaranjan (1991). *Comparative Aesthetics,* Calcutta: Sanskrit Pustak Bhandar.

13. Hota, A. (2006). *Sphota, Pratibha and Dhvani,* Delhi: Eastern Book Linkers.

14. Pollock, Sheldon (2012). "From Rasa Seen to Rasa Heard," in *Aux bords de la clairière,* Caterina Guenzi and Sylvia d'Intino,Paris: Brepols, 2012, Collections érudites de l'École Pratique des Hautes Études, pp. 189-207.

15. Pollock, Sheldon, (2012). *"Vyakti and the History of Rasa," Vimarsha,* Journal of the Rasthriya Sanskrit Sansthan (World Sanskrit Conference Special Issue), Vol 6, 2012, pp 232-253.

16. Pollock, Sheldon (2010). "What was Bhatta Nayaka Saying? The Hermeneutical Transformation of Indian Aesthetics", in Sheldon Pollock, ed., *Epic and Argument in Sanskrit Literary History: Essays in Honour of Robert P Goldman,* Delhi: Manohar, 2010, pp 143-184.

17. Mishra, Kailash Pati (2006). *Aesthetic Philosophy of Abhinavagupta,* Varanasi: Kala Prakashan.

18. Raja, Kunjunni K (1969). *Indian Theories of Meaning,* Adyar Library Series, Vol 91.

19. Sharma, Mukunda Madhava (1968). *The Dhvani Theory in Sanskrit Poetics,* Varanasi: Chowkhamba.

20. Coward, Harold G (1986). *The Sphota Theory of Language—A Philosophical Analysis, Delhi: MLBD.*
21. Patnaik, Priyadarshi (1997). *Rasas in Aesthetics,* Delhi: DK Printworld.
22. Singh, Jaideva (1988). *Abhinavagupta: Para-Trisika-Vivarana—The Secret of Tantric Mysticism,* Delhi: MLBD.
23. Chaturvedi, Radheshyama (2002). *Tantraloka of Abhinavagupta,* Vol I-V, Varanasi: Chaukhamba Vidyabhawan.
24. Furlinger, Ernst (2009). *The Touch of Sakti—A Study in Non-Dualistic Trika Saivism of Kashmir,* Delhi: DK Printworld.
25. Toshkhani, SS. (2003) "Kashmir's Contribution to Indian Aesthetics", *Kashmir Herald,* Vol. 3 (3).
26. Tripathi, Ramsagar (1973). *Dhvanyaloka with Locana, First Udyot,* Delhi: MLBD.
27. Krishnamoorthy, K (1988). *Dhvanyaloka-Locana Chapter,* First, New Delhi: Meharchand Lachman Das Publications.
28. Kieschnick, John (2003). *The Impact of Buddhism on Chinese Material Culture,* Princeton University Press.

SAMVAD

Chapter 16

Palindromes, Anadromes and Indian Culture

Most of us relish playing with words and numbers. It's fun to discover interesting patterns. Palindromes are always fascinating. What is palindrome? It's a specific characterization of any number, phrase, word, verse or even narrative which can be read in either direction. It's the antidote to linearity paradigm. Modernity erased every other mode of characterization in literature, mathematics, sciences, history and philosophy and built up the empire of linearity. Time flows in linear fashion. Light follows the linear path. Ideologies postulate a teleological purpose. Positivism of sciences and social sciences presupposes this universalization of linearity. Biological evolution is linear. Social evolution is linear even though that follows dialectical path in Marxist jargon. History is linear. Perception is linear. Thought itself has been linearized. Writing has to be done in linear ways. Reading has to be done in the same way. But, non-modern cognition contained manifold paradigm. Palindrome is one of the most fascinating ways to understand our ancestor's thinking process and to retrieve our indigenous roots in simulacral eco-cultural system.

One of the often referred earliest palindrome belongs to the Roman period. In 79 AD, a Latin word square was inscribed at Herculaneum as follow:

"Sator Arepo Tenet Opera Rotas"

This can be read in same way in both directions.

The story about Napoleon composing a palindrome phrase is widely known. While in custody at Elba, he is believed to have composed the following palindrome:

"Able was I ere I saw Elba."

This can be read same way in both directions. There are thousands of words in every language with this property. Most familiar and yet unnoticed are the words like 'radar', 'level', 'civic'. One Indian language, Malayalam being spoken in Kerala is a palindrome.

In biology, the property has seized the minds of the molecular biologists since the double-stranded DNA has palindromic sequences and these are under serious studies. Palindromes are found in proteins, the building blocks of our lives also. In DNA, the nucleotides complement in particular fashion. Thymine pairs with Adenine and Cytosine with Guanine. Thus, in a DNA helix, if there is a sequence in one strand as ACCTAGGT, the complementary strand will be a palindrome, TGGATCCA. DNA in its natural, double-stranded form may contain palindromes, sequences which read the same from either side because they are identical to their reverse complement on the sister strand. A recent publication by three Swiss scientists are making headlines for identifying palindromes in the DNA sequencing as the marker of species. Authors Estelle Lamperea-Burgunder, Philipp Ludin and Pascal Mase working at Roche Diagnostics have published the work titled "Species-Specific Typing of DNA Based on Palindrome Frequency Patterns" in *DNA Research*, 18, 117-24 (2011).The authors conclude that:

"Accustomed to reading DNA as linear sequences, we tend to forget that it is double-stranded in nature. In double-stranded DNA, the only sequences which are unique are palindromes. Here, we

confirm the notion that Short palindromes are underrepresented in all kinds of genomes. The frequency distribution of short palindromes exhibits more than twice the inter-species variance of non-palindromic sequences, which renders palindromes optimally suited for the typing of DNA. Here, we show that based on palindrome frequency, DNA sequences can be discriminated to the level of species of origin. By plotting the ratios of actual occurrence to expectancy, we generate palindrome frequency patterns that allow to cluster different sequences of the same genome and to assign plasmids, and in some cases even viruses to their respective host genomes."

Figure : 16.1

(Palindrome in DNA sequence)

In mathematics, palindromic numbers constitute major part of recreational mathematics. Numbers like 121, 111, 555 or large prime palindrome numbers like 32423 are fascinating for their properties. In 2003, a palindromic prime containing 30,913 digits was found by a mathematician, David Broadhurst. In India, palindromes have been part of mantra tradition.

Palindromes in Sanskrit

Indian tradition is marked with constant production of mantras. One thing that India has comparative advantage is this art of building mantra-verses. Palindromic mantras have been found in both Vedic and Tantric tradition. One of the most famous statements of the Upanishads, *So aham Asmi (I am He) that points to the* establishment of non-duality in existence has been remarkably used in the hamsa mantras. *Soham* (the conjunction of Sah and Aham) has its anadrome (the reverse palindrome or semordilaps where words spell different words in backward direction), *hamsa* (swan) combines together to constitute the most famous palindromic mantra, *hamsah so ham*. Similarly, one finds the palindromic mantras in operation while propitiating every major god in Hinduism by following a pattern of adding the alphabets in forward order at beginning of the seed mantra and in reverse order at the end. The operation itself is known as *anulomavilomena* or *kramotkramat*. It is to be noted that the alphabets are not mere the written words but the grosser form of the Divine potency. The word represents the manifested world. Hence, the alphabets are seen clubbed in different fashion in various mantras. In Sanskrit, the palindromes are constituted syllable wise. Thus a palindromic mantra containing powerful resonance can be created by such operations. There can be palindromic mantras like:

Aim hrim shrim chamundaye shrim hrim aim!
Ka ae ee la hrim tripursundaraye hrim la ee ae ka!

Many times these palindromes are sandwiched between the beginning seeds like Om and end syllable representing the sacrifice/ manifestation like swaha/phat. So, one can generate complete mantras by using, say, the first palindrome as follows:

Om aim hrim shrim chamundaye shrim hrim aim swaha!

But, mantra formation is not only such kind of pattern, there are ascending and descending resonances. It's a vast field of learning. I will just reproduce a famous Ganesha mantra:

Hrim ham hlaum ganapataye glaum gam hrim!

In Sanskrit poetries, lot of experiments were made with the verses and the ideas of chitra kavya (pictorial verses) emerged. Anandavardhana, the famous Sanskrit critic and the composer of the world's finest theory on Poetry (*Dhvanyaloka*) has put such compositions as the most inferior. But, paradoxically, he himself composed a hymn *Devishatakam*, a chitrakavyam, littered with palindromes. It is another matter that Anandavardhana considers *dhvani* (suggestion) and rasa as the basis of great verse.

At the time when Anandavardhana was experimenting with

paradox, Magha composed a great poem, *Shishupala Vadha* during the 8th century. The poet created the most beautiful palindrome stanza of all time. It was a *sarvatobhadra*, perfect in every direction.

George L Hart, a Sanskritist wrote a letter in *Scientific American* (1970), discussing about an article on palindrome by Martin Gardner, a writer on recreational mathematics by referring to a verse of Shishupala Vadha, as follows:

sa-kā-ra-nā- nā-ra- kā-sa
kā-ya-sā-da-da- sā-ya- kā
ra- sā-ha-vā vā-ha- sā-ra
nā –da- vā-da-da- vā- da- nā
(nā –da- vā-da-da- vā- da- nā
ra- sā-ha-vā vā-ha- sā-ra
kā-ya-sā-da-da- sā-ya- kā
sa-kā-ra-nā- nā-ra- kā-sa)

The last four lines, which are an inversion of the first four, are not part of the verse but are supplied so that its properties can be seen more easily. This verse is a description of an army and may be translated as follows: "[That army], which relished battle[rasāhavā], contained allies who brought low the bodes and gaits of their various striving enemies[Sakāranā nāra kāsakāyasādada sāya kā] , and in it the cries of the best of mounts contended with musical instruments[vāha sāranādavādada vāda nā].)"

I have come across one of the finest poetry in Sanskrit written in full in palindromic sequence. It is the composition by Kavi Surya Pandita named *Ramakrishna Viloma Kavyam* written in 14th century. Every verse is a palindrome and pertains to life history of two greatest epic heroes Rama and Krishna in different directions.

But once palindromes and chitrakavya were discouraged by the great aestheticians, the movement dwindled down. The pattern of verses gave way to the techniques to generate the rasa (jouissance/joy/emptions/flavours) through words/verses/punctuations/absences. Anandavardhana and later his successor the great cultural synthesizer, Abhinavagupta who wrote the commentary *Locana* on *Dhvanyaloka* led the movement to marginalize this genre of expression.

Anadromes

Anadromes is slightly different than palindromes. Here a word or phrase is read differently in backward direction with different meaning. A simple word like 'was' explains this. The reverse 'saw' is a different word with different meaning. Even 'God/dog' constitute such an anadrome which many call as semordnilap (an anadrome of the word 'palindromes'). I am of the view that anadromes have played vital role in constituting Indian culture. The emergence of idea of Rama itself seems to be intricately woven in such verbal construction. Valmiki, who was a robber named Ratnakar and who killed numerous passerby, was asked to meditate on 'mara' (death) since it was easy for him to concentrate on a theme he was familiar with. While repetiting the sound, the anadrome Rama emerged. An ant hill grew around him. But, he continued to enchant the name. From the ant-hill, his name Valmiki was derived and he was encouraged to write the story of 'Rama'. Interestingly, Rama is also an anadrome of Mara, the leader of the evil/desires who tormented Buddha. There was a mutual reciprocity and competition between two sects of Hinduism and Buddhism during those days, which narrative was weaved earlier and which one was written merely in response is yet to be fathomed with authority by cultural historians.

Another famous anadrome is Vashi/Shiva which gave rise to Vashi Yoga, popularized nowadays as the Kriya Yoga technique of Babaji. By repetiting the word vashi, one meditates on the power of Shiva. Vashi has meaning of 'resident'. Thus, the word connotes the residence of Shiva within the body in which breathing technique is utilized to achieve the maximum effect. Hams/soham is such an anadrome. Since soham is "I am He" and its anadrome is 'hams', a swan; the soul has often been eulogized as hamsa (swan).

These anadromic mantras have been adopted in a breathing tradition that replicates the same anadromic process. In India, the mastery over breath is considered the way to mastery over life-forces and the way to realize the ultimate truth, the root of existence. The breathing techniques have been generated by keeping this aspect of a process and its reverse. In Pranayam, it is also called anulomaviloma. One follows normal breathing and then the reverse breathing. In fact, our natural breathing itself represents an anadromic process. One breathes into and thence breathes out. There is no end of the process. There is no linearity involved. Everything ends and every end is a new beginning.

Similar pattern is found in the phoneme universe. Every manifestation dissolves into its end, but, every end syllable gives rise to the new beginning. The endless pendulating process continues. In tantras, it is called *kramot kramat*. Every krama (series) reverses. In rituals, it is the fundamental factor in mudras (gestures).

This gave rise to the cyclic nature of time. Evolution ends into involution. The inherent cyclicity postulates the non-dual view of universe. Since, no preferred directionality can be eschewed in such kind of thinking. The paradox can be overcome by presupposing the identity of Self/other in a cyclic universe. The anadromic primacy gets reflected in the belief system in which the Spandan (oscillation) gains predominance as mode of thinking in literature and sciences.

It is being established that the sequences like palindromes (possibly more of anadrome is yet to be deciphered) lies at the very root of our species-ness. New questions will arise as to whether repetition of palindromic verses produce certain effect over the DNA sequences? Whether science is catching up with Peter Gariaev's Wave Genetics? Whether higher density of palindromes in the DNA of an individual makes him more imaginative, since he/she can discern the world of diverse patterns easily? Whether certain geographies produce higher preponderance for palindromic sequence? Whether the ethnic mapping of palindromic gene sequences will establish diversity thereby, explaining cultural diversity? Whether Indian populace has higher density of anadromes/palindromes in genetic make-up making them to view the world in a cyclic karma-rebirth perspective as compared to the Semitic or Anglo-American world?

Whether modernity as a mode of looking into the perceptible universe is a parochial way of living? Can we enhance our livingry by replicating palindromic/anadromic way of existence?

Anadromes in Indian Culture

I have come across many anadromes which might contain the secret of various hidden aspects of Indian culture. The concept of 'deva/veda' itself seems to be an anadromic relationship. Vedas, the most ancient Indian texts contain hymns for various Devas (gods) like Indra, Brahma, Savita etc. There is concept of 'Aham/Maha' in Kashmir Shaivism constituting such a relationship. I can see the way to unravel the myth of Shiva drinking poison (visha) by seeing how the two words 'Shiva/visha' form an anadrome. Most of the time anadromes have different meaning. But, many a times anadromes have opposite meanings. If 'Mara' stands for death, the anadrome 'Rama' symbolizes life, hence, recitation of Ramanama is believed to bestow life-saving power. In similar vein, one can decipher Shiva as an antonym for Visha, the poison. Shiva utters boon for immortality. In the mythology of Krishna, one often comes across the Raslila, the bliss-permeated playful dance of the bhakta gopis with Krishna. In Sanskrit, the anadrome of Ras will be 'Sar', the summary, the gist of the Existence. Thus, the gist of existence is nothing but joy, love and playfulness in the tradition worshipping Krishna. In the ancient times, the worship of Yakshas was very popular and the Yaksha tradition was appropriated by the Buddhist sects in their own iconography and rituals. Yaksha and its anadrome Kshaya constitute an antonymous relationship in meaning. Yaksha were worshipped for their potentiality, for providing vitality. The anadrome Kshaya semantically stands for dissolution.

If one glances at the Jaimini astrology, one will be surprised to find emphasis given to anadromes. In Jaimini sutras of astrology, Katapayadi alpha-numeric system is followed. Every consonant has been assigned a numeric value. Now, if one needs to predict the fortune of 'Dara', Sanskrit term for wife, one has to put the numeric value of two phonemes 'da' and 'ra'. Da has a value of 8 and ra, 2. Thus, the number will be 82. Now, one has to write the value of anadrome 'Rada'. This is 28. The difference of two numbers has to be divided by 12 (the number of rasi/signs). The remainder is 6. Thus, the 6th House concerns Dara in Jaimini astrology.

In Indian tradition, every manifestation is believed to have absorption. There is no linearity, but an oscillatory movement of things across time, a rhythm. Thus, anadromes in one way denote the absorption back of the manifested entity and the pair constitute the cycle of expansion and dissolution; manifestation and re-absorption.

By taking the tool of anadrome, one can decode the name of Lakulisha. Lakulisha was the greatest teacher of the oldest sect of Shaivism, Pashupat. It is from the Pashupat that Kapalik, Kalamukh and other sects emerged. It is believed that Pashupat is the last incarnation of Shiva and when, he died as a child, Shiva himself permeated the body and grew up to spread the sect. The place where this transformation is supposed to have occurred is in the Vadodara district and the known as Kavyarohan to commemorate the said event. They were pure ascetics and precursor of the Bhakti sects that sprung during medieval ages.

Lakulish, if read in reverse direction reads as 'Shilakula'. 'Shila' stands for modesty. Since they were the ascetics who shun normal family life and ego, they were the modest par exceilence. 'Kula' stands for "lineage" and in later centuries, the term was widely used in the tantric literature. In my opinion, the name Lakulish was derived from similar operation of the prevalent Sanskrit vocabulary that described their whole characteristics. Lakulisha/Shilakula anadrome opens up new possibility to understand this important sect.

Though, grammar of anadromes is yet to be composed; one cannot ignore the occurrences of palindromes in various mantric traditions. It is to be noted that the formation of these relationship in English and Sanskrit are different. In Sanskrit, the palindromes are constituted syllable-wise. The words like 'tantra' and the 'Ganga' itself are palindrome in Sanskrit.

Since Sanskrit grammar developed in systematized form in early times and the grammar was based upon mathematical relationships, I am of the view that the manifest World was described by the relationships intrinsic to the Word as well as various operations of the phoneme, sentence and narrative etc. In Indian tradition, the world is considered as mere grosser extension of the word which itself is the grosser form of unmanifest power of the Ultimate Reality. Thus, in a textual universe, possible resemblances and contradictions, possible mathematical relationships were harnessed to develop vocabulary, concepts and meanings. In the cyclic, karmic view of things, it is difficult to say which came later—Veda or Deva, Lakulisha or Shila Kula. Or, were these created like bipolar Reality oscillating within Unity, the hallmark of Indian ontology. Duality under non-dual Reality of Words opens new vista for explorers into India's hoary past!

Chapter 17

Padmasambhava - A Pan-Asian Avatar!

Padmasambhava, popularly known as the Guru Rinpoche and the Second Buddha among the Himalayan people has left indelible mark across sacred geography in Asia. He is said to be from Oddiyana, a supposedly magical kingdom often mentioned as a sacred pitha in tantrik literature. Oddiyana has been variously located in Kashmir or the Swat valley. Though, in recent days the historians from Orissa are claiming Oddiyana as modern day Odisha and fortified their arguments after the inauguration of *Padmasambhava* monastery on January 12, 2010, consecrated by the Dalai Lama at Chandragiri in Gajapati district. There has been spurt of writing suggesting that Padmasambhava might have been born in Sambhal (presently Sambalpur) in Oddiyana (presently Odisha). This assumption is employed to explain the occurrence of nomenclature of mystical land of Shambala in Padmasambhava's biography and subsequent Buddhist tantra. Dr Bimalendu Mohanty, former founder Vice-Chancellor of the Utkal University of Culture, Bhubaneshwar has edited a voluminous work, *Padmasambhava* of *Oddiyana* (Odisha KIIT, 2012) using the recent finds in Udayagiri-Lalitagiri-Ratnagiri archaeological materials and regenerated the interest of the Buddhist world towards the importance of Odisha as the relaying point of Buddhism across Asia. But, most of the historians pit Oddiyana in the northwest. The most famous biography of Padmasambhava was written by Yeshe Tsogyal mentions Oddiyana in the west of Bodhgaya. Oddiyana is the land of big ponds where plenty of big size lotus bloom. Orissa is in the east of Bodhgaya. Hiuen Tsang, the famous Chinese pilgrim has mentioned about Oddiyana situated in the north west of India. Patrul Rinpoche, an authoritative teacher of the Nyingma tradition views Oddiyana in the region between Chitral, Gilgit and Swat where big ponds are located and locate Oddiyana in Kashmir. Apart from these narratives, the fact that Padmasambhava carried the ideas of the Sarvastivadin School makes Kashmir the most probable centre of Padmasambhava's early activities. His various hagiographies contain sufficient material to establish Kashmir as inspirational landscape in Padmasambhava's sojourn across the Himalayas. We will see in later section of this essay how Padmasambhava carried many of the ideas across which were sourced from the contemporary tradition and philosophy in Kashmir.

Born in the eighth century, he is regarded as the patron saint of Tibet and founder of the oldest Vajrayana sect, Nyingma. He was invited by the powerful Tibetan King Trisong Detsen (740-98 AD) after being advised by the Nalanda abbot Shantarakshita to pacify the evil forces. Padmasambhava was instrumental in the founding of the first Buddhist monastery at Samye. Padmasambhava did not limit his activities to the construction of Samye monastery, but also extended his influence across the Tibetan plateau and beyond. It is believed that he defeated the negative forces, spirits and demons and converted them as protectors of the Dharma. This reflects the narrative of appropriating the pre-existing belief system to propagate a Great Tradition like Buddhism, which many a contemporary scholars term as the Buddha-isation of Tibet.

Padmasambhava is credited with introducing the practice of Dzogchen (seeking to examine the fundamental nature of mind directly, without relying on visualizations and images) and hiding scriptures or 'terma' to be discovered by later practitioners or the tertons. The world-known text, *Tibetan Book of Dead* is such a term discovered by the terton Karma Lingpa. Similarly, there have been more than 150 biographies discovered by various tertons. The most popular biography was discovered by the terton Yeshe Tsogyal. The name of this book is *Padma Ka-hi-thang-yig* (Padma's Precepts). It is also called *Ke-rap Nam-thar Gye-pa* (Complete Birth History). The biography was published by W.Y. Evans-Benz with an introduction by Carl Jung in 1936 as *The Tibetan Book of Great Liberation.* Padmasambhava's influence over the Himalayan laity is immense. He is the protector of Dharma, prosperity and the Guru to ward off evil forces. He is propitiated more than any other Buddhist saint after Buddha and rightly called the Second Buddha. But, astonishingly, there is less exploration about his influence in shaping the modern Tibet and its neighbourhood in comparison with many other Vajrayana teachers and translators. This has to do something with the ascendance of the Gelukpa and Karma-Kagyu sect following the political upheavals in Tibet. There has been persistent resistance to introduction of Nyingma rituals in the practice of Tibetan Buddhism by the dominant Gelukpa followers. This has adversely affected the emergence of Padmasambhava as the greatest Indian missionary who accomplished his objectives in creating a syncretic sacred space expanding across Asia in single life time.

Padmasambhava is the only historic figure through which appropriation of a site through the taming of its local demons have been achieved on such a huge scale. The pre-existing Bon practices were, thus, amalgamated in the new Great Tradition. Similarly, the sacred sites of Shaivites were appropriated by conjuring the myth of victory of Samvara (Demchok) over Shiva in the battle at Kailash. The Buddhist sacralisation of the Himalayas was achieved through production of similar legends. Padmasambhava's name is associated in one way or the other with these transformatory cognitive practices. Padmasambhava is associated with most of the pilgrimage sites across the Himalayas. Padmasambhava is invoked in prayers. He is invoked in rituals of the folk religion and by doing this people believe that the fruits can be realized. He is credited with the invention of the Mongolian Fire cult and of non-sacrificial ritual practices in

India and beyond. People invoke Padmasambhava in a variety of everyday activities like hunting rituals, blessing of the yurt among the Mongols, warding off disease, starting a new venture, calling of the soul etc. Padmasambhava is the true 'Cultural Superman' of the Himalayas, the epitome of sacredness.

Padmasambhava —The Patron saint of Kaliyuga

In Buddha Nirvana calendar (zero point is 544 BC.), the advent of millennium (sahastrar years) occurs in the year 456AD. Aryabhata fixed the year 499 AD as the zero ayanamsha year and every astronomical calculations were to be derived from this particular point onward. There was lot of millenarianism in the air. New cults and new gods multiplied. The Hindu sects vied with each other to occupy the space to be vacated by the Buddhists in their millenarian perceptions. For most of the people steeped deep into ritual universe governed by the calendrical time, the yuga of the Buddha seemed to be passing away.

The problem of millenarian shift was compounded by the news of the invasion of the White Huns. The Huns destroyed the Taxila University in 455 AD, one of the greatest monastic institutions for Buddhist studies. The Guptas were the patron of the Buddhist institutions. The horde of Huns riding their horses destroyed cities as far as Bengal. Even the capital of the Gupta Kingdom, Pataliputra was sacked. There was a perception that the Huns were enemies of the Buddhist sect. This was fortified by the rise of Mihirkula, who, it is believed, converted to Shaivism and widely persecuted the Buddhists.

Buddhists must have felt the heat and began the counter-narrative. The idea of chakra (cycle of time) was appropriated in the ritual usage of tantra like ganachakra, *chakrasamvara* and later kalahchakra. The millennial age had passed. Each age ought to have a new avatar to stem over the looming crisis. Buddhist discourse centred on new emanations of Vajradhara. The wrathful deities were being imagined which could save the Buddhist from immanent disaster. The idea of Kaliyuga and the Kalki spread sporadically among each vying sect. The Kalki-avatar is derived from the word, 'Kalkin' which symbolized White Horse. (Interestingly, the Huns were known as the 'shweta-hun' in Sanskrit and they were well versed in cavalry). The appearance of Huns and their wrathful marauding of the Jambudwipa might have caused this spurt in creative imagination about tantrik deities.

Both, Hindus as well as Buddhists sect developed the rituals to propitiate a new avatar, Hayagriva. Hayagriva is the horse-necked form of the deities. It is not a mere coincidence that the Kalki avatar was predicted as a warrior riding the White horse.

The White horse had conquered the imagination of Hindu as well as Buddhist thinkers. In kingship ritual of ashwamedha sacrifice, white horses were preferred. In the Puranic literature, one of the rare objects that emerged while the devas and demons were churning the ocean was Uchaishravas, white horse. The white horse also symbolized the sun.

In Buddhist history, white horse has often been employed to describe the purity, renunciation and spread of dharmas. Kanthaka, Siddharth's horse was pure white. It is this horse which Siddharth rode while renouncing the world to successfully attain nirvana. There is a White Horse Temple or Baima Temple at Luo Yang built in 68 AD by the Chinese Emperor to commemorate the arrival of Kashyapa Matanga on white horse to spread the dharma in China. There is another White horse pagoda in China to commemorate the loyal horse of Kumarjiva who is credited with translation of much of the Mahayana sutra in Chinese.

Thus, when a yuga was perceived as being passing, the literature around righteous avatar associated with the White horse began to appear. People believed that the dharma will be revived and protected by the new avatar. Hayagriva, the avatar of Vishnu was worshipped as the God of knowledge and wisdom, with a human body and a horse's head, pure white in colour. It is said that Kamban, Ramanuja and Shankaracarya had visions of this horse-headed deity.

In Samvara and Guhyasamaj tantra, Hayagriva form of Buddha

emerged in wrathful aspect. Padmasambhava's hagiographers imposed every characteristics of Hayagriva over him. In the famous biography written by Yeshe Tsogyal, Hayagriva and Padmasambhava intermingle into each other. Hayagriva is the fierce form of the Avalokiteshvava and believed to liberate all and sundry, so do Padmasambhava who liberate sentient beings from the fear and evil spirits.

Padmasambhava is depicted as taught by "an ordained dakini, who dwelt in a sandalwood garden, in the midst of a cemetery, in a palace of skulls. In secret she also granted to him the Hayagriva initiation, which gives power to dominate all evil spiritual beings." Further, while residing in the Mandarva's kingdom (the famous consort from Sahor Kingdom), Padmasambhava is shown assuming the form of Hayagriva. He performed magical dances on the surface of a boiling lake, and all the nagas inhabiting the lake made submission to him. The biography describes how he took Mandarva "to the cave at Avalokiteshvara's heaven, and for three months and seven days made prayer and offerings to the Buddha of Long Life. Then Amitayus appeared, placed the urn of boundless life on the heads of Padma and Mandarva, gave them to drink of the nectar of immortality, initiated them, and conferred upon them immunity from death and birth until the end of the kalpa. Padma was transformed into Hayagriva and Mandarva into Vajra-Varahi." Both were blessed with the power of immortality and transformation into a rainbow. In the same episode, it is mentioned that when both of them were burnt on the king's command, suddenly a lake emerged with blooming lotus supporting the Padmasambhava and Mandarva in Hayagriva and Vajra-Varahi form.

There is another episode of the cowherd Guru in which a cowherd attained the form of Hayagriva after being initiated by Padmasambhava and meditating on the mantric syllable Hum. The cowherd developed a protuberance resembling the head of the Hayagriva.

Hayagriva is believed to be endowed with eight superhuman faculties. The structural correspondence with the eight forms of

Padmasambhava and Hayagriva is evident. Interestingly, in the biography by Yeshe Tsogyal, there is mention of the destruction of the famous Vikramshila University. The White Huns had destroyed every Buddhist institution and the monasteries in the Magadha region and in all probability, Vikramshila followed the fate of the Taxila and Nalanda, both destroyed by the Huns during Skandagupta times. The Buddhists needed an avatar in the form of Hayagriva since the horse was the most potent threat to the survival of Buddhism.

The first sahastrar had ended and new astronomical years had commenced. Padmasambhava was assumed as the avatar by the Buddhists due to his exploits in many regions and, hence, conferred the title of the Second Buddha. It is not a mere coincidence that this Second Buddha gained the characteristics as described in the literature about the future avatar. He bode farewell to the worldly activities in human world by riding a horse. Padmasambhava remains engraved in the imagination as the immortal avatar, the Hayagriva emanation of Buddha, by propitiating whom, one can keep away evil spirits and negative forces.

Hayagriva is worshipped by the Nyingma sect as a protector of the Dharma and the highest deity. Hayagriva enjoys high popularity among Mongolian shepherds, who offer him consecrated horses, possibly because it is a land of the powerful horses. In Tibet, Mongolia and rest of the Himalayas, Hayagriva and Vajravarahi are also linked to many sacred sites with caves and rocks. Many Buddhists still use these caves for intense spiritual practices. The mantra for Hayagriva contains this relationship. The mantra is as follow:

"Hri Padma datri Hyagriva hulu hulu hung phat!"

This fusion resulted into overcoming the crisis as well as the threat posed by the multiplying Hindu sects which vied with each other to regain the religious space in an imminent non-Buddhist future during the sixth century.

Padmasambhava and the sacred sites

Tibetans believe that the *Chakrasamvara* (Demchok) or the Great Circle of Bliss transcending both samsara and nirvana, find representation of their body, mind and speech in inner and outer geography. This is the homologisation of thought-structure with the physical landscape. Even human anatomy, cosmic structure, legends, historical figures and rituals get enmeshed in this kind of homologisation. Japanese philosopher Toshihiko Izutsu has used the concept of 'synchronical structuralisation' to explain such multi-polar and multi-layer structure whereby the concepts of one realm are transposed spatially into another realm.

In similar fashion, the believers have created structural correspondence with the Demchok's body and the known geography. The body of *Chakrasamvara* is represented in Mount Kailash to the west, speech to Tsa-ri in Central Tibet and mind in Lapchi. Now a days, Mount Kawa Karpo in the south east Tibet, now part of North West Yunnan is revered as the eastern most abode of Shri *Chakrasamvara*, also known as Khorlo Demchok in local parlance.

The figure of Padmasambhava evolved into an increasingly legendary character and his name is often associated with the most of the neri (power) places across the Himalayas. Yeshe Tsogyal mentions in Padma's biography that Padma "preached the Dharma to gods, nagas, dakini, and demons in their own respective languages and realms, and to men in many parts of the human world- in China, Assam, Ghasha, Trusha (near Samala), and elsewhere in India, and in Persia. He built many temples and monasteries, 824 of them in Tibet. In Devachan, the heaven of Avalokiteshvara, he constructed a stupa of crystal. Because of having done all these things, he was given the name Padma-Sambhava."

In the same work, the biographer mentions that Padma also went to the "country of Asafoetida, in Khoten, where he remained 200 years and established the Sutra, the Mantra, and the Mahayana forms of Buddhism Between the Khang-kar-te-say Mountains (near the Nepal frontier in southern Tibet) and Tri-shi-trik in China, Padma hid 108 large works, 125 important images, five very rare essences (of secret doctrines), the sacred works of Buddhism and of the Bonpos, and books on medicine, astrology, arts, and crafts. Similar caches were made by Padma in Nepalese caves and temples. Along with the texts, he buried such worldly treasures, magical weapons, and food as would afford support to the tertons who should take out the texts and give them to the world. Altogether, Padma is credited with having hidden away texts and accessory objects to the number of ten million."

The *Chakrasamvara* tantra dates back to the 8th century when Padmasambhava was active across the Himalayas. The stories that *Chakrasamvara* defeated Shiva on Mount Kailash, were invented. Since then, all sacred sites of Shaiva sect became sacred to Demchok. This is the mythical explanation of appropriation of categories from the early Shaivites. It is this fusion process that made Naropa to claim later that Buddha, Shiva and Jina are one and the same. As Padmasambhava is believed to be the emanation of Demchok, all such places also find legends about Padmasambhava's visit or meditational retreats.

Before Padmasambhava, the sacred places of Buddhists were limited to the northern plains of India like Rajgir, Varanasi, Bodh Gaya, Kushinagar and Nalanda. Buddhism spread in later centuries towards higher altitude as well as latitude. The sacred places multiplied manifold after the introduction of tantric practices since tantra required the drawing of mandala, a diagrammatic representation connecting different worlds structurally. The cave was considered a mandala since the pilgrim made entrance and exit in clockwise direction, thus, forming a sacred circle .The mandala can be depicted across topography, within the body or literally, in engravings, sculpture or paintings showing the correspondence between the realm of immanence and transcendence.

The pitha tradition emerged as an extension of the mandala doctrine. The body parts of the deity were believed to sanctify different landscapes. After Buddha, it is Padmasambhava who is credited with creating so many sacred sites. Tibetans believe that the Himalayan landscape and the varying topography has been caused by Padma's miracles. Padmasambhava is supposed to have taken almost every route that connects India to Tibet and China, Burma, Persia, Nepal, Bhutan, Sikkim and China to Mongolia. He left footprints or prints of other parts of his body in a kind of resemblance with the pitha tradition .

Origin of Samvara-pitha

The noun *samvara* is derived from the verb 'sam - vrri', meaning to bind or conceal. Indrabhuti, a commentator on *Chakrasamvara* Tantra sees the manifestation of Sri Heruka (Samvara deity) and his mandala as a process of emanation in this world. The *Chakrasamvara* tantra in 10th chapter mentions that the process begins from the body manifestation of Vajradhara from the Mount Sumeru and culminates in the manifestation of *Chakrasamvara* mandala of Heruka and his consort embedded in the landscape of Jambudwipa.

Non-dual union with Sri Heruka is essential for the realization of the trikaya which is equivalent to buddhajnana. In Chakrasamvara mandala, there is a central deity couple, Sri Heruka and Vajravarahi. They are surrounded by the four kinds of yoginis. Together these deities constitute the central jnanachakra of the mandala. They are surrounded by the three concentric wheels-blue coloured mind wheel (cittachakra), red coloured speech wheel (vacachakra) and the white coloured body wheel (kayachakra). Each wheel consists of eight deity couples. Thus, the wheels contain 24 couples, a number that also finds reflection in the narrative of Kapalika, Dattatreya and Matsyendranath. The mandala palace is surrounded by the 'eight great charnel grounds', which seems to be borrowed from the pre-existing Siddha/Shaivite sects. Each charmel ground is linked to one of the eight sacred mountains and particular species of tree.

There is multiple level of referentiality in symmetrical correspondences. The practitioner's body is linked to the outer cosmos via the three wheels of the mandala, which are correlated to the triple world cosmology. There are three worlds of heaven, earth and the underworlds (a realm to which nagas belong and often find mention in Buddhist mythology and cosmogony). Buddha has three bodies (trikaya)—dharamkaya (reality body), sambhogakaya (enjoyment body) and nirmankaya (manifestation body). Each of these 24 points of the cakrasamvara is correlated to 24 sacred sites scattered around Jambudwipa. Each of these 24 goddesses also correlate to a body part. Each of these wheels are arranged hierarchically along the body's central channel, avadhuti. Mind wheel occupies the head and upper most part of the torso. Speech wheel corresponds to upper torso and vocal organs, body wheel corresponds to lower torso, leg and feet.

The central deity, Heruka, has a set of three mantras-a longer moolamantra (root), a shorter hridayamantra and still shorter upahridayamantra. *Chakrasamvara* tantra has 51 chapters which seem to correspond with Sanskrit alphabets just like Shiva Sutra revealed to Vasugupta consists of aphorisms corresponding to Sanskrit alphabets.

The sites associated with Guru Rinpoche are dedicated to the cult of Samvara tantrism and constitutes the major pilgrimage network in Tibet. The three leading sacred sites of the Samvara and his consort, Vajra Vahini namely, Ti-se (Kailsash), La-phi and Tsari are the oldest systematized sacralised mountains, each having legendary presence of Padmasambhava. The sacred geography of vajra-kaya doctrine related to India was relocated to the Himalayas only after the appearance of Padmasambhava. This itself was emanation from subtle to grosser scale the various tantrik sites classified as pitha, kshetra, chandoha connected to internal body in anuttara-yoga tantras.

Prominent Sacred sites of Padmasambhava

Some of the sacred sites associated with the legend of Padmasambhava are outlined below:

Meili Snow Mountain

This range is located in Zhongdian, 10 kilometres northeast

of Deqin County of Yunnan Province, also termed officially by the Chinese authorities as Shangri-la. The mountain sits on the border of Yunnan Province and Tibet, where the three famous rivers, namely, the Yangtse (Jinsha), Mekong (Nu) and Salwen (Lancang) flow. These three great rivers of Asia run parallel to one another though separated by high mountain ranges. After this confluence the rivers diverge and empties in different direction. Salween empties in Indian Ocean through Burma, Mekong into South China Sea through Vietnam and Yangtse into the East China sea at Shanghai. There is another triad of the holy peaks, which is believed to be blessed by Padmasambhava who projected his divine light onto the range and named the three peaks after the three bodhisattvas.

The south peak Jambeyang is the avatar of Manjushri, the Bodhisattva of Wisdom. The east peak Chanadorje represents Vajrapani, the Bodhisattva of Wrath while the north peak, Chenrezig, the highest of the trio, symbolizes Avalokiteshvara, the Bodhisattva of compassion.

These three holy peaks are believed to be the patron saint of the Tibetans. Tibetans believe that pilgrimage to the holy triad three times in life can bless one with all the boons.

But, the most sacred region is the Kawagebo Peak, the highest in Yunnan Province rising about 6,740 metres. It is still a 'virgin peak' for no one has ever climbed at the top. Tibetans revere it as the eastern most abode of Shri *Chakrasamvara*, also known as Khorlo Demchok.

Kawagebo became the patron saint of Nyingma School after the encounter with Padmasambhava. As per local narrative, Kawagebo was an evil spirit with nine heads. Padmasambhava defeated him and made him the protector of Tibetan people. In visual representations, Kawagebo is shown to ride a white horse with a sword in hand. This reminds one of the presumed avatar of the Kaliyuga.

Tian Sheng Qiao

Padmasambhava is known as Lian Hua Sheng (Lotus Bom) in Chinese. On the anicient Tea and Horse route in Diqing region of Yunnan province, a natural stone chiff, Tian Sheng Qiao, is believed to have been sanctified by Padmasambhava. Shudugang river flows under the bridge. There is a sacred hot spring in the place and legends link the geothernal springs with exorcising powers of Padmasambhava.

Tsari

The Tsari mountain lies at the south-eastern end of the Great Himalayan range. It is one of the last peaks (5,735 m) before the Yarlung Tsangpo river (Brahmaputra) cuts through the range in the world's deepest gorge. The mountain is surrounded by the tributaries of the Subansiri River which drain into the Brahmaputra in Arunachal Pradesh to the south of the mountain. This is the place of Pure Crystal Mountain, and one of the three main mountain pilgrimage sites in Tibet. It is also one of the 24 great sacred places described in esoteric Buddhist texts. Every 12 years, in the Monkey year, this mountain is the site of pilgrimage. Here lies the mind mandala of Sri *Chakrasamvara*. And it is also the principal abode of the sky dancers, amongst whom Khandroma Dorje Phakmo is supreme. There are various secret caves where Padmasambhava is believed to have meditated. The obeisance to Amitayu Buddha and Hayagriva is made. Its identification as Charitra or Devikota includes it among the important mountain power places.

Tirthapuri

The only other point of pilgrimage considered essential to the traveller in the Kailash region is Tirthapuri, located on the Sutlej River. The traditional order of the pilgrimage is first to circumambulate Manasarovar, then Kailash, and then to go to Tirthapuri. The monastery contains the guru's footprint. Pilgrims dig for healing stones. There are many hot springs.

Tarboche

Saga Dawa is the most important annual festival of Mount Kailash. During this time, the giant flagpole is ritually taken down and the prayer flags along its length replaced. During the flagpole ceremony, as the pole's tip is raised and pointed east towards Gyangdrak Monastery, monks of that monastery perform a special ritual. After the Tarboche is fully upright, Tibetans scrutinize its position for omens. If the column stands straight, all will go well; if the pole leans toward Kailash, local inhabitants will suffer famine, disease and perhaps, untimely death. If the flagpole tilts away from the mountain, great alarm is generated.

Tarboche's importance is linked to the sanctity of the nearby cemetery of Drachom Ngagye Durtro, situated on a ridge east of the flagpole. Gotshangpa, first explorer of Kailash, and Guru Rinpoche are known to have blessed the site. The latter predicted that the trunk of an exceptionally tall, 'self-originating' (rangjung) tree would serve as the flagpole.

Bhutan

Figure 17.1

(Paro Taktsang Monastery)

Taktsang is one of the holiest places in Bhutan. The monastery is perched on a high granite cliff overlooking the northern Paro valley.

This place is especially venerated because of its association with Padmasambhava, who is said to have flown to Paro Taktsang in the form of Dorji Drolo, mounted on a flaming dakini-tigress in the year 747 AD.

According to the Neyig of Taktsang, compiled by Lopen Pemala, there are nine holy caves (Phug) sanctified by Padmasambhava around the Taktsang: 1. Machiphug, 2. Singyephug, 3. Pelphug, 4. Drolophug, 5. Yoeselphug, 6. Gadigphug, 7. Choegyelphug, 8. Kapaliphug and 9. Phagmoiphug.

Lhasa

The hidden lake temple of the Dalai Lamas behind the Potala called Lukhang is dedicated to Dzogchen teachings and has murals depicting the eight manifestations of Padmasambhava. It is believed that Padmasambhava also visited Garu Nunnery of Sera monastery, north of Lhasa.

Rewalsar, Mandi

It was in Zahor that Padmasambhava was first addressed as Lord *Padmasambhava*, the Lotus-born Guru, and was praised as the second Buddha.

Here, he was burnt along with his consort Mandarva. But, a lake was formed and both of them emerged on lotus flower in the form of *Hayagriva* and *VajraVarahi*. There is a huge statue to commemorate the tale and the lake is believed to be sanctified.

Samye

Santaraksita was invited by the Pala King, Dharmapala to take part in a peace mission to Tibet ruled by Tri-song Detsan, son of a Chinese princess and the Emperor of Tibet (755-797 AD). Santaraksita advised the Tibetan King to invite Padmasambhava. A mission was sent to Nepal to extend the imperial invitation. Padmasambhava subdued the negative forces and consecrated the site upon which Samye Monastery, Tibet's first Buddhist academy was established.

Sikkim

Padmasambhava visited Sikkim and converted the *Kanchenjunga* peak as the keeper of Sikkim . He concealed several sacred scriptures. Sikkim is regarded as sacred as is Padma's abode at Copper-plate Mountain at Tsari.

Pemayangtse

This Sikkim monastery is considered to be the premier monastery where 'Zangdopalri', a multi-tiered three-dimensional wooden structure symbolizing the copper mountain palace of Guru Padmasabhava, is placed.

Lake Khecheopalri

Pilgrims believe that the lake fulfils all wishes and is a site blessed by Guru Padmasambhava. The lake Khecheopalri in Sikkim resembles the foot print of Guru Padmasambhava when viewed from above and is revered as a lake of Tara as well.

Tashiding Gompa

This is one of the holiest stupas in Sikkim which was built on the spot where Padmasambhava's arrow is believed to have fallen.

Chungthang

The footprint of Padmasambhava on this sacred rock in Sikkim is believed to exist.

Four Sacred Caves of Sikkim

Padmasambhava is believed to have originally 'opened' 108 caves in Sikkim, but closed 104 of them, leaving 4 for the pilgrims.These surround Tashiding, the spiritual centre and heart of Sikkim in the four directions. These are:

(i) The Hidden Cave in the East at Sharchok Bayphuk.

(ii) The Secret Cave of the Dakini, or Womb of the Dakini, in the South at Khandro Sangphug (south cave) where there was hot spring water coming out of the side of the river which is known as Guru Padmasambhava's holy place.

(iii) The Cave of Great Bliss in the West at Dechen phu.

(iv) The Cave of the Heart of the Deity in the North at Tashiding-Cheminingpo.

Nepal

Padmasambhava is believed to have gained enlightenment in Nepal. One of his famous consort was the Shakya Princess. He is still highly revered in the region.

Maratika Caves

Halesi Mahadev has been a sacred site for the Hindus as well as the Buddhist. There are three caves that represent the three eyes of Shiva. Buddhist call these caves Maratika. It is believed that Padmasambhava and his consort Mandarva gained enlightenment and became immortal here. There is another cave Yanglesho where Buddhists believe Padmasambhava fought with snakes and turned them into stones. Padmasambhava is said to have attained the Mahamudra here.

Pharping

Padmasambhava went to Pharping, which lies in the hills to the southwest of Kathmandu. This is the place of enlightenment in the Kathmandu Valley. There is a very famous Buddhist temple dedicated to the feminine aspect of Buddha, known as Vajrayogini, the Divine Mother.

High on the mountain side above Pharping is the little cave of Lang-le-sho where Padmasambhava and his consort, the Nepalese princess SakyaDevi, lived together. The entrance to cave resembles the shape of yoni.

His handprint can be seen outside the entrance of Lang-le-sho cave to this very day, where he and his consort *SakyaDevi* attained simultaneous Enlightenment.

Caves of the Mustang Valley

In Mustang, near the town of Lo Manthang, various deities supposedly appear from walls. It is believed that these are the termas hidden by Padmasambhava which is revealed only to the righteous person.

Ladakh

Padamsambhava visited Zanskar. Padmasambhava is said to have dwelt in the Kanika and Sani monastery of Ladakh. The bushes of the cemetery in Sani are considered sacred. There is a Guru Rinpoche cave in Ladakh known as Urgyen Dzong at a distance of 50 km from Leh; the caves of Padmasambhava is located in the Takthok monastery.

Behind the Hemis Monastery in Ladakh, there is a sacred cave where Padmasambhava and Yeshe Tsogyal are believed to have meditated and a granite rock with their embedded footprints is present.

Ayui-yin Sume, Mongolia

Ayui-yin Sume, meaning 'Temple/Monastery of the Caves' is one of the most important Buddhist institutions in Southern Mongolia, built around a cave complex. Hayagriva, is the deity represented at Ayui-yin Sume. There are five sacred caves of the five dakinis. People believe that Padmasambhava engaged in tantric practices with five dakini sisters each dwelling in a different cave. Padmasambhava left a print of his left foot near the Hongyang cave. There is a dakini footprint in front of the cave of Tara. It is said that Padmasambhava made a statue of himself with his own hands, which is a major pilgrim attraction.

Womb-Caves of Padmasambhava

There are series of 'womb cave,' sanctified by Padmasambhava across Asia. Womb caves have narrow entrances that make visitor to either squeeze or crawl through. This is considered a purificatory rite essential in many pilgrimages.

The Maratika Cave where Padmasambhava is believed to have attained enlightenment is such a womb cave. Similar caves with legendary presence of Guru Rinpoche are the caves of Gur Du Monastery in Amdo, Ayui-yin Sume Monastery in Mongolia, the caves near the pilgrimage sites of Mt. Kailash and Mt. Amnye Machen in Tibet, Tarap in Dolpo, Gaden monastery in Central Tibet, and Paro Taktsang in Bhutan. In Jammu and Kashmir, the Ardhkunwari Cave in the Mata Vaishno Devi pilgrimage is such a womb cave.

Association of Padmasambhava with womb caves is an interesting twist to the sacralisation of the sites across the Himalayas, since Padmasambhava is believed to be the lotus-born. He did not pass through the earthly human womb and is believed to be reincarnated as an eight-year-old child appearing in a lotus blossom who was discovered by the Uddiyana King, Indrabhuti.

Octad, Pentad and Triads

In the narrative of Padmasambhava, there is greater emphasis on numerological correspondences. There are recurrences of octad, pentad and triad. Padmasambhava is credited with having eight Indian gurus belonging to eight different schools. In the prayers offered to him, he is prayed as a Heruka (someone naked with respect to samsaric things) accompanied by eight Matrikas, the Mother-Goddess of the Hindu pantheon. Padmasambhava is said to have taken eight forms or manifestations representing different aspects of his being—Guru Uddiyana Vajradhara, the vajra-holder; Vajradhara Guru Sakyasimha of Bodh Gaya, Lion of the Sakyas, who learns the Tantric practices of the eight Vidyadharas; Guru Padmaraja of Uddiyana, the Lotus Prince, King of the Tripitikas; Guru Padmakara, Lotus-arisen, the Saviour who teaches the Dharma to the people; Guru

Sthiramati of Kashmir, the Intelligent Youth, the one who gathers the knowledge of all worlds; Guru Suryabhasa or Suryarasmi, who illuminates the darkness of mind through the insight of Dzogchen and who holds a khatvanga which points towards the sun; Guru Vajra, the fierce manifestation of Vajrakilaya (wrathful Vajrasattva) known as "Diamond Guts", the comforter of all; Guru Simhanada of Nalanda University, the Lion of Debate, His various aspects are linked to different regions like Nalanda, Kashmir, Zahor, China, Tibet, Bhutan, Uddiyana and Bodh Gaya.

In the biography by Yeshe Tsogyal, there is mention of a dialogue between Mandarva and Padmasambhava. When she raised the issue of Padmaa's parentage, he replied:

> *"I have no parents. I am a gift of the Voidness. I am the essentiality of Amitabha and of Avalokiteshvara, born of lotus in the Dhanakosha lake; and being of the same essence of as the Adi-Buddha, Vajra-Dhara, and the Buddha of Bodh-Gaya.... I am the master of the Eight Fathers of Generation, of the Eight Mothers of Birth, of the Eight Places of Travel, of the Eight Places of Abode, of the Eight Cemeteries for Meditation, of the Eight Kinds of Gurus, of the Eight Classes of Wisdom, of the Eight Highest Lamas [or directors of religion], of the Eight Classes of Magical Illusion, of the Eight Sorts of Garments, of the Eight Tantric Deities Difficult to Propitiate, of the Eight Parts of Yogic Dress in Cemeteries of the Eight Past and Eight Future Events, of the Eight Classes of Past Error and of the Eight Classes of Future Error. I have collected all perfection doctrines, and I know the past, present and future in completeness...."*

Padma went on a mission to eight countries. He is associated with the eight great charnel grounds. In chakrasamvara mandalas, there are eight cemeteries, eight trees and eight stupas, eight bodies of water, eight nagas and eight gods. Eight is the number of completion in Vajrayana mandala space. There are eight sacred mountains. Padma himself incarnated as an eight-year child. He consecrated the work of building of Samye monastery on the eighth day of the eighth month of the earth-male-tiger year.

But, the transformation of the eight consciousnesses into the five wisdoms is the secret way. Within the Eight Solitary Places of Realization, there are five Power-places of the Guru. These are five caves of Guru Rinpoche. Each one is associated with a different aspect of Padmasambhava: Body, speech, mind, qualities and action. Drak YongDzong is the cave of his Buddha-body. The cave of Samye Chimpu is the power-place of his speech. Yarlung Shetak is the power-place of his qualities. This is a crystal cave. This is an example of an 'eagle's nest" hermitage. Senge Dzong is the power place of his action and located across the Tibetan border in the Mon region of Eastern Bhutan. Padmasambhava had five consorts or 'Wisdoms,' of Guru Rinpoche—Mandarva of Zahor, considered an emanation of Vajravarahi's Body; Yeshe Tsogyal of Tibet, emanation of Vajravarahi's Speech. Belmo Sakya Devi of Nepal is considered an emanation of Vajravarahi's Mind; Belwang Kalasiddhi also of Nepal, emanation of Vajravarahi's Quality; and Mangala (Monmo Tashi Khyeudren or Tashi Chidren) emanation of Vajravarahi's activity. There were five dakinis with whom Padmasambhava practised tantra in five different caves at Ayui-yin Sume shrine in Mongolia.

Similarly, there are triads associated with Padmasambhava. Heruka whose emanation he is believed to be, itself is derived by conjunction of three root syllable each connoting different mode of emptiness. '*He*' is the emptiness of phenomena, '*ru*' is the emptiness of person and '*ka*' is the union of bliss and emptiness. Herukas are the embodiment of the 'male' qualities of Buddhahood—the dynamic aspect of Enlightenment.

There is unfoldment of concept of trikaya of Buddha just like Trika philosophy of Kashmir Shaivism. The three trikayas are represented by the three sacred mountain peak of Tsari, Kailash and Lapchi. There is a triad of bija syllables. OM is in bright white light on forehead, AH in bright red light on throat and HUNG is in bright blue light on the heart. The rainbow body of Padmasambhava is supposed to be created by the emanation of different colour of light from three centres of body.

The threefold OM, HUM and PHAT corresponds to the three

main forms of Vajra-Yogini on three different planes of experience. It is mentioned that Padmasambhava received the 'initiation of body (kaya), speech (vak) and mind (chitta)'.

Kashmir and Padmasambhava

Octad, pentad and triad of categories are important characteristic of belief-system in Kashmir Shaivism also. Trika philosophy is built upon this intricate weaving of mathematical models that fits into diagrammatic representations of things, viz. mandalas. Abhinavagupta's *Para-Trisika-Vimarshini* has explored the three set of numbers in detail. It is well known that the trika philosophy revolves around triads and there are the eight Matrika Goddesses deployed to describe the world of speech. Shankaracharya composed '*Ashtakam*' (an Octad to Tripurasundari). Panini grammar deployed to develop mantra shastra itself is based upon such octads. There are eight series of Sanskrit vowels and eight series of consonants. Matsyendranath whom Abhinavagupta makes obeisance in the famous Tantraloka, is famed as the founder of the Kaula school of tantra. Much of his works in the sphere of rituals have been appropriated in esoteric Shaivism in Kashmir. The Kaula-chakra system is eightfold. There are eight lotuses each with eight petals and these became inspiration for the 64-yoginis cult.

Similarly, there are pentads. Pancastavi is the pentad of Hymns to Bhavani/Mother Kundalini. There are five functions as the Self in the *Pratyabhijnahridayam* namely, *abhasana* (to make something appear), *rakti* (thinking process), *vimarsana* (experience from involvement with the object of thought), *bijavasthapana* (proliferation) and *vilapana* (dissolution). There are five states of consciousness—jagrat, svapna, sushupti, turiya and turiyatita. There are five undifferentiated states—kriya, jnana, iccha, ananda and chitta. There are seven sets of pentads that describe the philosophy of Kashmir Shaivism. Pratyabhijna Sastra itself consists of pentad discourse viz.Isvara Pratyabhijna, Vrtti, Vivrti, Vimarsini, and Vivrti Vimarsini. Para Shiva has pentad Shakti: Cit Sakti, Ananda Sakti, Ichcha Sakti, Jnana Sakti and Kriya Sakti (Consciousness, Bliss, Will,

Knowledge and Action). Shiva maintains five functions. These are Srsti, Sthiti, Samhara, Vilaya and Anugraha.

Shiva Sutra revealed to Vasugupta mentions various triads, there are three Upayas (means) suiting the aspirants in spiritual development—Sambhava Upaya, Sakta Upaya and Anava Upaya. There is triad of three states—para, apara and parapara.

Para itself consists of a triad, Shiva, Sakti and their union (Prakasa, Vimarsa and Samarasya). Apara consists of triad Shiva, Sakti and Nara (Shiva, Sakti, individual soul). Trika System itself is based on three sacred texts—Agama, Spanda and Pratyabhijna.

The iconography of Padmasambhava holding a khatvanga with three severed heads denoting the three kayas of Buddha, viz. the dharmakaya, sambhogakaya, and nirmanakaya, is well discussed. It is well established by the scholars that attributes used to decorate Padmasambhava like bone ornaments, animal skin, marks of human ash, a skull-cup, damaru, thighbone trumpet and the skull-topped khatvanga were directly borrowed by the Buddhist from the Shaiva-Kapalik. Particularly, the transformation of khatvanga as a vajra is remarkable. The hagiography of Padmasambhava often narrates about his sojourn to charnel grounds in Kashmir. This points to the import of practices and philosophy prevalent in Kashmir.

An image of a 12-armed *Chakrasamvara* has been found in Kashmir (circa 725 AD) and put up in the Los Angles Country Museum of Arts (*John C Huntington and Dina Bangdel*, 2003, p. 252). The Chakrasamvara is represented in blue colour with 4 faces, 12 hands and 2 legs. He holds vajra, bell, damaru, axe, trident, khatvang, skullcap, and the four-faced head of Brahma, necklace of 50 human heads and tiger skin. The severed head of Brahma in the 6th hand seems to be the direct borrowing from the iconography of Shiva in Kapalika sect. Since, this image dates back to a time of Padmasambhava, it can be safely assumed that Padmasambhava adopted many things from the pre-existing things and appropriated to expand the influence of Buddhism. Similar strategy is evident in adoption of Bon religious sites, practises and beliefs, to Buddh-ise the

Himalayas. Samvara is conceived as the demchog, the circle of bliss which is beyond samsara and nirvana. This is similar to the Kula rites.

There is no doubt that Padmasambhava and his Nyingma sect and various schools of Kashmir Shaivism shared a common cultural matrix. It is why Sixteenth Karmapa used to mention that the *chakrasamvara* tantra is the northern lineage while Kashmir Shaivism is the southern lineage of same belief and practises.

Trikuta, Womb Cave and Padmasambhava's Terma

The landscape of the Himalayas have been appropriated by many traditions to establish their hegemony over the Indian sub-continent.We have seen how the Himalayas has been fitted into mandala concepts. The eight sacred mountains of the Samvara tradition are associated with the eight-folded mandalas. Three peaks are considered the most sacred. Kailash (Kang Rinpoche) in the West Tibet, Tsari in Central Tibet and Lapchi in eastern Tibet represent Vajrakaya's body, speech and mind, respectively. But, we have seen how the power points are always subsumed under pentad category. Whether the triad of the holy peak constitutes another pentad, further subsumed by the octad of sacred mountains? There is likelihood of building a pentad of the holy mountains in Himalayan topography that can fill the missing link. Location of three sacred peak of the Meili snow mountain in the eastern most corner of Tibet in the area now known as Shangri -la adds to the dilemma. Interestingly, on the other spectrum of the Himalayas, there is another set of three holy peaks of Trikuta in the Katra region of Jammu and Kashmir. The flanking of three holy peaks of Kailash, Tsari and Lapchi by triad of the holy peaks create a pentad that reiterate the pentad characteristics of the power-spaces found in abundance in Padmasambhava's hagiography. The five dakini caves, five shakti-consorts, five holy caves have this correspondence with the five holy mountains. This create a mandala structure and puts Tsari , the Copper-coloured mountain and the abode of Padmasambhava, in the middle of the mandala.

The Trikuta Mountain is one of the most important power

places in the Indian sub-continent. A pilgrim has to pass through a womb cave at Ardhkunwari about which the local belief is similar to the Buddhist beliefs about other womb caves in Asia. From the main cave at the Bhawan, water stream burst forth. Similar caves associated with Padmasambhava with water streams are found as far as Sikkim and Mongolia. The Trikuta caves contain three sacred stones that enhance the sanctity of this place. Seeing in the pan-Asian perspective, it is clear that the Trikuta hills contain most of the characteristics of various kind of sacred landscape found in Asia. Surprisingly, Padmasambhava, being active in Kashmir, Mandi and Ladakh did not notice the prominent Trikuta peaks with this unique combination of the womb-caves, three holy stone and water stream. Or, did history witness obliteration of imagination about certain landscape essential in the construction of Vajrayana Buddhist external mandala after the rise of antagonistic Hindu sects? Did Trikuta hills ever constitute a pentad completing the pan-Himalayan mandala of Tibetan Buddhism?

References

1. *The Tibetan Book of the Great Liberation*: Or the Method of Realizing Nirvana Through Knowing the Mind Includes: The Epitome of the Great Guru's Biography or 'Padma's Precepts' and The Last Teachings of Phadampa Sanga, Yeshe Tsogyal, discovered by terma, Sang-gye Ling-pa and translated in English in 1936 available at http://www.arfalpha.com/One Mind/The Great Liberation.PDF
2. Huber, Tony (2003). Where exactly are Caritra, Devikota and Himavat? A sacred geography controversy and the developmemt of Tantric Buddhist pilgrimage sites in Tibet; in A McKay (ed.), *The History of Tibet*, Volume II: The Medieval period: c. 850-1895. The Development of Buddhist Paramountcy, London: Routledge Curzon, pp 392-424.
3. Huntington, John C and Dina Bangdel (2003). *The Circle* of

Bliss: Buddhist Meditational Art, The Columbus Museum of Art.

4. Gray, David B. (2007). *The Chakrasamvara Tantra*, The Discourse of Sri Heruka; A Study and Annotated Translation. New York: The American Institute of Buddhist Studies at Columbia University.
5. Thurman, Robert and Tad Wise (1999). *Circling the Sacred Mountain: A Spiritual Adventure Through The Hinalayas*, New York: Bantan Books.
6. Cook, John and James Low (1997). *The Yogins of Ladakh: A Pilgrimage Among the Hermits of the Buddhist Himalayas.* New Delhi: MLBD.
7. Govinda, Lama Angarika (1960). *Foundations of Tibetan Mysticism*, New Delhi: B.I. Publications.
8. Davidson, Rondd M. (2002). *Indian Esoteric Buddhism: A Social History of the Tantric Movement*, Columbia University Press.
9. Wayman, Alex (1973). *The Buddhist Tantras: Light on Indo-Tibetan Esotericism.* New Delhi: MLBD.
10. Izutsu, Toshihiko (2002). *The Structure of Oriental Philosophy*: Collected papers of the Eranos Conference, Keio University Press.
11. Dowman, Keith (1988). *The Power Places of Central Tibet: The Pilgrims Guide*; A hands-on guide to pilgrimage in Central Tibet following the 19th century pilgrimage route of Khyentse, Routledge & Kegan Paul.
12. White, David Gordon (2003). *Kiss of the Yogini: 'Tantric Sex' in its South Asian Context*; University of Chicago Press.
13. White, David Gordon (1988). *The Alchemical Body: Siddha Traditions in Medieval India*; University of Chicago Press.
14. S Sutherland et al. (1988). *Saivism and Tantric Tradition*; Alexis Sanderson, in *The World's Religion*, London: Routledge.

Chapter 18

Declare Vindhyachal Shrine as India's Prime Meridian!

In reply to an unstarred question in the Rajya Sabha upon the setting up of different standard time for different regions in India considering the geographical and climatic conditions, the then Minister of State (Ind), Science and Technology, Kapil Sibal replied on 22nd July, 2004 that considering the fact that India is located between 68° 7' E to 97° 25' E and 8° 4' N to 37° 6' N, the Indian Standard time (IST) has been chosen with reference to a central station located at 82° 30' longitude E and 23° 11' latitude N. Since the expanse of the Indian State is not large, no need has been felt for different time zones.

The government may be right in its logic, but what if the central station is shifted to the famous pilgrimage centre of Vindhyavasini Devi (25° N, 82.5° E) that will involve marginal change in the IST, but that would be in consonance with Indian cultural geography and Indian history?

It is not that India's quest for IST has been achieved in a single go and is so paramount that no adjustment could be made with it. When in 1884, the International Meridian Conference in US set up uniform time zones across the world, India got two time zones, one at Calcutta and another at Bombay. But, by 1880s, the railway companies began to use Madras time as 'Railway time.' Thus, emerged third time zone for India and still the nascent state grew without any confusion over the time zone.

British government officially adopted the standard time zones for India in 1905, by marking the longitudinal meridian passing east of Allahabad at 82.5° E longitude as the central meridian for India. This was implemented from January 1, 1906, onwards. But, Calcutta and Bombay time continued to be functional as separate time zone until 1948. In 1947, the new government of independent India continued with the British delineated IST as the official time for the whole country. The Central Observatory which was established in 1792 by Michael Topping of the East India Company was moved from Madras to a location near Mirzapur at 82° 30' longitude E and 23° 11' latitude N.

During freedom movement, many nationalists like VD Savarakar demanded Ujjain to be made the prime meridian for India since Ujjain was used as the astronomical prime meridian from early Gupta period. *Surya Siddhanta*, a treatise on astronomy, dating back to 4-5th century mentions about the city. But, the elaborate discussion was initiated by Aryabhata in his famous treatise, *Aryabhatiya* (499AD). In Chapter 4 on Gola section, Aryabhata discussed how the astronomical prime meridian passed through Ujjayani, the capital of Avanti. The prime meridian intersected the equator at Lanka. The prime meridian or the Meru danda linked Lanka to Meru mountain at the Northern most point and the Badavamukha at the southern most point. In fact, Aryabhata stirred much debate among next generation of astronomers with his precise earmarking of different cities. If at the Equator, Lanka is the city at prime meridian (o degree longitude), Yavakoti is at 90 degree east on the equator, Romanka is at 90 degree west of Lanka and Siddhapura is at 180 degree from Lanka and, hence, diametrically opposite to Lanka. Ujjain was considered 22-1/2° north of Lanka. Since Ujjain is at 23°10′58″N, 75°46′38″E, and almost 700 km west of the central station chosen in accordance with India's expanse (68° 7" E to 97° 25' E), many could have argued against reviving ancient prime meridian.

But, take the case of Vindhyavasini Temple in the Mirzapur district. This is a famous shaktipitha. Since, the prime meridian already passes through the Mirzapur district, slight adjustment to coincide with the Vindhyavasini pitha would have done wonders to the post-colonial indigenous perspective for our nationhood.

Vindhyavasini temple is located at 25° N, 82.5° in the eastern part of the Vindhya Mountain range and is also on the banks of the river Ganga, the river at the heart of Indian civilization. It is few kilometres away from Mirzapur city. Prof. Rana P B Singh of BHU has done extensive work on the cultural geography of area. He has traced the tradition of the sacred pilgrimage site to the temple complex to 6th century AD. The sacred complex finds reference in the *Devi Mahatmya*. 'Vindhyavasini' term itself incorporates multiple layers of Indian tradition. Associated with the mount Vindhya (this mountain range also finds reference in national anthem and frequently found in the great epics, the Ramayana and the Mahabharata) which is one of the abode of Shiva's wife, Parvati, along with the Himalayas,Vindhyavasini is the sacred site of the goddess Durga.

According to Rudraymal Tantra, back of Sati (meru) fell at this place. Its homonym, Binduvasini (one who abides in bindu, the dot) is also clearly manifest in this sacred complex. Vindhyavasini Devi manifests in form of Binduvasini (goddess living at the central point). Binduvasini is the name of the ultimate source of creation, which is often depicted in Indian yantras and mandalas as the dot inside the triangle, the three dots of the triangle itself represent three other creative powers of action, will and knowledge (kriya, iccha, jnana) or Mahalaxmi, Mahakali, Mahasarasvati. Indian thinking is based upon triadism. Since, Indian geography itself is perfectly peninsular, the geophilosophy that emerged paved way for the 'trinities' in every conception.

The sacred complex of Vindhyachal is enclosed by water channels on three sides. While on the eastern side is the river stream Ojhala (Punyodaya), in the west is the river Karnavati and on the north is the river Ganga. The central part of the Vindhyachala territory has three shrines of goddess. The temple of Vindhyavasini is in the east, that of Kali in south and Astabhuja in the west. These three Shakti temples themselves constitute a sacred triangle. Similarly, there are three sacred sites for different form of Shiva-Vankhandishvara in the east, Mukteshvara in the west and Rameshvara in the north. This forms a scared triangle with apex pointing northwards. Interestingly, the downward triangle and the upward territorial triangle intersects just like in a Laxmi yantra diagram. At the centre is the Anandamayi ashram where the primordial shakti, Vindhyavasini manifests in the form of Binduvasini, nowadays represented by the present circular platform attached to the Anandamayi ashram. The three edges of Shakti shrines together with superimposed triangle of three forms of Shiva constitute the hexagram with central part at Anandamayi Ashram. Thus, the Vindhyavasini shrine appears to represent the navel point of Indian cultural geography. The back of the Sati is believed to have fallen here and the place is being sanctified as the central point of India's backbone.

Figure 18.1

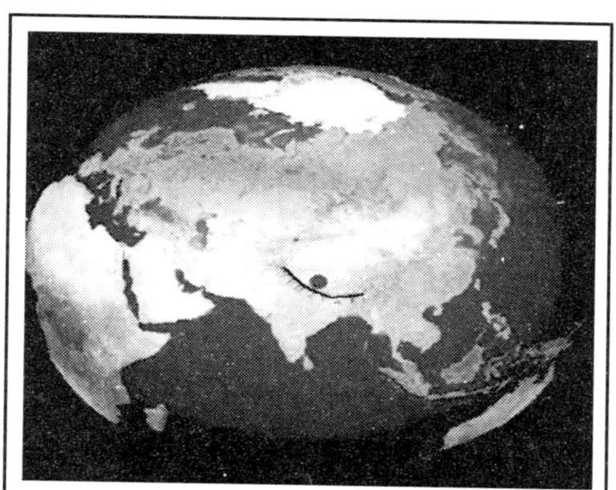

(Mt. Kailash appears as dot above the crescent shaped-Himalayas)

Figure 18.2

Matra of Chandrabindu

Let us extend our purview northwards to the Himalayas. The Himalayas appear as an arc over Indian territory. It can be viewed as a crescent moon. The Mount Kailash can be seen as the dot over the Himalayas. Thus, the Himalayas along with the Mount Kailash appears as a 'chandrabindu' of Sanskrit matras. In Sanskrit alphabets, the phonemes are the great mothers. Matras are the Matrika (mothers). We also know how the digits of the Moon are associated with the various vowels in Sanskrit. Chandrabindu that appears as a crescent moon holding within the bindu, dot (primordial potentiality of creation) itself is one of the most sacred symbols in Indian tradition.Chandrabindu is associated with the crown chakra, the highest realization, the digit of immortality. The Himalayas along with Mt. Kailash sustains the perpetual existence of Indian territory, prospering and flourishing, and sustaining Indian population like the immortal digit of the Moon.

Figure 18.3

(Rib/Meru of Mt. Kailash)

Mt. Kailash is the axial mundi for ancient Indian astronomers as it is also identified with the Mount Meru, the axial mundi of the earth and the cosmos. Interestingly, Mount Kailash does have rib like structures on southern face and thus, the homonymic play of Meru (spinal cord/ mythical *axis mundi*) is fully represented by Mt. Kailash. It stands like a single dot. In the epic Mahabharata, there is a description of the Bindusagar (sea of dots) at mythical Mount Meru. There is the sacred lake of Mansarovar near Mount Kailash and in all probability, the composer of the Mahabharata got it absolutely right. There is also a channel known as Ganga Chu in the vicinity of Mountain Kailash. Thus, like Vindhyavasini complex, Mt. Kailash has close association with the bindu, the central dot. What appears amazing is that the Kailash and Vindhyavasini are located on almost the same meridian. Mt. Kailash is located at 81.3°longitude East, 31°Laltitude N, while Vindhyavasini shrine is at 25° N, 82.5°. Therefore, it will be appropriate to have India's prime meridian pass through Vindhyavasini complex that meaningfully could also revive close connection of Tibet's holiest mountain with India.

Reference

1. Singh, Rana PB (2011). *Sacred Geography and Cosmic Geometries: Interfaces in Holy Places of North India and link*

to Leonardo da Vinci's images. Asiatica Ambrosiana saggi e ricerche di cultura religioni e società dell'Asia [Accademia Ambrosiana, Piazza Pio XI, 2 - 23123 Milano, Italy], No 3, pp 31-82.

http://www.iflaonline.org/images/PDF/ISOLA2011/369-11aa-3sacredgeoprrana16may11fin.pdf

2. Clarke, WE (1840). *The Aryabhatiya of Aryabhata: An Ancient Indian Work on Mathematics and Astronomy,* Kessinger Publishing.

Chapter 19

Is Ganga a Mantra with Roots in Buddhism?

River Ganga is sacred stream flowing from the Himalayas, creating the vast Gangetic plains in India's heartland and ending its journey into the Bay of Bengal. For centuries, Ganga has chiselled contours of Indian civilization. Ganga is not only a river that carries the amrita (elixir of life), it is also the Goddess Ganges in anthropomorphic form whose vehicle is the crocodile. Ganga is a consort of Shiva as well as Vishnu in different mythology. Gangajal is believed to be purifier of all sins. A dying man is offered a drop of Gangajal. Even after cremation, ashes is offered into the Ganga so that the dead man attains liberation from the cycle of transmigration. Every Hindu considers oneself to be lucky to have taken bath in the river. Gangajal is kept in the puja rooms in each home. Ganga is the confluence of two different world-philosophies of Hinduism and Buddhism. Ganga is the confluence of matter and word, samsara and nirvana, peaks and valleys, mountains and seas, birth and death.

The Ganga Bhajans and Ganga Arti is what binds millions of pilgrims who visit the sacred bank of the Ganga. There have been *Gangapurana, Gangashatakam, Gangamahatmyas, Gangalahari* composed by the best of Indian brains in praise of Ganga. If water is the connecting fluid inside human body, Ganga performs the same function inside body of Indian civilization. Ganga holds the key to understand uninterrupted continuity of Indian civilization.

Every major text or scripture of Indian civilization has eulogized Ganga. In the Gita, Krishna mentions: "Among streams, I am the Ganga."

An authoritative text of Agama Shastra, Devi Bhagavatam mentions: "He who utters 'Gange, Gange', becomes purified from all sins, and attains Vaikuntha, the world of Vishnu."

The great practitioner of Ayurveda, Dhanvantari mentioned: "When the body is afflicted by senility and diseases, the holy water of Mother Ganga is the medicine."

The belief in healing property of the Ganga river, both from physical ailment as well as moral and existential ailment stems from the mythology of descent of the Ganga (avataran). Ganga descended from the heavens just like avatars of various Gods. Ganga in that way is more sacred than avatar themselves since the Ganga continue to exist physically and it is the same without changing forms. Ganga is also the tripathagamini. She travels across three worlds-Devaloka (land of gods), Bhuloka (land of human beings) and Patalloka (land of the nether wolds) and purifies the sentient and subtle beings. Avatara and avataran has same roots, "tr", (त्र) to cross over. Ganga like the avatar facilitates the believer to cross over the cycle of existence. Ganga is a healer as it is believed to possess the power to bestow grace like avatar.

The mythology of the avataran of Ganga has many versions in different sects like Shaivism or Vaishanavism. The most popular is how King Sagara performed austerities for child. One of the queens bore 60,000 sons. Sagara performed the Ashvamedha sacrifice to declare himself as the greatest sovereign. The sacrificial horse entered a cave where sage Kapila was meditating. Sagar's 60,000 sons disturbed the meditation of Kapila assuming that the sage hid the horse. Kapila burnt all the 60,000 sons of Sagara by curse. Bhagiratha, the great grandson of Sagara, wanted to perform the shraddha of his ancestors but there was no water available for the ceremony. Bhagiratha, therefore, prayed to Gods to end the drought. The Ganga began its descent to the earth from the heavens. The force of the descent would have destroyed the earth, so the Ganga first flew down from the Pole Star across the Universe as the Milky Way (Akash Ganga), then it descended onto Shiva's head whose abode is at the Meru mountains. Shiva made cascading Ganga to move in zigzag trajectory on his matted long hairs and slowed down the descent. The Ganga descended the Himalayas and down the plains at Haridwar where the temple of Bhagiratha has been built at Har Ki Pauri. Bhagiratha performed the shraddha for his ancestors and they were finally cured of the curse of Kapila.

This is how Ganga in popular imagination has got intertwined with the post-death rituals and the Gangajal as the holiest thing to purify one's sin.

Out of the 18 major Puranas, *Brahmanda Purana* is the most extensive one and covers every aspect of Indian geography and astronomy. A cursory glance over the section on the descent of Ganga will make the story of avataran better:

> 39-41. On being released, the river began to flow in seven channels. Three of them flowed towards the east and three to the west. The river Ganga flows through seven channels. The Nalini, Hradini and Pāvanī are those which flow towards the east. The Sita, the Caksus and the Sindhu flow towards the west. The seventh among them followed Bhagiratha towards the south.
>
> 42. Hence that river is Bhagirathi. It joined the salt sea. All these seven (channels, rivers) sanctify the sub-continent named Hima. [1]

Etymology of Ganga

Ganga is derived from root, 'ga,' (ग) means to go. 'Ga' is the root of terms like gaman, gaya, gati, gate. The great Prajnaparamita mantra is *gate gate paragate parasamgate bodhi svaha* ("Gone, gone, gone beyond, gone far beyond, Enlightenment dawns!"). Thus, we see the root 'ga' being profusely used in one of the most popular mantra of Buddhism. Interestingly, Buddha attained enlightenment at Gaya in Bihar. Gaya has same roots, ga (to go). It will be worthy to discover the concept of sacred Ganga in ancient India.

Ganga finds rare mention in early Vedas, since Vedas were the hymns composed by western people. The Nadistuti Sukta (Hymn 10.75 of the Rigveda) mentions ten rivers, begining with the Ganga and moving westwards. The mention of the Ganges appear in the travelogue of Greek ambassador to Maurya Kings in Magadha, Megasthenes (ca. 350-290 BCE). He mentions in *Indica*:

> "India, again, possesses many rivers both large and navigable, which, having their sources in the mountains which stretch along the northern frontier, traverse the level country, and not a few of these, after uniting with each other, fall into the river called the Ganges. Now this river, which at its source is 30 stadia broad, flows from north to south, and empties its waters into the ocean forming the eastern boundary of the Gangaridai, a nation which possesses a vast force of the largest-sized elephants." (Diodorus II.37)

Many writers trace the origin of term to Tibeto-Burman language. Nirmal Chandra Sinha (1977) writes how in Tibetan languege, the river is celebrated as Ganga, and it is derived from term Gangri (snow mountains) and Bumo (daughter). In fact, Kailash mountain which is identified as source of origin of river in Indian mythology is located in Gangdise range. There is Ganga chu canal that connects Mansarovar lake with Rakshas Tal. Terms like Gunggal is widely used among Tibeto-Burmans for describing heaven. Even term `Kang' for snow-mountain and `Gang' indicate common origin of term in Tibeto-Burman languages.

But, the first iconographic record is available only after 4th century at the Udaygiri caves. In Cave V, God Vishnu is shown in boar avatar, Varaha, flanked by two river goddesses, Ganga and Yamuna on their respective vehicles, makara and kurma (tortoise).

During late 4th and 5th century, the avatar phenomena grew as the time line in the Buddhanirvana calendar was approaching the millennium edge and millennium (sahastra) was the highest number for earthly manifestation. This was the time when the Puranas were being composed and new gods were imagined. Hindu religion revived with fresh enthusiasm in the hope that with the end of the first millennium, the new yuga would commence in which Buddhism would not have much impact.

Thus, the geographical river Ganga was morphed into the sacred goddess Ganga corresponding with various avataras of concurrent times.

Ganga as a Mantra

Etymologically 'ganga' appears as a mantra more than a name. It is why enchanting the name of 'Ganga' is considered a sacred ritual to attain liberation. This is one of the seven sacred ways to worship Ganga. Word, 'Ganga' has mantric structures. Basically, it is alliterative as well as a palindrome. These are two of the basic structures in a mantra unravelled by Robert A Yelle in '*Explaining Mantras*'.[2] Ganga can be phonetically examined. It has four parts—bindu, ga, ga and aa.

Ganga (गंगा)
. Bindu
ग Ga
ग Ga
आ aa

Bindu is sacred in mantra. It's the resonance. It's the unity of sound, light, consciousness, matter. It's the sign of potentiality. It's the sign for the source. So, bindu in the term 'Ganga" explains the primordial and the continuous, eternal source of the sacred water. Interestingly, there is story of Bindusagar associated with the descent of Ganga as we have seen in the reproduced section from the Brahmanda Purana.

Ga is like the beeja (seed) mantra. In mantras, the seed letters are energized with bindu, the potentiality. 'Ga' root can be seen in Sanskrit words like gata (dead/past), gatagat (to and fro), gati (speed), gaman (movement, to go), gatayu (one whose longevity has come to end). The term Ganga consists of two phonemes—gan+ga. It is an alliteration of the phoneme 'ga' with the meaning of going, movement. It is also a palindrome as discussed earlier and can be seen as homologous cousin to mantra like 'soham-hamsa,' 'shiva-vashi,' 'aham-maha.' Bindu (dot, anusvar) is also the fifteenth vowel and a culmination of vowelic power of the Vac. It corresponds to fifteenth kala (digit) of the Moon and associated with amrata (nectar), power of renewal. It is not only a coincidence that the Ganga is depicted as flowing in the matted hair of Shiva where the Moon (ardha-chandra, which appears in Chandrabindu, another vowel) is shown to be shining. Aa (आ) is the second vowel, and the primordial ananda. During the emanation of Vac, the first phoneme that appeared was the first vowel a. 'A' saw its mirror image and that gave the Primordial Shakti the first taste of joy, Aa. Thus, if one interprets the word, 'Ganga' गंगा, it emerges as a powerful simple mantra in the context of work by grammarians as well as in the language of Tantra. Ganga signifies "the incessant flow from the primordial source to eternal joy!"

Ganga, in all probability, gained sacredness during the creative boom of later Gupta period. Pali texts mention about Ganga and there is a Gangasutta in which tale of Buddha swimming to cross a flooded Ganga has been narrated. But, there is no evidence of sacredness vested with the river. The first literary reference can be traced in the *Kumarasambhava* by Kalidasa written during 5th century where Ganga is eulogized as Shiva's water: "Sambhor ambujamayi murti". Possibly 'Ganga' as a signifier of sacred water was appropriated by Hindu revivalists from the Buddhist tradition of 'gata'—Gaya during this period. In the emerging proliferation of mantras for individual anthropomorphic deities, the seeds were structurally arranged to produce powerful resonating influence over human psyche. The seeds like *'klim, shrim, hrim'* in the emergent mantric/tantric tradition signified various characteristics of deity simultaneously. One can then trace the origin of 'Ganga' as a mantra to the famous Prajnaparamita sutra. One can reduce the famous Buddhist mantra "gate gate paragate parasamgate bodhi svaha" into seed form. Since 'ga' is the seed of the whole mantra, and anusvara is attached with each seed syllable to give it a nasal sound, the seed 'ga' becomes 'ga-ng' (गं). The repetition of another 'ga' signifies the endless 'going.' This entails endless act of movement in taking beyond samsaric realms. Just as each mantras end with 'svaha' which denote the emission; '*aa*' is also the first emission that also produces bliss. *Aa, ha,* and *visarga* correspond at different levels. Svaha of mantras are the combination of all three emission-phonemes—Ha, aa and visarga. The most condensed form of the ending of a mantra would be 'aa' as the first phoneme for emission corresponding with visarga. This release (visarga) is etymologically correlated with the process of visarjana. Visarjana (offering into Ganga) is the most pervasive ritual in Indian civilization where from the idols of gods and goddesses, the left-over of the sacrificial fire, the ashes of the dead ancestors, sacred thread, various offerings are immersed into the waters of the Ganga to propitiate the Ganga. Like the dot over the seed 'ga' signifying going beyond the samsaric realm; Gangajal is believed to possess the potency to purify other waters. A drop (corresponding to dot/bindu) of Ganga water is believed to make water as purifying as the sacred river Ganges itself.

'Ganga' (गंगा) becomes the most compressed mantra for the Prajnaparamita Mantra. Ganga becomes the miniaturized expression of the most compressed sutra of Buddhism. Ganga turns out to be the syllabic confluence of Hinduism and Buddhism, word and water. Since, Ganga symbolizes state of 'gata,' passing over; Ganga has so much significance in post-death rituals in contrast with the birth ritual. Ganga becomes a layman's substitute for intense hankering after nirvana. Ganga that emerges in Gangotri (Ganga+tri—Ganga which crosses over) ends its journey into Gangasagar after mythological avataran. It is a phonetic structured whole that is believed to be bestowed with the magnificent power to take beings beyond the trans-migratory world.

Ganga—A Sacred Geography that Duplicates like its Name

Ganga is not only the singular river imbued with mythologies and praises in verses that flow from the source of the Himalayas into the Bay of Bengal. Ganga is a paradigm for sacred water, stream or no stream. Ganga is paradigm of not only water-stream but of any apparent flow, stars and nebula, prana and ideas. Diana L Eck, a Professor of Comparative Religion and Indian Studies at Harvard University writes about the sacred Ganga:

> "The Ganga as goddess is more than a single river. She functions in India as the archetype of sacred rivers. Other rivers are said to be like the Ganga, others are said even to be the Ganga (such as the river Kaveri, the 'Ganga of South India'). But, the Ganga remains the paradigmatic sacred river in which they are likened. The river Ganga is not confined to the course she takes across the plains of North India but participates in that spatial transposition that is so typical of Hindu sacred geography, pervading the sacred waters of all India's great rivers." [3]

> As discussed earlier, Gangajal is believed to have transformative potency. Even a single drop is supposed to turn whole water body sacred. But, like alliteration in mantras, there is duplication of the whole concept of sacred Ganga and the world-view gets disseminated like visarjan over the Indian geography. I will put up a list of many Gangas within and beyond India.

We can see transposition of the paradigm of sacred Ganga at different levels, from within body and beyond into the cosmos. From the microcosm to macrocosm, the river Ganga becomes iconic signifier for sacredness of liquid-flow.

Kashmir	Banaganga at Katra, Vaishno Devi Shrine, Kishanganga (Sharda Peeth now in POK is situated on its bank), Gangabal (lake near Harmukh peak considered as sacred as Prayag), Gangajatan (in Badgam district where Ganga Ashtami is celebrated), Guptganga (adjacent to Nishat garden), Gangachoti (mountain peak in POK)
Mongolia	Saran Ganga (Sajan-kang-ka at Dornod, Mongolia), Ganga Nuur Lake (near Dariganga), Muharin Ganga, Ulan Ganga (mountain peak), Dzegestiyn Ganga (Hill at Dornod)
South India	Gautami Ganga or Dakshin Ganga (Godavari), Panchganga that meets River Krishna at Narsobawadi near Sangli, Dakshin Ganga (Kaveri, Narmada, Tungbhadra)
Tibet	Ganga Chuu stream that connects Lak Mansarovar with Lake Rakshastal.
Human Body	Nadi (here 'da' ड is third in third series of Sanskrit consonants) and nadi ('da' द is third in fourth series of consonants) have similar sounds. One is the subtle channel and another is the river. But, in Indian esoterism, two have fused. Just like river streams, there are confluences of different layers as well as directions of meanings. Ida is a subtle nadi that courses from the right testicle to the left nostril and corresponds to the Ganges river. It is believed to controls all the mental processes.
Cosmos	Akashganga (Milky way)

Saptanada Ganga

In fact, duplicating characteristics is incorporated in the myth of origin of Ganga itself. Structure of Indian thinking reveals that Indians believe in the underlying unity of everything. In such a world-view, One is assumed to Become Many. The non-dual becomes dual and thence the whole diversity of creation. But, just like the often-repeated metaphor of fire, which is assumed to be same in the sun, moon or inside human body, the basic nature of Many is same as what was contained in the One. This allows for proliferation of diversity and retention of unity at the same time. It is how India developed Unity in Diversity.

There are narratives about recurring seven-divisions of the Ganga. In the Brahmanda Purana, it is mentioned how Ganga is a Saptanadi. On being released, the river began to flow in seven channels. Three of them flowed towards the east and three to the west. The Brahmanda Purana describes how the streams Nalini, Hradini and Pavani are those which flow towards the east. The Sita, the Caksus and the Sindhu flow towards the west. Bhagiratha being the seventh channel flowed towards the south. This idea of Saptaganga is all-pervasive.

It is also mentioned in Puranas that when Ganga was descending, first it reached the Dhruva star (Pole Star) and then purified the seven planets near Dhruvaloka. Thus, Ganga before its mythical descent over earth had a journey of sapta-grahas.

One can find mention about Saptanadi in the Vedas also. The river Sindhu is known as Saptasindhu. It is difficult to trace the exact origin of sevenness in Indian tradition. But, one can seek some support from Yaska's etymology.

/Sapta srpta samkhya/
Number seven creeps like a snake.

/Saptaditya rashmaya iti vadanti//
Rays of sun always creeping.

There are seven rays of sun in ancient Indian world-view, which is so accurate even in contemporary context. They characterized the sun rays with riding seven horses (present day seven colours) as rays appear to creep like snake. Snake is sarpa. Sapta is derived from sarpa. I feel that the concept of seven crept into the description of river streams as the rivers in its zig-zag flow appear as long, liquid terrestrial snake. Thus, Sindhu is sapta-sindhu. Ganga is sapta-Ganga. Kaveri is believed to divide into seven streams. There is saptadhara kunda in Rajgir where even Buddha frequently visited. There can be innumerable references to sapta-dhara across Indian geography. The moving constellations are identified with seven sages and known as Saptarishis. It is why seven life-cycles becomes the critical time period in Indian rituals. Life is also viewed as flow of prana, samskara, karma. The marriage bonds are valid for seven life times. The sons have responsibility to offer pindadaan for salvation of seven generations. Marriage is barred by law of sapindaa (seven generations).

It's like each entity multiplying into seven and the process goes on. One can see shadows of fractals that occur in non-linear dynamic theories where same pattern recurs ad infinitum.

Indian thinking appears to be inherently fractal. Indian mentality always tends to compress wisdom into minimum possible size on one hand, while hankering simultaneously for infinite expansion in space and time for any entity, tangible or presumed. It is simultaneous act of expansion and contraction of imagination and consciousness that propels the topophilia. The story of Ganga contains the seeds of Indian thinking. By planting it in proper minds and nourishing with sacred waters, we may be able to bring confluence of ancient wisdom and modern thinking.

Notes

1. Tagare, GV (trans). (1983). *Brahmanda Purana,* Delhi: MLBD, Chapter 18.
2. Yelle, Robert A (2003). *Explaining Mantras: Ritual, Rhetoric, and the Dream of a Natural Language in Hindu Tantra,* New York: Routledge.
3. Eck, Diana L (1996). "Ganga: The Goddess *Ganges* in Hindu Sacred Geography, in John Stratton Hawley, Donna Marie Wulff (eds) (1996). *Devi: Goddesses of India.*

Reference

1. Sinha, Nirmal Chandra (1977). *India and Tibet : Geographical Considerations,* Gangtok, Sikkim: Namgyal Institute of Tibetology, pp. 11-13.

Chapter 20

Sri/Shri in Indian Tradition

In India, Sri/Shri is still the most common honorific prefixed before male names. If English people have 'Mister', Spanish 'Senor', French 'Monsieur,' Indians have used for centuries, the prefix 'shri.' One can often come across holy people with the title `Sri'. Many pilgrim centres have 'Sri' in their name. Sri Sail, Sri Rangapattam, Sringeri, Sri Badrinath, Sri Jagannath Puri, Srihatta (Sylhet), Sri-dih (Shiridi)... and the list can be endless. There are administrative capitals in India with the name starting with Sri like Srinagar. Sri is prefixed before vidyas and holy texts. Srimad Bhagwad Gita and Sri Vidya are the most sacred text/method for the Hindus. Many objects used in rituals have Sri in their name symbolizing the sacredness. Sriphala (coconut) and Sringataka (water chestnut) still play prominent roles in rituals. Sri is so much inherent in Indian psyche that it rarely raises query from various corners. But, the influence of Sri crossed seas. The island south of India is known as 'Sri Lanka'. Sri Vijaya was a powerful Hindu empire in Indonesia.Thai transliterate the word as 'Si' and prefix it before important places like Si Ayutthaya.

In recent years, secular India has given stamp of approval to the sacredness of the term by itself appropriating it to honour eminent people with the title, like 'Padma Sri.' Sri is used as a symbol in letter pads, ledger books of business dealings. What is the significance of the letter? What does the letter symbolize?

Figure 20.1

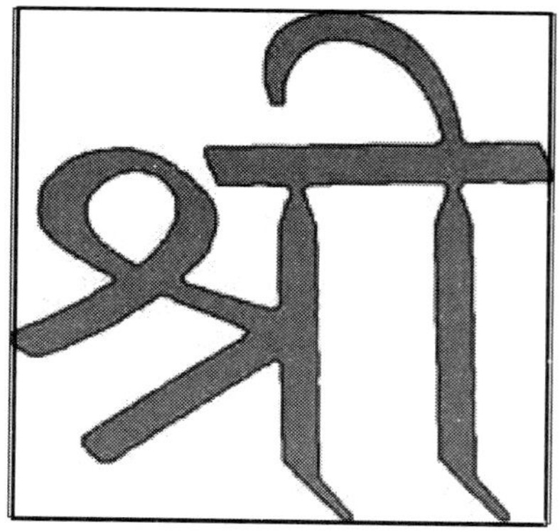

Sri in Sanskrit

In Sanskrit, 'Sri' stands for prosperity. Sri refers to the Goddess of wealth, Lakshmi. The word 'shra' is a conjoint consonant and created by joining 'Sha' (श) and 'ra' (र). 'Sha' refers to Shiva while 'ra' to fire, desire, love, vibration, play'. Shra (श्र) in union with 'ee' creates this powerful letter (श्री). 'Ee' denotes Lakshmi. It is also the syllable for immortality. By applying this version, we get the meaning of 'Shri' as the union of Shiva and the Feminine energy in form of Lakshmi, the fusion of male and female principles, the non-dual aspect of the Existence.

Shri in Tantra

But, the genealogy of the letter leads to the exploration of Tantra philosophy. Shri is the most auspicious term in the tantras. It is the tantra rituals and theories which had lasting influence over Vedic rites during medieval periods and the Indian civilization as we know it, was shaped. In Tantrik lores, Sri-Vidya is the highest and most complex sadhna. It is said that only those who have taken the last birth gets opportunity to practice this highly esoteric and philosophic sadhna. In Sri Vidya, there are 15 alphabets corresponding to 15 kalas (digits) of the Moon (lunar tithis) known as Panchakshari. In Indian tradition, the transcendental aspect is often kept separate as an undivided unity beyond the divided (krama) immanence. It is, therefore, assumed that the Moon has 16th transcendental kala from which the new cycle of Moon arises. It is believed that after the 15th lunar tithi, on the new moon, the sun and the Moon come down to the earth and engages in union which leads to new cycle of emanation. This sixteenth kala is the secret of immortality in which everything dissolves and everything emanates. This permeates and sustains preceding kala and yet, transcend them. The phoneme correspondence has been worked out excellently in Sanskrit grammar.

There are 16 vowels, each corresponding to a lunar tithi. The sixteenth vowel is the visarga (:). The visarga is the manifestation of the Vac/sound in the external Universe. Visarga contains in its womb the power to manifest into any phoneme. Since, it was believed that on the sixteenth lunar day, the power of immortality emerges, the practitioners created rituals on the New Moon to harness this power. The vedic people developed the cult of soma-drinking attuned to the digits of moon, to achieve immortality. It is said that this plant of immortality grew one leaf on each day during waxing moon and shed similarly in the next fortnight. The sixteenth kala idea had a deepening influence over evolution of Indian culture. One can find the ubiquity of sixteen in rituals, youthfulness, grammar etc.

Shri (श्री) in Sri Vidya tradition is the phoneme corresponding to the sixteenth kala. It is linked with not only movement of time/moon outside but also inside breath. In mantra tradition, every root syllable becomes a bijamantra by assuming a form which ends in nasal sound of 'ng', produced by placing a dot/bindu over the seed syllable. Bindu is the 15th vowel and it is considered to be the Shabda Brahma—creator of Vac/word, since it contains the potentiality. Shri when placed with a bindu becomes Shrim. Shrim is employed along with other two important phonemes, 'aim' and 'hrim'. While aim stands for knowledge, hrim for the immanence; Shrim stands for the transcendence. Shri is the expression of grace of the Transcendental energy. It is the sixteenth kala, the Kamakala. It represents the union of Shiva and Shakti, solar and lunar principles, union of immanence and transcendence. Thus, Shrim is the secret to attain prosperity as well as liberation. Shri is considered to be not merely a mantra root but the form of Mother goddess itself. Just as the Moon has only fifteen lunar tithis yet having the sixteen digit, the Mother Goddess has fifteen aspects corresponding with the lunar aspects, and the Shri is pervasive like the sixteenth digit of Moon and provides the sustenance to the world of *Vac*. Shri is the syllable of immortality that sustains the phoneme—universe.

Shri and Kundalini Awakening

In esoteric practice of Kundalini awakening, there are seed syllables that resonate with different body chakras. 'Aim' (ऐं) influences the lowest chakra, mooladhar. The shape of 'ai' with a dot above it, is triangular just like the triangular base in the coccyx where the Kundalini energy is supposed to lie dormant. 'Hrim' (ह्रीं) is the root syllable for awakening heart chakra. One can compare the shape of 'ha' with a cavity. Klim (क्लीं) is the root syllable for the higher centres of the body and influences the ajna chakra (forehead). 'Shrim' (श्रीं) is the root syllable for the highest centre, the crown of the head where the Sahasrar chakra is supposed to exist. It is believed by the practitioners that the Shiva and Shakti, the sun and the Moon energies enter into conjunction at the crown of the head that produces the nectar of immortality. This corresponds well with the narrative of sixteenth digit of the Moon. Shri has a shape of a whirl. There are nine gates in Srichakra corresponding with nine gates in human body. The key to the tenth gate, the gate to transcendence is the syllable Shrim. In human body, it is supposed to be in the crown, i.e. the sahasrar chakra, while in the Srichakra it is supposed to be at the centre transcending the yantra-diagram itself. Therefore, to amplify the practice, many practitioners believe that one should visualize Shrichakra at the Sahasrara itself while using the empowered mantra holding in its womb the secrets of the power of Shri-beeja.

Figure 20.2

(Sri Yantra)

Indian tradition represents this beautiful correspondence between writing, speech, physical body and cosmos. It is more than morphological correspondences or analogies It is something novel that characterized India's unique mantra-tradition in the world. In many of the tantric traditions, the four root syllables are sequentially used (krama) to cause vibrations of the corresponding subtle points and provide smooth passage of the Kundalini energy from the base of spine to the crown of head, from 'ai' to 'Shri.' It is a journey of Shakti to fuse with Shiva, a journey to attain non-duality.

Journey of 'Shri' from Esoteric Ritual to Social Usage

How and when did the usage of 'Shri' percolate in the wider social realm? I propose a conjcture. Shravak (श्रावक) was the word used to address non-Vedic practitioners. Buddha and Mahavira Jain were called shravak and not yogis. In discourses of Buddha as preserved in Pali sources, one often finds how Buddha differentiated Brahmanas and Shramanas. Shramanas were those who loved seclusion and indulged in contemplation, practicing austerities. Brahmanas mediated between human and the divine realm through yajna, fire rituals. Chanakya dedicates his *Chanakyasutrani* to the Goddess 'Shri', the ruler of aishwarya. It was the duty of a king to not only make the kingdom safe and prosperous, but also, radiant with the 'Shri'. Shri in this context is the positive aura of opulence and dynamic creativity. There is a strong possibility that 'Shra' from this tradition entered the earlier tantric discourses emanating from Nalanda. When the chakra movement gained prominence during ninth-tenth century, 'shra' was appropriated to refer to the highest Chakra symbolizing Enlightenment. It is at this time that thousand-name verses were being composed for various deities. There is such a strong resonance of 'shra' with 'sahasrar' (thousand). All these verses always began with Shri. Though, the movement dwindled, the usage of Shri entered the vocabulary of bhakti movement. The name of Ram or Krishna or Hanuman began to be prefixed with 'Shri'. The syllable got engrained in Indian psyche, since the chanting of powerful names was recommended as the easiest way to achieve salvation. What a better way to multiply the enchanting of this powerful syllable than to prefix it with proper names. Exploring this journey of Shri from heterodoxy and esoteric tradition to become the most auspicious signifier of mainstream tradition can open new vista to write genealogy of current cultural practices.

'Sh' (श) is the root of Lakshmi, the Goddess of prosperity, 'r' is the wealth, 'I' is satisfaction and the bindu (.) represents overcoming. Thus, Shrim stands for prosperity for another sect of practitioners. They consider the syllable imbued with the power of sustenance and prosperity. Shri can be prefixed before every name, male or female. This is the tradition in South India also. But, in North India, Shri has been appropriated exclusively by the male world. It is an outcome of deeply ingrained patriarchy where the supposed auspicious power of a syllable has been reserved for the male and the holy men. Let Sri be used by everyone in proper way. Indian woman should regain the syllable from chauvinist male-society. There can be millions of '*SriDevis*' in north India even. We should create opportunity to create Shree-dom, a gyno-piety space to renew a kind of material-spiritualism, which will provide us prosperity in this world and salvation in post-death realm.

Shunya

Chapter 21

Zero and Indian Tradition

There is a consensus about the origin of zero. Zero as a numerical notation was discovered in India. But, when did it occur, remains to be answered conclusively by the historians. The Bakhshali manuscripts dating back to 200 AD does represent 'sunya' as both dot and a small circle. But, the first inscriptions with the notation of zero as circle can be found in Malay inscriptions at Kotakapur (686 AD). Since these were based upon Saka calendar and Hinduized kingdoms, it is presumed that the idea emerged in India. The first record of use of zero in India dates back to 876 AD. This inscription is found on tablets in Gwalior. The chronology is quite relevant while tracing the spread of this revolutionary notation.

The greatest ancient Indian mathematician Aryabhata who built new calendars by fixing beginning of sidereal time in 499 AD. composed *Aryabhatia* at around same time. But, in all likelihood, he was not aware about the operation of zero, nor any notation determined for zero. He did develop alpha-numeric system. He apportioned certain values to 33 consonants from 1-25 and later 30-100. The vowels attached to the basic consonants changed the numerical value as a series of power of 10. Using these signs, the numbers up to 10^{18} were calculated. The Aryabhatia system is summarized below:

Figure 21.1

अ	इ	उ	ऋ	लृ	ए	ऐ	ओ	औ
10^0	10^2	10^4	10^6	10^8	10^{10}	10^{12}	10^{14}	10^{16}

(Vocals)

Figure 21.2

य	र	ल	व	श	ष	स	ह
30	40	50	60	70	80	90	100

(Avarga Consonants)

Figure 21.3

Ka क 1	**Kha** ख 2	**Ga** ग 3	**Gha** घ 4	**N'a** ङ. 5
Cha च 6	**Chha** छ 7	**Ja** ज 8	**Jha** झ 9	**Nia** ञ 10
Ta ट 11	**Tha** ठ 12	**Da** ड 13	**Dha** ढ 14	**Na** ण 15
T त 16	**Th** थ 17	**Da** द 18	**Dha** ध 19	**Na** न 20

Pa प 21	Pha फ 22	Ba ब 23	Bha भ 24	Ma म 25
Ya य 30	Ra र 40	La ल 50	Va व 60	
Sha श 70	Ssha ष 80	Sa स 90	Ha ह 100	

(Varga Consonants)

Let us take a number. 64 can be written in alphabet as gha (4) + va (60) or ghava (घव) Thus Aryabhata developed the versification of mathematical works. This system clearly lacked any positional value and a numerical notation for zero.

Stephen Chrisomalis concludes in his monumental work, *Numerical Notation: A Comparative History* (2010) that "the concept of shunya or 'emptiness' existed in the fifth century AD and may have prefigured the use of positional numerals in India, but no good evidence survives for an actual ciphered-positional numeration system prior to the seventh century AD, long after Aryabhata's death."[1] But, Aryabhata did use the word '*kha*' for numeric position and it was used later as the name for zero. Since `*kha*' in Aryabhata's system denotes mere number 2, which for there were existing notation, what actually favoured the use of '*kha*' to designate 'zero' in words and then as the sign of small circle? Before delving upon this 'kha'-movement, we may sum up how did the use of 'kha'/small circle for zero begin?

It was not Aryabhata, but a succeeding mathematician, Brahmagupta, who is credited with discovering zero and giving sutras for the operation of zero in 628 AD.

In chapter 18 of his work *Brahmasphutasiddhanta* (Corrected

Treatise of Brahma), Brahmagupta describes about Zero as the numerals which stood for nothing. His formulations are as below:

> *The sum of zero and a negative number is negative, the sum of a positive number and zero is positive, the sum of zero and zero is zero.*
>
> *A negative number subtracted from zero is positive, a positive number subtracted from zero is negative, zero subtracted from a negative number is negative, zero subtracted from a positive number is positive, zero subtracted from zero is zero.*

Similarly, he gave the operation of zero as a multiplier correctly. But, he could not handle the formulation of zero as divisor. For Brahmagupta, it would give 0 which was fallacious. This problem was taken up by Mahavira two centuries later in his treatise *Ganita Sara Samgraha*. But, even he fumbled and stated that if 0 is the divisor, the number would remain unchanged. Bhaskara wrote *Lilavati* during 12th century and he could put in proper perspective various operation of 0. One thing is to be noted prominently. 'Kha' became synonymous with zero beginning from Aryabhata and later the terminology was used in spiritual tradition much widely than in the mathematical world.

'Kha' Effect

Aryabhata uses the word 'kha' to denote emptiness. Suryadeva commenting on Aryabhata's kha, says that, "*khani sunya upa lakshitani*". In Brahmagupta's work, the word gets prominence. 'Kha' and sunya (void) is used synonymously. In *Lilavati*, when one comes across the chapter on description of Sunya (zero), it's a veritable cornucopia of 'kha'. The verse reads as follows:

> *Yoge kham kshepsamam, vargado kham, khabhajito rashi Khahara syat, khaguna kham, khaguna nishchantayashcha sheshvidhau!!* (verse 46)

Ananda Coomaraswamy had written an exploratory piece on the concept of 'kha' in connection with the Indian Metaphysics of space.[2]

He has tried to trace the origin of the use of 'kha' for space in the Rigveda in the context of the "hole in the nave of a wheel through which the axle runs." He states that sunya (void) as well as purna (full) have a common reference in the Vedas. Since, the Vedic seers were enamoured by the wheel (chakra), the names of various parts of wheel were used to explain metaphysical concepts. Now, 'kha' is the nabhi of the wheel, the space within the hub. Nabhi is also the navel, navel of beings and things. Thus, 'kha' is the central space of things and beings. In the Rigveda, 'kha' or nabhi "of the world wheel is regarded as the receptacle and fountain of all order, formative ideas and goods."[3]

I find it unlikely that the Vedas could influence mathematical formulations during a period when there was growth of plethora of new sects, a synthesis of Buddhism and Shaivism was going on and various tantra sects were emerging. Moreover, it was also the millennium moment from the *Buddhamahaparinirvana* calendar which resulted into refixation of nakshatra chakra by Aryabhata in 499 AD.

Rather, mathematicians had adopted reverse approach towards the Vedas. While in the Vedas, there are instances of numbers denoting things like number 12 denotes the 'year', the mathematicians like Aryabhata opted to formulate alpha-numeric system where now the numbers were versified. This was a severe reversal of Vedic approach.

I would like to emphasize that some momentous churning occurred during the period between Aryabhata's time to Brahmagupta's time that made zero (sunya/ kha) to emerge as a conceptual category. The notation of small circle emerged only during the later half of the seventh century. This was the period of the rise of Siddha tradition in India which had significant impact over structure of Indian culture. The Siddhas were adept in bodily techniques and oblique statements. The Siddha movement and the emergence of circle to denote zero seems connected.

If one juxtaposes the greatest tantra literature, *Tantraloka* and the *Para-Trisika-Vivarana* by Abhinavagupta written at the time when *Lilavati* was composed by Bhaskar, one will be amazed at similarities of many ideas. 'Kha' is the mantra of absorption. Since, the Universe is viewed as a pulsating process between manifestation and absorption, emergence and dissolution, the great thinkers of the time began to work out the methods for achieving the state of permanent quietude, purna Shanti.

Kha became a mantra. It became the mantra to realize ten succeeding inner spaces of peace, the ten khas. By using the mantra of kha, the yogis were taught to awaken the Kundalini energy in the median nerve. The ultimate kha is empty space of heart wherein consciousness shines alone without any covering.

From 'kha', another concept, *khechari*, developed. Khechari is "which moves in 'kha' (space)". 'Kha' is the symbol of undifferentiated ultimate consciousness. It is the *samvid-sakti,* consciousness-power. Abhinavagupta's definition of *khechari* is very similar to Bhaskar or other mathematicians view on *Kha. khe brahmani abhedarupe sthitva carati iti khechari*" - khechari is that which while stationed in Brahman/ Absolute, in unity, moves about", states Abhinavagupta. It's the nature of mathematical zero. Though, it is indistinguishable from the void, it moves about and gives power to the numbers. *Khechari* like zero is dynamic. Abhinavagupta even explained about various dynamic modes of khechari like *vyomachati, gochari, dikchari, bhuchari* just like the number of zero that while succeeding a numeral adds to the power of number. It is clear that the 'kha' pervaded literature of tantra as well as mathematical treatises simultaneously.

Khechari Mudra and 'Kha'

The Nath sect is believed to have emerged during 9th century. They were instrumental in spreading hathayoga techniques. In *Hatha Yoga Pradipika*, the Khechari Mudra is described as below:

Verse 32: T*he Khechari Mudra is accomplished by thrusting the tongue into the gullet, by turning it over itself, and keeping the eyesight in the middle.*

The same text mentions the benefits of khechari mudra for

yogis. Khechari saves one from poison, diseases, death and old age. Khechari is the panacea for the physical ills and also the path towards freedom.

Khechari mudra were meant to accomplish mastery over space, the void by doing which the Nath Yogis believed, they could achieve the ultimate realization. What is interesting is that though, small circle is present in Devnagari script in many letters like tha, tha, va, ba, ma, bha, but only the letter 'kha' assumed significance in denoting sky/space/hole/circle. It has to do with khechari mudra. Once a yogi folds the tongue, the mudra assumes the form of a 'kha.' Based upon spiritual experiments, they might have realized that this gesture makes them feel lighter and experience the expanse of consciousness.

ख

The correspondence between the structure of phoneme 'kha', the gesture of khechari mudra appears to be a journey of phoneme mysticism. In Indian tradition, phonemes are always considered as mere subtler form of the grosser Reality. The word is the World. Thus, the phoneme 'kha' and the khechari mudra became one by the relationship of hierarchy of manifestation.

What is interesting that like mathematical conception of 'kha', the mystical conception of 'kha' incorporates paradoxical ends of void and expansion of fullness. Thus, one finds in the texts like *Tantraloka,* Purnatasparsha and 'Kha' fuse at a point. The fullness of the touch of Reality and the pervasion of inner most space of heart is achieved in one go. The eternity and the nothingness becomes one and the same. It is like a wheel, without end.

Sunya, Chakra and Siddhas

After the attack by the Huns during middle of the fifth century, Indian sub-continent was gripped by the millennium fever. The millennium had approached from Buddha Parinirvana calendar. There was a spurt in composition of literature like Puranas to describe the coming avatars. At this time, the idea of chakra spread all across. If one cycle was ending, another cycle was about to begin with new avatar commanding the righteous society. Chakras entered into tantra rituals. Practitioners believed that by performing chakra-worship, they would be able to sail across the millennium time. Various kinds of sects centred around rituals like ganachakra, kalachakra, srichakra, chakrasamvara emerged. The circle became important in popular usage. The circle, triangle and dots were used to construct mystical diagrams in various rituals. But, it was the circle which won the race, as the cyclicity represented by the pattern of circle enamoured the thinkers and the royalty who were caught in the millenarian fever. First, Aryabhat recalculated nakshatrachakra and fixed sidereal time as zero in 499 AD. Subsequently, the chakra ideas peaked and so did the conception of zero and later its notation as circle became common during middle of the seventh century.

Emergence of notation for zero was dictated more by the religious needs rather than mathematical exploration. The idea of 'kha', shunyata, khechari and chakra fused together to provide the most wonderful gift to the modern world. Shunya emerges as the syntagm of civilizational grammar in India.

Endnotes

1. Chrisomalis, Stephen (2010), *Numerical Notation: A Comparative History*, Cambridge, p 208.

2. Coomaraswamy, Ananda K (1934). *Kha and other Words denoting Zero, in Connection with the Indian Metaphysics of Space*, Bulletin of the School of Oriental Studies, VII.

3. ibid.

References

1. Coomaraswamy, Ananda (1934). *Kha and Other Words denoting Zero, in Connection with the Indian Metaphysics of Space*, Bulletin of the School of Oriental Studies, VII.

2. Chrisomalis, Stephen (2010). *Numerical Notation: A Comparative History,* Cambridge : Cambridge University Press.
3. Silburn, Lilian (1988). *Kundalini—Energy of the Depths,* NY: SUNY.
4. Singh, Jaidev (1988). *Abhinavagupta Sara Trisika-Vivarana, The Secret of Tantrik Mysticism,* New Delhi: MLBD.
5. Sarma, K.V. (eds) (1975). *Lilavati of Bhaskaracarya with Kriyakramakari of Sankara and Narayan,*VV Research Institute.
6. Datta, BB and AN Singh (1935). *History of Hindu Mathematics,* Asia Publishing House.
7. Mukherjee, R.N (1976). *Background to the Discovery of the Symbol for Zero,* in Proceedings of the Symposium on the 1500th Birth Anniversary of Aryabhata I, New Delhi, 1976, *Indian J Hist Sci* 12(2), (1977), 225-231. downloaded from http://www.new.dli.ernet.in/rawdataupload/upload/insa/INSA_1/20005af8_225.pdf

Chapter 22

Japanese 'Ma' and Indian 'Kha'

Emptiness in Asia and West

Asian traditions have incorporated the concept of 'vacuity' in myriad ways. All of us are aware about the development of Shunyata in the Mahayana Buddhism and later discovery of the symbol of zero as a hollow circle. The space in Asian tradition has been conceptualized differently than the Western tradition. The absences, ruptures, silence, gaps, emptiness are not something to be dreaded. Rather, these are the loci of cultivation of powerful aesthetic, spiritual and ethical experiences. In the western culture, there is ubiquity of the axiological principle of utilitarianism-everything has to be counted for the utility value. Since, vacuum abhors calculative thinking, vacuum became the major hindrance in universalizing calculative thinking. Space had to be bound, enumerated and fitted into mathematical calculations. The persistent attempt since Galileo finally reached the apogee when Albert Einstein formulated the General Theory of Relativity and space-time continuum lost the autonomy from categorization and merely reduced to an appendage of the gravitational bodies. Nowadays, cosmology is fixated at renormalizing infinities and establishing vacuum space as container of wave-particles like gravitons, dark matter, dark energy, Higgs bosons etc. Similarly, time in Asian tradition is cyclic while the western calculative thinking has reduced it to a linear flow of matter. Space-time is mere geometrical entity in western paradigm. But, across Asia, space-time in its vacuity has been an experiential state. It is not an object but an admixture of subjective experience and objective existence. Both, 'kha' in Indian tradition and 'Ma' in Japan depicts similar experiential state apart from signifying an objective existence.

Figure 22.1

In Asian civilizations, there is greater emphasis on harmony and co-existence. Opposites can co-exist. There is no need to obliterate the 'other'. While in the western culture, there is always the faith in the universalization. The tendency to capture, control and establish a rule of law, a rule of geometry or a rule of science is the most pressing aspect of western thinking. The western civilizations do not trust empty spaces. Their own version of truth must establish monopoly. Thus, capitalism has to overcome the crisis by extending and deepening into the barren lands of the planet. The cyberspace has to be created to expand exploration and manipulate space. Science has to explore everything unknown. All unknowns have to be stripped naked of their unknownness and the cloak of western meaning has to dress those. On the other hand, Asian tradition allows for the existence of unknown and the known. The harmony can be established by each following his own dharma. The balance has to be maintained either through the Middle Path or through the Yoga or through the proper flow of chi. The vaccum is the source of creative potential. In Sanskrit linguistics, anusvar, the dot '.' is the unknown creatrix which resonates the auditory universe. It was this dot which later emerged as a circle. From here emanated the concept of zero which was thought to be the creative unknown—the limitless potentiality. Kisho Kurokawa, a Japanese architect-philosopher, sums up, "In the West, dualisms are transcended through the dialectical method of resolving (*aufbehen*) opposites on a higher level. The two opposites are unified into a single entity, or one of the two is negated and rejected. In contrast, the philosophy of symbiosis creates a relationship between the two elements while allowing them to remain in opposition. That relationship must be a dynamic, ever-changing one. To create a relationship between two opposing elements, it is usually effective to place spatial distance (a neutral zone) or temporal distance (a cooling-off period) between them."[1]

'Ma' refers to the state of in-between-ness, an interval in space as well as time. Life is an interval between two junctions of birth and death. It is a 'ma' in time. 'Ma' is an interval in motion. The time between preparing and sipping tea can be thought of as the interval of waiting for the savouring. 'Ma' refers to intervals of space and time that becomes meaningful only when filled with motion. It is not a static vacuity. The interval must be dynamic to be termed as 'Ma'.

Concept of 'Ma' and Contemporary Japanese Philosophers

The concept of 'Ma' as essence of Japaneseness was highlighted by Arata Isozaki (1931-), a Japanese architect and philosopher who organized an exhibition—*Ma: Space-Time in Japan* (1978-82) in

Paris and New York. Isozaki tried to trace the roots of the concept of Ma to the notion of *utsu* (void), an 'interval' between two (or more) spatial or temporal things and events. Isozaki writes:

"Utsu signifies the void inside a certain substance, a cave in a rocky mountain, the hollow inside an old tree, the 'dug-out' of a canoe, or the cavity of a pit dwelling—the sacred spirit was thought to lodge in all of these voids. As the view towards the void became more ritualised, even a solid gem was believed to contain a void, a sack of cloth, without holes for hands and feet, was thought to be inhabited by the sacred God. The more severed from exteriority, the more sacred the internal void."[2]

Thus, 'ma' is also used in the sense of a gap or opening, the in-between space and time. Isozaki explains in this work how the ancient Japanese viewed such spaces with this particular characteristic as the abode of the spirits. Japanese people developed various rituals and formal structures to represent this descent of the spirits *(kami)*. This act of waiting is the 'ma' in time, while the hollow sacred space, 'Ma' in space.

Isozaki describes the native tradition of Kami to explain the concept of 'ma'. Kami were believed to descend to fill the sacred voids with chi. The performer or the observer has to perceive the instant at which this occurred. Thus, the moment of 'Now', the in-between past and future became the main focus for religio-aesthetics in Japan.

In every religious experience, the participants have to first prepare an interval of space to be occupied by the kami and then to spend an interval of time waiting for the kami to descend. It was the dual spatio-temporal gap which was believed to generate the events that filled them with meaning. Extending the same notion, each empty interval of space and time came to be perceived as prelude to some sort of action. These junctures became 'ma'. In the Japanese art, 'ma' became a means for inviting the action of the audience as participants in the artwork like in the Noh drama or ink-paintings or the rock gardens where the audience-observer has to fill the meaning. Thus, the true meaning became more than mere literal or representational or intentional meaning. The true meaning germinates only during the act of participation or performance. True meaning became relational and implicit. True meaning has to be experienced and not literally explained.

In other words, one can see the world as a relationship between eventful and non-eventful events. The non-eventful interval that gives meaning to the whole structure is the 'Ma'. The relationality vs. rationality holds the key to understand Asian and western paradigms. In Asia, the concept of shunyata as dependent origination has a tremendous influence over the shaping of culture. Shunyata incorporates both existence and non-existence. What matters is the relationships. Every object exists in relationship across space and time and this inter-connectedness gives meaning to experience and observation. In the west, it is the individual-centric paradigm and the things are considered as objective beings. Relationality is not important, individual is. In Asia, the non-event and event are part of the whole. And it is the non-event, the gap, which is the abode of transcendence. This is why the in-between gained credence in Asian traditions. The transcendental experience is the ultimate realization and it is the experience of the void as the interstices of the experience. To attain the state of transcendence, all forms of technology are being deployed. One counts mantras on rosary beads by keeping hands in a linen bag. The linen enclosure with the single opening becomes sacred. It is the reason that sages meditated inside the mountain caves, since the caves are enclosures with single opening and it is neither inside nor outside. It is an in-between. While breathing in pranayam, emphasis is put on in-between, to hold down the breath *(kumbhak),* neither inhaling *(pooaka)* nor exhaling *(rechak).* This state of space and silence between breath is worked upon in the Japanese music, *honkyoyu* and called shakuhachi breathing.

All these working with in-between state of Being are 'ma'. The moments of silence in music or empty space in ritual, interstices in architecture *(kenmen-ho),* non-meaning in haikus, pauses in performance, sumi-e in ink-paintings, wrinkled space in *ojiya-chijimi* linen, piercing in sushmi, *tokonama* (vacant space) inside homes—all these are mere expression of the concept of 'ma'. Without 'ma', events cannot take on the meaning. It is the experience of the 'ma' that the highest meaning can be revealed. Therefore, we find the obsession in Japanese culture with zen-silences, and the act of waiting, may it be in the floral arrangement like Ikebana or the tea ceremony. The use of pauses in Japanese music and puppet-theatres are in the similar vein. Zeami Motokiyo, the codifier of Noh theatre stated "*senu tokoro ga omoshiroki*" meaning thereby what the actor does not do is interesting. Kisho Kurukawa, the great Japanese philosopher-architect sums up brilliantly:

> "In writing Chinese ideographs, it is more important to pay attention to the space between the lines than the lines themselves. This space is not nothingness. It has as much significance as the lines, it speaks as much. Ma is also important in folk songs and Noh chants. The engawa is a space, a ma, inserted between nature and building, exterior and interior. This type of intermediate zone functions as ma to permit two opposing elements to exist in symbiosis. Intermediate space makes a discontinuous continuum possible, so that a plurality of opposing elements can continue in an ever-changing, dynamic relationship. The nature of intermediate space is its ambiguity and multivalency. It does not force opposing elements into compromise or harmony; it is the key to their living and dynamic symbiosis."[3]

Kurokawa uses the imagery of everyday life to depict the value of 'Ma'—"Those who properly space (ma) their words are effective speakers who create a deep impression. When two factors are in fierce opposition to each other, it often becomes surprisingly easy to adjust their conflicting claims by inserting a ma -- that is, after a period of waiting."[4]

Kurokawa is known for his bold claim "No Plaza in the east and No Street in the west". It is this street-ness in Asia which is the expression of 'ma' in our market. Kurokawa writes, "the Eastern city has no plaza, while the Western city has no street ... a special feature of Eastern cites is that though they lack plazas, their streets perform the functions of the plaza. But that is not all that I want to say. Not only do the streets of Eastern cities perform the function of the plaza in the Western city, that of binding the life of the private citizen to the life of his city, but the Eastern street also possesses, at the same time, an ambiguous meaning, for it has double nature: it is simultaneously public and private space, city space and residential space."[5]

Roland Barthes, the great French literary theorist took a detour of Japan and penned down *Empire of Signs*.[6] He experienced the flashes everywhere and the text he wrote, he explained, was like a *satori*—an emptiness of language. Barthes wrote, "And it is also an emptiness of language which constitutes writing; it is from this emptiness that derive the feature with which Zen, in the exemption from all meanings, writes gardens, gestures, houses, flower arrangements, faces , violence."[7] It is this pervasiveness of emptiness which is 'Ma'.

While investigating the City-Centre of Tokyo, Barthes was intrigued. He contrasted the West where "all its cities are concentric; but also, in accord with the very movement of Western metaphysics, for which every centre is the site of truth, the center of our cities is always full: a marked site, it is here that the values of civilization are gathered and condensed-spirituality (churches), power (offices), money (banks), merchandise (department stores), language (agoras: cafes and promenades)."[8]

In Tokyo, Barthes discovered the paradox as it did possess a centre, but the centre is empty. Barthes explains, "the entire city turns around a site both forbidden and indifferent, a residence concealed beneath foliage, protected by moats, inhabited by an emperor who is never seen, which is to say, literally, by no one knows who." He equates this part of Tokyo with the 'visible form of invisibility' which merely hides the 'sacred nothing'.[9] Trapped in typical western mode, Barthes tries to fathom the functionality of this empty centre—'to give the entire urban movement the support of its central emptiness, forcing the traffic to make a perpetual detour."[10]

'Ma' is an aesthetic-spiritual sensibility, an experiential encounter with Nothingness, an engagement with immediacy. In Japan, the interval, 'ma', has been incorporated in all juncture of life and cultivated to enrich the experiences which makes one to keep renewing the sense of dwelling in an immediacy, in event or non-event, in karaoke or silence, in war or peace.

It is very similar to the concept of rasa-dhvani in Indian literature that relates the temporal and transcendental realm in the immediacy of experience.

'Ma' and 'kha'—Paradox of Common Similie

While tracing the origin of the concept of 'Ma', many philosophers have suggested it to be a Chinese import. Lao Tse described this concept of 'Ma' in Tao Te Ching written during 6th century BC:

Thirty spokes share one hub,
but the empty space between them
is the essence of the wheel.
Pots are formed from clay,
but the empty space between it
is the essence of the pot.
Walls with windows and doors form the house,
but the empty space within it
is the essence of the house.
Thus, what we gain is something (yu),
Yet it is by virtue of nothing (wu)
That this can be put to use."

Similarly, the concept of 'kha' has its roots in the earliest Vedas, the Rig Veda Sukta VIII.91.7 which mentions: *"In the axle hole of the chariot, in the axle hole of the cart, in the hole of the yoke, O Wise Indra, have purified Apala thrice and have given her a skin like the Sun."*

(khe rathasya khe anasah khe yugasya shatakrato!
apalamindra trishputvaykrinoh surya tavacham!)

'Kha' was the term for the hole in the axle upon which depended the proper motion of the cart. Similarly, there was 'kha' everywhere, 'kha' as a central hole. It was considered to be within human bodies, in the sky, in the things. 'Kha' came to signify any hole or opening through which something may pass that by extension applies to fountain-head or canal or river-bed and later on the bodily apertures. Any sky or antariksha, the space that pervades between this world

and the other-worldly (heaven) either internal or external is known as 'kha' in ancient Indian tradition. Even the cavity within heart is called 'kha'. The vacant space inside which a mediator experienced is 'kha' *(chidakash)*. 'Kha' is pervaded by the Brahma. One can see the analogy between Kami spirits and Indian Brahma. 'Kha' is the state to be experienced. It was 'kha' which was the symbol for zero. Only later on when the concept of Shunyata held sway, Shunya as emptiness was represented at first as a dot, then a circle signifying the relatedness across the Universe. Many argue that the concept of 'Ma' may be influenced by the Shunyata principle which had origin in India. But, in all likelihood, the common Asiatic mentality led the leading philosophers to postulate about the State of Vacuity as an experiential immediacy across Asia independently. Similar ideas find resonance across similar environment. Thus, it is not appropriate to seek the genealogy of the concept and reduce it into a linear pattern of diffusion.

Figure 22.2

間

(Japanese 'ma')

'Ma' is graphically represented by its Chinese ideogram as a gate with the character for sun (*hi*) or moon (*tsuki*) passing through. The light shining through (literally and/or metaphorically) the opening (ma) is revealed during moments of intervals and non-action. This light is the light of consciousness and renewal of self. The sun/moon shining through the gate evokes the sense of something hidden. It is not the complete Truth. It is neither black nor white. It is grey and this is the reason for abundant use of grey colour in Japanese visual aesthetics. Similarly, 'kha' appears as a central hole inside a cavity in the graphic representation. 'Kha' is also the sound that is uttered from the throat where there is another cavity, glottis. 'Kha' and 'Ma' signify similar aspect of the creative emptiness. But, while 'Ma' was used to capture through aesthetic expressions the experience of emptiness in Japan, in India this was limited to spiritual practices. Realizing 'kha' became the central theme in the Tantras and the Yogas. In everyday lives, it got hidden under the compound words like 'su-kha' (happiness) and 'du-kha' (tragedy)".

'Ma' as well as 'kha' captures 'in-between world' when one extinguishes the self into the interstices of space-time, when there is intermission, visarga. While in 'Ma', this emptying takes place in the external, temporal intervals, in 'kha', it occurs in the atemporal vacuity of internal space. But, both creates symbiosis of aesthetic (poetic) and religious (spiritual) dimensions of life. It is by experiencing the immediate, the nothingness that mankind can take a detour from the western calculative thinking which has unleashed havoc against our propensity to live harmoniously. We need revolution in Asian thinking to experience un-thoughts, to rever the sacred spaces and relish delight in the immediate moments. That is the sacredness and in sacredness, lies our salvation!

Notes:

1. Kurukawa, Kisho (1994). *The Philosophy of Symbiosis*, Academy Books, London. An elaborate discussion has been made in the chapter VIII, 'Intermediary Space', available online at http://www.kisho.co.jp/page.php/305.
2. Isozaki, Aratai and Ken Tdashi Oshima (2009). *Arata Isozaki*, Phaidon Press, p 158.
3. Kurukawa, n.1.
4. Ibid.
5. Ibid.
6. Barthes, Roland (1970). *Empire of Signs*, translated by Richard Howard (1982), New York: Hill & Wang.
7. Ibid, p 4.

Index